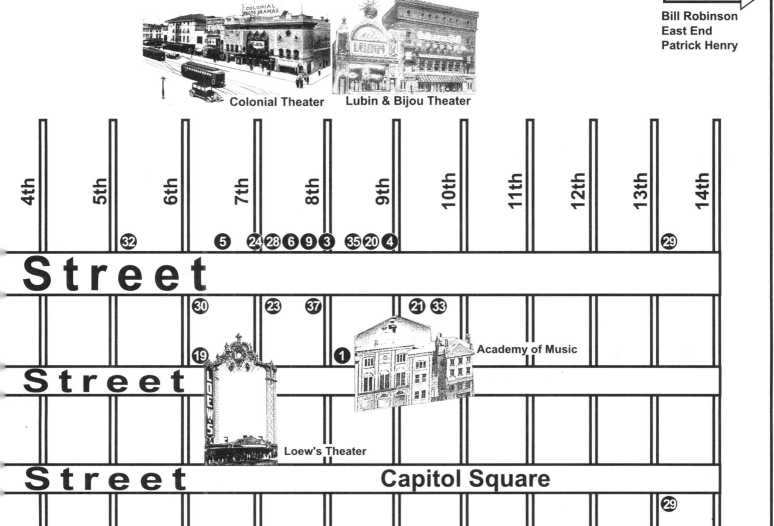

Colonial Theater   Lubin & Bijou Theater

Bill Robinson
East End
Patrick Henry

4th | 5th | 6th | 7th | 8th | 9th | 10th | 11th | 12th | 13th | 14th

Street

Street

Loew's Theater

Academy of Music

Street   **Capitol Square**

Hull St.

Mayo Bridge

Henrico

Colonial Heights
Hopewell
Petersburg

19. Loew's/Carpenter Center - 600 E. Grace St.
20. Lubin/Isis/Park Theater - 808 E. Broad St.
21. Lyric/WRVA Theater - 901 E. Broad St.
22. Majestic Theater - 23 W. Broad St. (Nickelodeon)
23. Marshall/Richmond Theater - 701 E. Broad St.
24. National/Towne Theatre - 704 E. Broad St.
25. New Theater - 206 E. Broad St.
26. Pastime Photoplay - 1224 Hull St.
27. Rayo Theater - 411 N. 2nd St.
28. Rex Theater - 700 E. Broad St. (Nickelodeon)
29. Richmond Theater/Monumental Church - 1300 E. Broad St.
30. Superior/Odeon Theater - 211 N. 6th St.
31. Theater Comique/Putnam's - 1313 E. Franklin St.
32. Theato - 500 E. Braod St. (Nickelodeon)
33. Thompson's Musee Theater - 909 E. Broad St.
34. Venus Theater - 1412 Hull St.
35. Victor Theater - 800 E. Broad St.
36. Victoria/Ponton - 1316 Hull St.
37. Virginia Theater - 711 E. Broad St. (Nickelodeon)

CELEBRATE RICHMOND THEATER

CELEBRATE RICHMOND THEATER

Compiled and Edited by

Elisabeth Dementi • Wayne Dementi

Written by

Kathryn Fuller-Seeley

First Printing, 2002

Copyright© 2002
ISBN: 0-87517-116-8
Library of Congress Catalog Number: 2001094237

The Dietz Press
Richmond, Virginia

ACKNOWLEDGEMENTS

A Faculty-Grant in Aid awarded by the College of Humanities and Sciences of Virginia Commonwealth University aided in the collection of primary documents and the production of this book.

The Dementi Studio staff team members were tenacious in bringing the manuscript together. Thanks to Rebecca Crumley, Tayloe Moore, Josefa Mulaire, Cory Hudgins, Mark Mitchell, Laura Kinney and Jeremiah Sargent.

A special thanks to Brian and Pat Dementi for their support and assistance in locating several wonderful photographs, which are included in this publication.

Kristin Thrower and Douglas Gomery wrote the essays that are included in Chapter Four. Kristin conducted interviews, and unearthed some elusive primary research documents. The book is much improved by her efforts and suggestions.

Roy Proctor, *Richmond Times Dispatch* theater critic, has devoted 25 years to the study of Richmond's theatrical history. We are grateful for the research notes he generously shared, and for the many newspaper articles he has written over the years. The late *Times Dispatch* theater and film critics Edith Lindeman and Carole Kass also gave encouragement to the city's theater and film communities in print for more than 60 years, and their work made our research pleasurable.

For their research guidance and opening of many doors, we'd like to thank Kelley Brandes at the Library of Virginia; Theresa Roane at the Valentine Museum; Dr. James Ryan of the Historic Petersburg Foundation; Charles Berthea and staff at the Black History Museum; Ray Bonis at the VCU Library Special Collections department; Harry Kollatz of the Firehouse Theater Project and *Richmond Magazine*; Todd Schall-Vess at the Byrd Theater, John Whiting of Whiting's Old Paper, Joel Katz of the Carpenter Center for Performing Arts, Rita McClenny of the Virginia Film Office, Jarene Fleming at New Millennium Studios, Bruce Simon at the Richmond Public Library, and the staffs at the *Times Dispatch* archives, and Historic Richmond Foundation.

We wish to thank the following interviewees who shared their stories of Richmond theaters and moviegoing: Lucille Borden, Carolyn Brown, Bob Burchette, George Burnet, Nelson Calisch, Robert Coulter III, Nikki Calisch Fairman, Dr. Francis Foster, Harvey Hudson, Dr. Joseph Galeski, Robinson Horne, Jim Johnson, Edward Nunnally, Roland Rackett, Miles Rudisill, Jackie Samuels, Scott Terbush, Geneva Thrower, Harold Thrower, Dr. E. Randolph Trice, and Charles Hughes and the western film fans group that meets at Meadowbrook Library. Thanks also to members of the 5400 Club, Old Dominion Postcard Club, Shepherd Center, and students in history courses at Virginia Commonwealth University.

We are also appreciative of Jane Payne and Michael Ireland, assistants to Warren Beatty, who coordinated so kindly with us in facilitating Warren Beatty's composition of the Foreword.

Thanks to the kind friends who read drafts of the manuscript and cut through miles of red tape for us: Q. David Bowers, Wanda Clary, Margit Dementi, Kevin Finucane, Maria Mazzenga, Karan Sheldon, and Mort Thalhimer. Cynthia Ray, of Art & Graphic Studio, designed the book jacket, and Bobby Holliday, of Eclectic Graphics, designed the Richmond theater map for the flyleaves.

For their vision for Richmond Arts, and consequent representation in this manuscript, we extend a special thanks to Stephanie Micas, Philip Davidson and Brad Armstrong.

And to our respective family members Kenny, Harry and Kendall Seeley, Mary Lou Helgesen, Dianne Dementi, Margit Dementi, and Rob Dementi for all their love and support.

INTRODUCTION

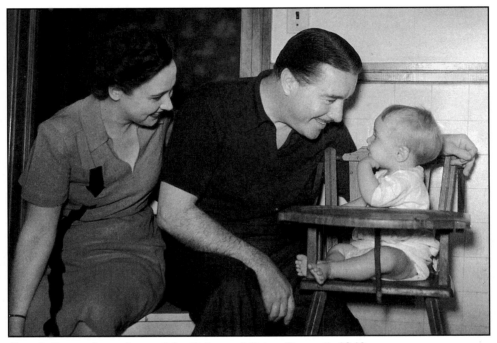

Connie Dementi, movie star John Boles, and Brian Dementi, 1940s.

I t's Saturday morning!
A double-feature, plus "Tom & Jerry", "Bugs Bunny",
and "The Roadrunner" are all waiting for us! The guys will meet
down by the creek at 9:30 in the morning so we can bike three miles
to the Bellevue Theater to enjoy a day at the movies. We are sure to
meet up with our other friends from school. So, I know it's going to
be a great day!

It was a tradition. We did Saturday at the movies for years as we
came along. The big screen strengthened our friendships, as we would
journey together through the wild west, become soldiers in practically every war ever fought, take down every monster ever created,

THEATER GROUP SOCIAL AT THE DEMENTI'S, *in Richmond's Lakeside Neighborhood, 1940s.*

Bottom row: Unidentified woman, Frank Dementi. Top row: Bob Dementi, Woolner Calisch, Edith Lindeman Calisch, Connie Dementi, movie star John Boles and Kathleen Sims, 1940s.

and enhance every line ever spoken by comedy heroes like Abbott and Costello and Dean Martin & Jerry Lewis.

I am most grateful to the people who made Richmond one of the greatest theater cities in America. I realize now how special we had it as we were growing up!

Growing up as a photographer's son made growing up around the theater even more special. As it happened, my Dad was frequently called upon to photograph visiting celebrities. Every now and then, my brother and I would get a chance to meet them. The occasion illus-

trated in this group photograph actually predates me. However, the time was so special to Mom and Dad that I heard the stories repeatedly growing up. Prominent actor John Boles was in town. *Richmond Times Dispatch* movie critic Edith Lindeman had arranged for Dad, and his nephew Bob Dementi, to photograph the occasion. All of the people involved were having such a nice time that they ended up at our home for what appears to have been a festive gathering! That's my Mom sitting in John Boles' lap! She loved that memory!!

Other special "celebrity" moments in the

Dementi household include the occasion of John Boles' visit, photographically illustrated here with my Mom and my brother, Brian, enjoying a moment with him. Mom enjoyed re-

Frank Dementi and movie star Eva Gabor, 1978.

calling fixing a breakfast for him, for which he was most complimentary! I think my Dad especially enjoyed the photo op with Eva Gabor! Look at the smile on his face!

These wonderful memories make the occasion of joining with my cousin Betty Dementi to compile this publication very special. Not only have we ventured to create a collection which serves to Celebrate Richmond Theater, we have rekindled personal memories, which validate the notion that Richmond Theater deserves to be celebrated. I am convinced that the distinction of Richmond as the entertainment capital of the upper South for 200 years is still intact, and will be significantly reinforced with the efforts currently underway to make Richmond a world class city for theater and the Performing Arts.

Richmond has always been a great city for the Theater, and today, we are enjoying our best display ever! And, just wait....over the next few

years we will experience Theater as few ever have before! The dream of our Performing Arts Complex to become a unifying force for all Richmonders, and the centerpiece for Historic Richmond, is worthy for all of us to embrace!

It is our hope that after you read this book, you will have a smile on your face, representing the same feeling we are having – a joyful spirit which justifiably announces that we all may join together to Celebrate Richmond Theater!

Wayne Dementi
President, Dementi Studio

Frank Dementi and movie star Martha Scott, 1940.

FOREWORD

Actress Polly Bergen joins Harvey Hudson on the Loew's Theater stage during a visit to Richmond, 1960's.

On stage at the Lyric Theater, 1955.

Theaters in the Richmond area have been so much a part of my life that I can hardly comprehend what they really have meant to me, so when I heard that a book was being written about them, I wanted to be a part of that project.

As I read the early proofs of *Celebrate Richmond Theater*, the memories of so many childhood delights returned. Luckily, my father and mother loved the movies. What a treat it was to walk the five blocks from our home in the northside to the Brookland Theater to see the early musicals and to be fascinated with the organ presentation there! (Yes, the Byrd and Loew's were not the only places that had great theater organs; the Brookland Theater had one and so did the Mosque.)

After the movies, we often went to the local drugstore. Sipping on limeades and cherry smashes, we talked about the movie feature and the added "short subjects"—cartoons, Laurel and Hardy, the Three Stooges, and newsreels, among others.

Who will ever forget the Saturday "kiddie" shows? Ten cents bought you a rip-roaring cowboy movie with stars like Buck Jones, Tom Mix, Ken Maynard (remember his white horse called Tarzan?), Hoot Gibson, and Bob Steel. Always before we left the theater, we were treated to another nail-biting episode of a cliffhanger serial. We had to come back every Saturday to discover how the hero escaped from sudden death! Wonderful stuff.

How I remember my father and mother taking me to see Al Jolson at The Capitol Theater on West Broad. "Talkies" had just arrived, and, when Al sang "Sonny boy," everybody cried—yes, even me. Later, as I grew older, my father would take me to see vaudeville shows at the National Theater – real professionals, a full orchestra, a stage full of singers, dancers, dog shows, magicians, and of course, comedians.

Because I loved show business so much, I applied for a job as an usher at the crown jewel of Richmond theaters, the Mosque. I got the job as usher for one of the middle aisles in the mezzanine. I didn't get any money (I even had to bring my own flashlight!), but I saw the shows, and the stars—from Paul Whiteman to the Ziegfeld Follies, and, of course, there were the big bands with singers like Nat Cole. During that same time, I was given a job (again with no pay, but I could use the same flashlight) at the famous old Lyric Theater at Ninth and Broad Streets. From its days as an entertainment center and regular vaudeville theater, the Lyric became the home for many fine shows like *Tobacco Road* and *Brother Rat* and performers like Cornelia Otis Skinner.

During my college days, there was a "hitch-a-ride" downtown every Thursday. To get a milkshake at Arnette's Ice Cream on Fifth Street or an Angelo's hot dog near Marshall and Fifth and to go on to the National Theater at Seventh and Broad for the new vaudeville show and a movie—that was living!

My radio career gave me the opportunity to interview the headliners on my morning show on WRVA (before Alden Aaroe). This led to special appearances on the stage and later full weeks' bookings. Several years ago, I had the privilege of going back to the National Theater where much work has been done to preserve that great institution. I walked back into the dressing room I had shared with several of the stars, walked fondly around the edge of the stage and in back of the curtains, and could still smell the greasepaint.

Although many people think of Loew's Theater's live performances by the beloved organist, Eddie Weaver, Loew's also hosted some superlative vaudeville shows from time to time with guest appearances by many stars. I was selected to introduce those stars and some of the shows at both the Loew's and the Byrd Theaters. The Byrd's stage was very small, yet we managed to do very well with it, and I fondly remember introducing at the two theaters Polly

Bergen, George Murphy (the dancer), Milton Berle, Denise Darcel, and Joseph Cotton, who was originally from nearby Petersburg.

In recalling the story of Richmond theater, this extraordinary book will bring back your childhood fascination with movies, with vaudeville, movie theaters, and movie stars of a bygone era. Join me for a marvelous journey along the "Passing Parade" of entertainment in Richmond.

Harvey Hudson
Richmond

Richmond native Harvey Hudson is eminently qualified to comment on the theater in his native city, having been a part of the radio, television, and theater scenes both here and across the country for many decades. The well-known morning personality was a fixture on WRVA in the 40's and WLEE in the 50's and 60's. The Junior Miss Pageant in Roanoke, the Miss Richmond Pageant and the Azalea Festival of North Carolina have all enjoyed his leadership as master of ceremonies for many years.

He continues to use his considerable talents as a sales and management consultant for several major Richmond corporations. A member of numerous civic clubs, Hudson has also received many awards including the Radio and TV Hall of Fame Award. He has also appeared in WCVE's "Memories of Richmond" series and currently can be heard on "Harvey Hudson's Passing Parade," a five hour program on WTVR radio. Hudson and his wife, the former Barbara Dement, reside in Richmond.

The Publisher

VIEW OF RICHMOND FROM MAYO'S ISLAND, *artist unknown, ca. 1822. From* Richmond Virginia in Old Prints.

PROLOGUE

Richmond Theater
1800–1900

Richmond has been the entertainment capital of the Upper South for more than 200 years, welcoming the great stars of stage, motion pictures, music and dance to its theaters. Through these performances we have been thrilled, inspired, comforted, amused, occasionally shocked, and distracted from our cares. Theaters have been the places where Richmonders have gathered as a community where we have laughed, cried and argued together. The story of Richmond's theaters, audiences and performances tells us about the city's aspirations, its blind spots, and its dreams for the future. It also illustrates Richmond's important role in the evolution and expansion of American popular culture.

From Richmond's earliest colonial beginnings in 1742, the village of 250 people entertained itself with chamber music, dramatic readings, charades and traveling players' performances; these were staged not in public amusement places but rather in private homes, meeting houses and in second-floor halls. Religious leaders (especially the Puritans farther north) forbade the theater as injurious to public morals, but Virginians were generally not as disapproving. Their scattered rural communities, however, could rarely support commercial amusements. When Richmond became the capital of the new Commonwealth of Virginia in 1780, the lively social whirl of Williamsburg moved westward to the city as it grew from 600 to 2,000 inhabitants. The Hallams and various other small troupes put on plays in school buildings, carriage houses or in any available space they could find. Theater historian Martin Staples Shockley found

that the first theatrical production that can be documented in Richmond was the play *Douglas*, staged in 1784 by Dennis Ryan's American Company of Comedians in a space called the "New Theatre."[1]

In 1800, Richmond was a bustling capital city 1.5 square miles in area, where 5,700 government officials, shopkeepers, blacksmiths, seamstresses, dockworkers, lawyers, clerks, laborers, free black artisans and slaves worked and lived in close proximity. When courts and the legislature were in session, the town's population swelled as hundreds of planters, farmers and their families came to town to conduct business, to shop and visit friends, and the atmosphere was ripe for theatrical entertainment. Both of Edgar Allan Poe's parents, Elizabeth Arnold Poe and David Poe, Jr., were actors at the Richmond Theater and other local performance spaces. Little is known of Poe's parents; his father may have died of yellow fever in Norfolk in the summer of 1811. Elizabeth died in early December 1811, just days before the great theater fire, leaving her two-year-old son an orphan. She is buried at St. John's Church.

Richmond's first theater building was erected in 1806 near what is now 13th and Broad Streets. It was first dubbed the New Theater (one in a series of buildings given that name, adding to historians' confusion), then was variously known as the "Brick Theater" or Richmond Theater. Nearly everyone in the small capital city attended the Richmond Theatre, rich and poor, black and white – it was the social center of the community. Like most theaters of the day, the Richmond had three levels

The BURNING of the THEATRE in RICHMOND, VIRGINIA, on the Night of the 26th December 1811,

By which awful Calamity upwards of ONE HUNDRED of its most valuable Citizens suddenly lost their lives, and many others were much injured

Published Feb 23th 1812 by B. Tanner N° 74 South 8th St. Philadelphia

THE BURNING OF THE THEATRE IN RICHMOND, *by B. Tanner, print, 1812. Valentine Museum.*

of seating – boxes for wealthy men and women, orchestra pit seats for the middle class and working class tradespeople, and the galleries for poor folks, drunkards, "loose women," free blacks and a few slaves. Seats ranged in price from a dollar to 75 cents to as little as 25 cents for the cheap bench seats in the gallery. The rowdy audiences clapped, cheered and booed, sang along with performers and stamped their feet demanding encores. The crowd was so raucous that manager William Maule issued rules and regulations for patrons' behavior at the Richmond Theatre that might surprise modern theatergoers who claim manners have deteriorated since "the good old days":

Gentlemen are most earnestly requested to dis-

continue wearing their hats in the first tier or dress circle. Persons in the Theatre will not be permitted to put their feet on the seats, over the backs of the benches or the front of the boxes. Smoking in any part of the Theater positively prohibited. Conversation in a loud tone will not be allowed in any part of the Theatre during the time of performance. Whooping, hallooing, whistling, or other disorderly noises, positively prohibited.[2]

The Great Theater Fire of 1811

On the night after Christmas, December 26, 1811, the Richmond Theatre was filled with more than 600

2

playgoers, the largest and most elite audience of the year, to see the most gala performance of the season. One attendee estimated that "every family in Richmond" was there, including that of Governor George W. Smith. The Richmond Theater was considered to be a modern, safe building. Its exterior was brick, but it had just had a new roof installed — shingles nailed to pine boards which were still wet with pine tar. There were only a few entrances to the building; winding, cramped and narrow stairs led to the balconies and to the upper and lower boxes, which merged at one small exit door. Dozens of painted hemp-cloth backdrops hung above the stage, and oil lamps served as stage lighting. *Richmond Times Dispatch* theater critic Edith Lindeman pronounced it, in retrospect, "the most treacherously constructed building ever designed for public entertainment."[3]

The play given that night was *The Father, or Family Feuds*, and the afterpiece was *Agnes and Raymond, or The Bleeding Nun*. When a stage manager brushed some painted scenery against one of the candle-lit chandeliers in the auditorium, the fabric caught on fire, and in less than ten minutes, flames engulfed the hall. Total chaos ensued — the women in elaborate gowns could not negotiate the treacherous stairways. Exits from the upper galleries and boxes were quickly blocked. Dr. James McCaw dropped 12 women and children out of an upper-story window into the arms of Gilbert Hunt, an African-American slave blacksmith, who had been sent to the theater when the fire alarms sounded to search for the daughter of his employers. Hunt gained nationwide fame for his heroism in saving the women, and also Dr. McCaw, as they tumbled from the fire-engulfed building.

Many more theatergoers could not be saved, however. In the tragedy, 72 people lost their lives, including Governor Smith (who had escaped, but ran back inside to rescue one of his children), 50 women in the box seats, and 20 African-Americans who had been seated in the top galleries.[4] Another tragic story involved young naval officer James Gibbons, who was engaged to Sallie Conyers, a South Carolinian in town visiting Mr. and Mrs. Joseph Gallego, owner of the local flour mill. James and Sallie quarreled on the night after Christmas (he was due to sail out the next day), so Sallie and Mrs. Gallego went out by themselves to join friends going to the Richmond Theater for the big show. When the fire alarms rang out, James raced to the theater and clambered inside the burning building to find his fiancée. The bodies of the lovers were discovered the next morning in the wreckage, their arms entwined around each other.[5]

Richmond was in shock after the fire, and the sensational news quickly traveled across the U.S. Distraught city leaders declared a four-month period of public mourning in which "no show, spectacle or dancing assembly" could be held. A growing evangelical fervor across the South contributed to a near abandonment of theater. In fact, there were virtually no shows performed in Richmond for eight years. The publicly funded Monumental Episcopal Church was built atop of the ashes of the theater to honor the fire's victims. John Marshall, then chief justice of the U.S. Supreme Court, headed the church's building committee. The church's designer, Robert Mills, was the first American-born professional architect; he is best known for his designs for the Washington Monument and the U.S. Treasury Building. The Monumental Church opened in 1814.[6]

Eventually, scars healed as the city grew, and Richmonders revived their fondness for theatrical entertainments. A building called "The Theater" was erected in 1818 on the southeast corner of 7th and Broad St (a theater would be at that location for nearly 80 years). Famed actor Junius Brutus Booth made his American debut in Richmond at The Theater on July 6, 1821, playing Richard III. (One story claims that during a return engagement here in 1824, the morning after appearing as Othello, the temperamental Booth attempted to murder the stage manager with a dagger.)[7] Booth would appear in Shakespearean plays with the Richmond Theater repertory company on occasion for 30 years. Theater-going was again an important part of the community's entertainment. A Richmond visitor attending the theater with James and Dolley Madison during the Virginia Constitutional Convention peered out from the box seats to see in the audience former president James Monroe and the entire Richmond Cavalry decked out in full uniform. In 1838, dingy and dilapidated from frequent use, The Theater was renovated and renamed the Marshall Theater, to honor the late Virginia jurist and fourth Chief Justice of the Supreme Court, who had been a theater aficionado.

After a long economic recession abated in 1845 (during which time there were only a few performances each season), Richmond's prosperity and size made it a major stop for any theatrical star on a national tour. By the 1850s, Richmond was the largest eastern city between Baltimore and Charleston, the 25th largest US city in population, and the 13th largest in manufacturing output. Richmond's population grew spectacularly in this decade, to 38,000, rising by one third as slaves hired out to work at city jobs joined immigrants from the northern states, and others from Ireland and Germany, as new residents. Two thirds of Richmond's population was white, and a third was African-American. It was a time of commercial and industrial expansion in the tobacco trade, flour milling, iron manufacturing, and coffee im-

MONUMENTAL CHURCH, *1313 E. Broad St., 1940s.*

porting.

Richmond's theaters were busy during this time of prosperity, and all the famous performers of the American stage "trod the boards" at the Marshall Theater, including Anna Cora Mowatt, Edwin Booth, William Charles Macready, John Howard Payne, Charlotte Cushman, young Dion Boucicault, even the scandalous Lola Montez, Irish-born dancer and former mistress of the King of Bavaria who toured the U.S. performing in plays based on her amorous escapades. In Richmond and other cities, Montez attracted large, all-male audiences curious to view first-hand her modest talent and huge notoriety. Edwin Forrest holds a record for longevity on the Richmond stage. Forrest made his first appearance in supporting roles at the Richmond Theater in 1824, had returning engagements in Shakespearean roles at the Marshall in 1840s and 1850s, and a final appearance at The Theater in 1870 (he would die in 1872 at age 66); his performances spanned 46 years. Junius Booth's son (and Edwin's younger brother), John Wilkes Booth, was

a member of the Marshall Theater stock company in 1858-59, and Booth hurriedly left from the Marshall to catch a train to view the hanging of John Brown in December 1859. Anna Cora Mowatt, who appeared in Richmond in January 1852, was an actress famous for being the first American woman of high social standing to perform on stage, and for writing the comic play *Fashion*, the first successful American social satire and best American play written before 1850. William Foushee Ritchie, mercurial publisher of the *Richmond Enquirer*, attended the performance and was entranced with Mowatt; he quickly courted and married the actress. Mowatt retired from the stage and lived in Richmond for several years, becoming a prominent figure in the city's social and cultural life, before she and Ritchie parted company in 1859.[8]

Dramas, tragedies, comedies, pantomimes, minstrel shows and opera were all popular with Richmond audiences. Often, elements of each were combined in the

MONUMENTAL CHURCH, *2001.*

same evening's performances. Odd Fellows Hall, at the corner of Franklin and Mayo Streets, another popular Richmond amusement hall, was open from 1842 to 1858. Thomas D. Rice, who created the "Jim Crow" minstrel show character, performed a "Negro Othello" there, and Swiss bell ringers, dancers, magicians, lecturers, General Tom Thumb, and acts like "The Singing Sisters in Bloomer Costume" also graced its stage.[9]

December 20, 1850 saw perhaps the most celebrated performance in the city's history. Famed vocalist Jenny Lind, "The Swedish Nightingale," appeared for one night as part of a nationwide concert tour organized by impresario P.T. Barnum. On the afternoon of the show, tickets were put up for auction, and the bidding reached such a feverous pitch that one gentleman paid $105 (worth $2,030 today) for a single ticket. At the concert the next evening, the house was packed, and promoters set up tiers of chairs on the stage behind the singer. One eager listener poked his head through a hole in the ceiling where a chandelier had hung. As Lind entered the Marshall Theater, hundreds of Richmonders outside joined the audience waiting inside in cheering for many minutes. Lind "glided into the intricate beauties of an Italian song with as much ease as a bird," a reviewer noted, and the audience was transfixed. Jenny Lind's performance netted more than $12,000 (worth a quarter of a million dollars today), which local boosters noted was the largest profit made in any city of comparable size on the entire tour.[10]

The Civil War Years

In the spring of 1861, Richmond was in turmoil. The aftermath of the bitter presidential election, the secession crisis, the firing on Fort Sumter, and start of the war spelled economic and social chaos. East Coast theatrical stars and dramatic companies became very reluctant to tour the South, and most players with Union sympathies went back north. Both the Marshall Theater,

FIREHOUSE BUILDING, *1609 W. Broad St., 1944.*

which was renovated and renamed the Richmond Theater in 1860, and the new Metropolitan Hall on East Franklin Street were shuttered for lack of business.

However, by the autumn of 1861, when Richmond was selected to become the capital of the Confederacy, the population tripled, skyrocketing to nearly 150,000. Thousands of Confederate officials and their families, military officers, hangers-on, refugees and spies jammed the town. The theaters reopened and several new ones blossomed in converted empty buildings, along with saloons and disorderly houses. The Richmond Theater mysteriously burnt down during the night on January 1, 1862; manager John Hill Hewitt suspected arson, but luckily, no one was injured in the blaze. Hewitt moved his theater to the closed Trinity Church (at 1417 E. Franklin St.) and renamed the building the Richmond Varieties. The burnt theater was quickly rebuilt at 7th and Broad St. and named the New Richmond Theater. Historian Ernest Furgurson writes, "The New Richmond was a gleaming four-story structure with promenade, dress circle and cast-iron scrollwork. Above its curtain was a heroic portrait of Robert E. Lee."[11] On the night of the New Richmond's opening in February 1863 (the play was Shakespeare's *As You Like It*) the full house glit-

tered with high society belles, officers, gamblers and speculators. It became known as the South's most lavish theater.

During the war, the Richmond Theater, Richmond Varieties, the Metropolitan, and the Richmond Lyceum were filled to capacity nearly every night. John Wilkes Booth continued to perform at the Richmond Theater, but few nationally known stars ventured to cross the blockades and battlegrounds to reach the South. The Richmond Theater and Richmond Varieties filled in by recruiting local performers through newspaper advertisements, and local actresses Sallie and Mary Partington became favorites (C.S.A. president Jefferson Davis was a big fan of the sisters).[12] Newspaper advertisements in May 1862 list the Varieties offering the "grand drama," *The Corsican Brothers,* featuring Mary Partington, followed by a "laughable farce." At the Lyceum was a play, *Black Eyed Susan,* with singing and dancing and concluding with the drawing of a lottery ticket. Metropolitan Hall mounted a show depicting "The Great Southern Victory at Hampton Roads" (which had occurred two months before). Its impressive-sounding "pantechnoptomon" special effects apparatus recreated the naval battle in miniature, using detailed models of the ships involved,

FIREHOUSE THEATER,
1609 W. Broad St., 2001. Creative Adaptation of a Richmond Landmark

INTERIOR OF FIREHOUSE THEATER, 2001. *Audience viewing production of* **Heads***, a play by Richmond author Philip Bly.*

HANOVER TAVERN, *Hanover Courthouse, 2001. The Barksdale Theater Company renovated and used this historic building for their productions and dinner theater from 1956 to 1995.*

with firecrackers and smoke representing cannon barrages; the tiny navies maneuvered about in front of large panoramic paintings which filled the stage. In an era before photographs were widely available, this show must have been quite a spectacular sight for its viewers, who paid 50 cents and 75 cents for reserved seats.

The Confederate Army requested that the theaters close for a week out of respect for those killed at the nearby battle of Seven Pines in June, 1862; it was one of the few times the entertainment ceased. Government officials actually encouraged the shows, in hopes that an entertainment outlet would keep the populace occupied and show the Yankees that Southerners were not panicking. Jeb Stuart swooped into city theaters on several occasions to scoop up errant cavalrymen and hustle them back to camp. While local ministers continued to fulminate about the low class people and war-shirkers who

dallied at the city's theaters, business continued to be brisk. By 1864, theater box seats sold for $35 (equivalent to nearly $500 today.) While some frivolity-seekers patronized such expensive amusements, other Richmonders were feeling pinched and held "cold water" or "starvation" parties instead. The price of food and clothing in Richmond continued to skyrocket due to wartime scarcity, and many working families faced starvation. Nevertheless, the Richmond Theater had taken in a million dollars in receipts by 1865. The beleaguered city's theaters were in operation right up until the evacuation of the city on April 2, 1865. Fortunately, the amusement halls escaped the fires that leveled most downtown buildings. Closed for one night, they opened again on April 4th, and extended special invitations to President Lincoln and the occupying Union Army officials to attend.[13]

BARKSDALE THEATER, *Willow Lawn Shopping Center, 1601 Willow Lawn Dr., 2001.*

RICHMOND THEATER, *701 E. Broad St., 1880s. Streetcar tracks were being dug along Broad St. in front of the theater. The new transportation system enabled residents to travel downtown more easily to conduct business, to go shopping and to see a show.*

Theater in Richmond 1870-1900

After the devastation of the war's end, Richmond rebuilt itself more quickly than most Southern cities, rebounding in the 1870s and 1880s. The city's population expanded from 51,000 in 1870, to 65,000 in 1880, to 83,000 in 1892. Few of the city's newcomers were European immigrants, however. Most were rural white and black Southerners seeking urban jobs. Richmond remained the South's second largest city (behind New Orleans) up until the turn of the century, and its cigarette manufacturing and commerce thrived, bringing prosper-

ity to enough people to resume a lively entertainment scene. Nationally known stage performers like Laura Keene, Charlotte Cushman, Mary Anderson, Edwin Booth (who returned in 1876 after a 17-year absence), Dion Boucicault (who played here in 1884, 28 years after his first appearance), Lily Langtry, Sarah Bernhardt, Helena Modjeska, Mme. Janauschek, Richard Mansfield and E.H. Sothern entertained Richmonders at the Richmond Theater with their traveling companies for half- or full-week stands.[14] Oscar Wilde gave a lecture on home decoration there on July 11, 1882, and more Rich-

INTERIOR OF RICHMOND THEATER, *1881. The Readjustor Convention political delegates enthusiastically nominated their candidate for Governor while meeting at the Richmond Theater. From Earl Lutz,* A Richmond Album *(1937).*

monders probably attended to gape at the flamboyant English playwright and novelist than to listen to him.[15]

Richmond Times Dispatch theater critic Bruce Chesterman recalled that in his youth during the 1870s, he saw shows at the Richmond Theater in the company of his play-loving mother. Small children were often in attendance. Chesterman's mother recalled a performance when a crying baby so disturbed the concentration of the great actress Mary Anderson that she stopped her lines and announced, "Now what can I do to quiet that child?" The embarrassed parent removed the small of-

fender, and the play continued. Chesterman remembered that the Richmond Theater had three gallery levels – dress circle, peanut gallery and above that, the "Buzzard's roost." The heights were ruled by tough young men called the "gallery gods," who talked and laughed boisterously throughout the performance, and were known to clang their "chestnut bells" and harass actors they thought were not giving the show their best effort.[16]

Although some of the city's prominent African-Americans were able to sit in the most desirable "dress circle" theater seats in the postwar period, because of increasing segregation, by the mid-1870s it was becoming more rare. Black Richmonders instead found entertainment instead through their churches and community groups.[17] A few shows, however, still gave opportunities for black and white Richmonders to be entertained together. On March 3 and 4, 1876, the Hampton Colored Students, a band of 13 former slaves who were students at the Normal College at Hampton, Virginia presented three concerts of spirituals at the Richmond Theater.

Joseph Jefferson, the most beloved actor of the late 19th century, gained valuable theatrical experience in Richmond before the war, when he held a position as actor and stage manager at the Marshall Theater for two seasons. Once he doubled as the character of "Lanky Lugg" in the Richmond premiere of a comedy called *Delight, or the Old Dominion in 1765*. Leaving for the bright lights of New York City in 1857, Jefferson soon created his famous role of "Rip Van Winkle." Jefferson returned to Richmond to perform the play in 1860, and after the war, Jefferson came through town with "Rip Van Winkle" annually until 1901, nearly equaling Edwin Forrest's record with 45 years of Richmond performances. Edith Lindeman writes that Jefferson "never forgot Richmond because it was here that a young reporter barged in upon him when he was bathing and the old man, clad only in soapsuds and a large smile, granted the interview."[18]

Increasingly, plays became more "serious" and the comic and bawdy portions of early 19th century theatrical entertainment shifted to the variety houses, where burlesque and vaudeville developed. The Theater Comique (formerly the Metropolitan Theater) was located at the heart of Richmond's hotel and boarding house district southeast of Capitol Square, on Franklin Street between Governor and Fourteenth streets. Although this early advertisement from 1870 stressed the Theatre Comique's appeal to genteel audiences, its fare was largely for male pleasure-seekers:

> Metropolitan/Theatre Comique Now Open for the Season. Houses Packed. Ladies Delighted. Ladies' Night every Friday. A Success. The House Crowded Last Night with a large and respectable Lady Audience. The Company pronounced to be the best ever in this city. A tremendous Saturday Night Bill. Miss Eloise Clyde, by special request, will sing "Wearing of the Gray." Miss Belle Graham in new songs and dances. Johnny Brasset in new Negro acts, songs and dances. The performance to conclude with the great moral drama of Jack Sheppard, introducing a thrilling and starting hanging scene, a warning to all – an example to none.

The Theater Comique, with its barroom in the basement, was known as Richmond's home of burlesque, dancing girls, liquor, and baggy-pants comics. Mary Wingfield Scott spoke for refined Richmond when she termed it "a rather questionable variety house." It was demolished in 1882. In 1873, New York-born ship builder and bar-owner W. W. Putnam opened the Lyric Theater burlesque house on the second floor of 923 E. Broad Street. In 1879 he moved into 1311 Franklin (across from the Comique) and renamed it Putnam's Theater, adding an orchestra and actors to the troupe of comely young women who danced, sang and solicited business for the bar Putnam operated a few doors down the street. Putnam's Theater became the centerpiece of the neighborhood southwest of the capital, which also became filled with tough bars and gambling joints. By 1900, however, the area had become the city's red-light district, and Putnam's had not aged well. In 1905, Putnam died, and while his wife and son attempted to carry on, the city shut the theater down as a hazard and nuisance in 1908.[19]

Family-oriented vaudeville shows were gaining in popularity. By the mid-1880s there were a half dozen small variety houses in Richmond, including the Pavilion Theater on Broad between First and Foushee streets, the Broad Street Opera House, Thompson's Musee Theater at 909 E. Broad Street, the Casino Theater next to City Hall, and Barton's Grand Opera House at Broad and 8th streets. These small theaters offered everything from minstrel shows, concerts, ventriloquists, animal acts and contortionists, to chorus girls on swings. They were clustered on Broad Street, which was becoming the new commercial hub of the city, attracting both female shoppers and businessmen. Advertisements in 1889 for the Broad Street Opera House announced: "Strict order maintained, and no improper characters admitted," which might suggest that the lack of restraint among the rowdy patrons caused the strict order to be imposed. On the other hand, this variety house wished to become more respectable in order to expand its appeal to audiences who desired gentility – middle class women and families.[20]

At the same time, the city's elite, following the lead of the urban upper class across the nation, became more protective of who controlled "refined" entertainment. In 1876, a group of Richmonders formed the Mozart Association to promote classical music through public concerts as well as private functions. They raised funds in the mid-1880s to build an elegant opera house for the city to replace their dowdy old Mozart Hall, which had been home to Dime Museum vaudeville shows as well as their weekly musicales. The new Mozart Academy of

Music opened in January 1886, on 8th Street between Franklin and Grace streets.[21] What was soon known as the Academy of Music Theater would become Richmond's largest and most prestigious theater for the next 40 years.

It was the end of one theatrical era, and the beginning of another. When the aging Richmond Theater closed in 1892, a saddened newspaper reporter mourned the old hall as "one of the most popular places of amusement in the South," and lamented the loss of "the merry song and dance of the opera-bouffe artist or the witticisms of the comedian" that would be heard there no longer.[22] When the Richmond Theater was razed in 1896, local theatergoers were so fond of the old building that they took home bits of the rubble as mementos. Still, a remnant of the theater remained, for the back wall of the building and original foundations were incorporated into Greentree's menswear store. The Greentree family found ancient playbills hidden in basement crevices, and amassed an extensive collection, which they donated to the Valentine Museum.

RICHMOND SKYLINE, *ca. 1910.*

CHAPTER 1

Theater, Vaudeville and Nickelodeons
1900–1920

In 1900, Richmond was a city of 85,000 inhabitants with a metropolitan population of 160,000. Washington D.C. and Baltimore to the north had grown to twice Richmond's size, and other southern cities like Nashville and Atlanta were beginning to surpass Richmond in population and manufacturing output. Nevertheless, the upper South looked to Richmond as its political, economic and cultural center. State and local government buildings, banks, shops, cigarette factories, tobacco warehouses and office buildings filled the downtown, and Richmond's sidewalks were thronged with workers, shoppers, visitors and amusement seekers. The social class, gender and racial divisions of Richmond (which in 1900 was 70 percent white and 30 percent black) were evident in Broad Street's shopping district. The south side of the street was home to the department stores, fine shops, jewelers and restaurants that drew in the middle class and elite white women, who were otherwise not welcome in the hustling male world of business. The city's largest dry goods merchants, Miller & Rhoads and Thalhimers, were evolving into elegant department stores to attract wealthy and middle class female shoppers. The Marshall, Richmond, and Academy Theaters were located on or near the south side of Broad. The north side of the street, however, was home to saloons and barbershops, which were still places patronized exclusively by men. Shops serving the African-American community in Jackson Ward were also on that side.[1] The opening on Broad Street's north side of increasingly elaborate theaters, which sought to attract the white middle class family trade, plus the traditional male amuse-ment seekers and black families, represented a new bridging of Broad Street's social divide. These new theaters intermingled the previously separated spheres of male and female, rich and poor, black and white.

Richmond's major theater in 1900, the Academy of Music, would be augmented by new showplaces along the new Theater Row on Broad Street. The city's trolley lines (opened in 1880) not only brought more people downtown to seek entertainment, but also spurred the development of summer amusement parks in the outlying suburbs that offered vaudeville shows on outdoor stages. In addition to these amusement places, there were more than 60 meeting halls on the second or third floors of buildings around the city, which hosted concerts, amateur productions and lodge meetings. Soon to come were more than a dozen nickelodeon movie theaters. Between 1900 and 1920, Richmond would witness an explosion of entertainment choices and venues, a bounty that would significantly alter the theater-going practices of the city's residents.

The Academy of Music's Heyday

Edith Lindeman recalled, "From the turn of the century until sound movies presaged the decline and fall of touring companies, Richmond was considered one of the best theater towns of the East. Some plays even staged pre-Broadway engagements here, as when a young and glowing Ethel Barrymore opened in *Captain Jinks of the Horse Marines* (1902), which was to become her earliest rousing success." The 1,600 seat Academy of Music Theater was Richmond's premiere showplace, home to half-

ACADEMY OF MUSIC THEATER, *100 N. Ninth Street, 1926. Richmond's most prestigious playhouse from the 1880s through the 1920s.*

week and one-night engagements by famous theatrical stars, to touring productions of great and mediocre plays, and to stock companies in residence for several months each year. Lindeman described the Academy as "a rococo gem of a place...[which] boasted plush seats, boxes with painted walls and velvet draperies. Above the auditorium was a gently sloping balcony. Above that was the 'peanut gallery' of almost perpendicular tiers where the seats were not reserved and the thrifty stood outside a separate entrance to 'go rush' up the iron steps when

the door opened."[2]

The outstanding performers of the day played at the Academy, including James O'Neill (Eugene's father), "Diamond Lil" (Lillian Russell), Mrs. Leslie Carter, William S. Hart, Ada Rehan, Jeanne Eagels, George Arliss, Alla Nazimova, William H. Crane, Frederick Warde, Anna Held, Richard Mansfield, Julia Marlowe, stars of the ballet Anna Pavlova and Nijinsky, Laurette Taylor, Otis Skinner, a 17-year-old Douglas Fairbanks, Sr., in one of his first roles, dancer Loie Fuller, George M. Cohan, the great Polish conductor Ignace Jan Paderewski, John Drew, and Billie Burke.

Sarah Bernhardt appeared at the Academy in 1891 as "Camille." She returned to Richmond in 1911 to reprise the role and performed here again on January 1, 1917, during her final farewell national tour. The "Divine Sarah" arrived like visiting royalty in a special five-car train with an entourage of 43 cast members, four servants, a St. Bernard, a mastiff, a parrot and 140 trunks. In her final Richmond performance, the 74-year old actress recreated death scenes from three plays while reclining on a platform, because the loss of her leg due to diabetes had made it impossible for her to move about the stage. Although Bernhardt spoke her lines in French, she nevertheless succeeded in "reducing [Academy] audiences to successive rains of tears." The career of Lily Langtry (if not royal, at least the former favorite of Britain's King Edward VI) also took a memorable turn in Richmond. Returning to town 22 years after her initial appearance here in *She Stoops to Conquer*, Langtry appeared at the Academy in November 1915 in a new play called *Mrs. Thompson*, in previews on its way to Broadway. Unfortunately, the play flopped here so badly that she abandoned the cast and show on the spot.

Famous sports celebrities appeared on stage in Richmond, although responses to their acting were decidedly mixed. Former heavyweight champion "Gentleman Jim" Corbett performed in a minstrel show that featured him fighting a round or two. John L. Sullivan, the last bare-fisted fighting champion, played a boxer on stage at the Academy in the play *Honest Hearts and Willing Hands*, but his off-stage dust-up with a waiter in the restaurant at Murphy's Hotel, in which he was subdued by a heaved coffee pot, was more memorable. Baseball star Ty Cobb appeared at the Academy in 1911 as a varsity football player in a comedy called *The College Widow*, but his acting efforts struck out with the critics.

Well-known theatrical stars were the drawing card for audiences in the early 1900s, and the Academy's managers booked their touring companies as often as possible. Watson James, Jr. recalled his joy, as a small boy, in viewing these stars from the lofty vantage point of the peanut roost at the Academy Theater. James especially remembered actress Maude Adams, who was called "the most beloved actress of her generation in one *News Leader* appreciation.[3] Watson described the unforgettable moment in Adams' *Peter Pan* (which she performed at the Academy from 1907 to 1916) when Adams stepped over the footlights, announced that Tinkerbell was dying, and pleaded that if anyone in the audience believed in fairies they could save Tinkerbell's life by applauding. The audience arose *en masse* in response, Watson wrote: "What

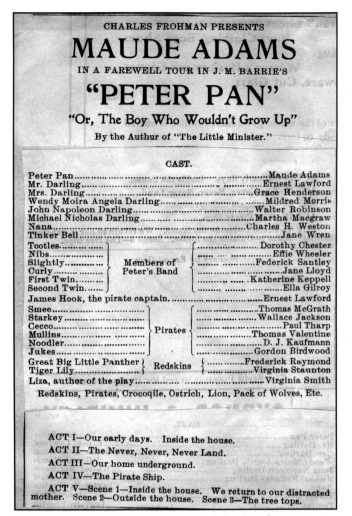

PLAYBILL, *PETER PAN starring Maude Adams, Academy of Music, 1909.*

a thunderous answer followed, waving handkerchiefs that were later used to wipe unashamed tears from the eyes of those who still remembered the magic of fairyland from their long-ago childhood years."[4]

The other regular fare at the Academy Theater was touring company productions of melodramas, the ever-popular "war horses" of the 19th century American stage. The Academy hosted everything from tear-jerkers like *The Two Orphans, Mazzepa, East Lynne* and *Way Down East*, to local favorites like *The Secret Service*, which was set in Civil War-era Richmond, to musical comedies like *The Black Crook* that relied on a bevy of blonde chorus girls in pink tights to draw interest. When *The Black Crook* first debuted in Richmond in 1867, middle-class and wealthy women were so shocked at what they had heard went on in the theater that they crossed the street rather than walk under the theater's marquee. By the play's umpteenth performance in Richmond in 1907, strict stan-

MME. SARAH BERNHARDT

AND HER OWN COMPANY

From the Theatre Sarah Bernhardt, Paris,

Under the direction of WM. E. CONNOR.

La Dame Aux Camelias

Piece en 5 Acts, by Alexandre Dumas, Fils.

MARGUERITE GAUTIER,
                    MME. SARAH BERNHARDT

George Duval	M. Maxudian
Gaston	M. Denenbourg
Armand Duval	M. Tellengen
Gustave	M. Barry
St. Gaudens	M. Favieres
Le Docteur	M. Canroy
Varville	M. Coutier
De Giray	M. Dorval
Arthur	M. Dieck
Un Domestique	M. Pierrat
Nanine	Mme. Seylor
Prudence	Mme. Boulanger
Nichette	Mme. Duc
Olympe	Mme. Desroches
Un Groom	Mme. Thomas
Anais	Mme. Ringel
Une Dame	Mme. H. Romain
Adele	Mme. Lauren
Le Commissionnaire	M. Ruber

PLAYBILL, *CAMILLE* starring Sarah Bernhardt, *Academy of Music, 1911. The famous French tragedienne appeared in Richmond at least three times in this role.*

dards of propriety had loosened a bit, and *The Black Crook* was seen as quaint.[5]

Uncle Tom's Cabin, beloved by Northern audiences from the late 1850s through the 1910s, was an adaptable show in which the melodrama of Eliza's escape from overseer Simon Legree could be varied with the comic turns of Topsy, the Victorian sentimentality of Little Eva's death and spirituals and minstrel songs sung by Uncle Tom. For decades, Southerners shunned the show for its abolitionist themes, so performers who unexpectedly found themselves booked below the Mason-Dixon line dared enact only the comic or musical scenes of their "Tom shows." In 1898 one troupe bringing *Uncle Tom's Cabin* to the Richmond Theater advertised that it per-

formed a special version adapted to Southern tastes.[6]

Touring melodramas vied with each other to incorporate ever-more elaborate stage effects into their shows (rainstorms, snow, ice floes and real fire engines drawn by horses), for audiences at the turn of the twentieth century loved spectacles and realistic reproduction of events on stage. One theatrical producer engaged the Richmond Fire Department to fill a huge tank of water on stage for a play, *After Dark,* in which an actor made a dramatic dive at a pivotal moment. Three days later, the firemen were called in to pump it back out. The most popular touring show to play Richmond was the stage production of *Ben Hur,* which enthusiastically sold out the Academy from 1905 to 1917. At $2 per ticket, it was also a champion moneymaker. Annually, the backstage crews struggled to install the treadmill necessary to recreate the show's climactic chariot race, with its crashing vehicles and real horses on stage.[7]

Jake Wells, Richmond's Vaudeville Impresario

Jake Wells, a professional baseball player turned theater executive, changed the face of entertainment in Richmond. He built most of the showplaces that lined Broad Street's Theater Row. He brought the new family-oriented vaudeville to the city, and sponsored repertory stage companies, outdoor theaters at summer parks, and early movie shows. Between 1899 and the mid-1920s he and his partners Wilmer and Vincent controlled nearly every major legitimate theater, vaudeville show and large movie house in Richmond. Using Richmond and Norfolk as his bases, Wells established a theatrical circuit that encompassed 42 theaters in nine states, one of the largest chains in the South. He shaped the entertainment scene in Richmond for 25 years, and paved the way for the picture palace era.[8]

Born in Memphis, Tennessee in 1869, Jake Wells was a talented baseball player, described as tall, handsome, gentlemanly and a great hit with the local fans. He led the Richmond Virginians to winning seasons from 1894 to 1898 as catcher, then as first baseman and manager. Traveling with the team throughout the Eastern states, Wells had seen the American entertainment scene changing. Vaudeville was quickly growing to be the most popular entertainment in the Northeast, yet it had not made inroads into the South beyond Washington, D.C. A typical vaudeville show consisted of between eight and 12 acts, including a mixture of comics, singers, performing dogs, contortionists, dancers, magicians, famous people and novelty stunts – anything that could hold an audience's attention for five to ten minutes. There was something for everyone to enjoy in a vaudeville show. The performers played between three and five shows

BIJOU THEATER, *810 E. Broad St., 1929. Jake Wells started his theatrical empire, and Richmond's Theater Row here. He built Richmond's first family vaudeville theater, the Bijou, in 1902.*

per day ("2-a-day" was the most prestigious circuit for performers) for a week or half-week stand in one city, then they traveled an organized "circuit" route to theaters in other cities. Theatrical impresarios in New York City such as B. F. Keith had created booking firms in order to organize the movements of hundreds of vaudeville acts; in doing so, they were consolidating theater circuits into powerful and profitable national organizations. Yet the big circuits largely overlooked the South. The population of the South was still overwhelmingly rural, agricultural and cash-poor. Traveling distances between Southern cities were long, and circuit managers decided that the small profits could not cover the expense of transporting performers and scenery between bookings. Jake Wells took in this situation during his baseball travels and saw an opportunity to form his own circuit in Southern towns.

Jake Wells' start in the theater business came in the fall of 1898 when, at the end of the baseball season, he entered Spence's Trunk Shop in the 800 block of Broad Street to purchase a trunk strap to hold his bats together. He noticed that the old building had a sloping floor and

RICHMOND'S POPULAR PLACE OF AMUSEMENT,

❖ BIJOU FAMILY THEATRE ❖

JAKE WELLS, - Directeur.

Devoted to Polite Vaudeville; the essence of refined entertainment, and Musical Comedy Productions of the highest class. Seats may be secured at **Box Office from 9 A. M. to 10 P. M.,** or can be ordered by Mail or Telephone, and held until called for.

ADVERTISEMENT, *ca. 1905. Jake Wells stressed that the new style of vaudeville program offered at the Bijou Family Theater was suitable for women and children.*

a raised stage. Inquiring, he was told that the building was the old Barton Opera House, a failed variety hall, which at one time had also been a depot for the Richmond, Fredericksburg & Potomac Railroad, and Ford's Opera House. Wells saw potential for the building to become a good place to start a popularly priced vaudeville show. He leased the building and opened the (original) Bijou Theater on January 9, 1899. Prominent performers including magician Harry Houdini headlined shows at the Bijou in its first several seasons.

Wells put on "polite" or family vaudeville in Richmond, which featured variety acts that had none of the Putnam's Theater fare of bawdiness, off-color humor, and sexual suggestiveness. There was nothing in the show that would be objectionable to audience members. In the theaters of the nation's larger cities, vaudeville kingpin B.F. Keith had transformed variety into polite vaudeville by setting strict guidelines for the performers' dialogue and behavior, and also by providing audiences with clean, well-lighted, modern theaters staffed with corps of ushers to shush and remove rowdy patrons; no alcohol was served, and no chorus girls buttonholed male audience members to buy them drinks. Keith created an atmosphere attractive to middle class families and especially to women, who often made the entertainment choices for the family. Keith helped turn vaudeville (and by extension much of public entertainment) from being primarily a part of the "male sphere" of saloon-type bawdiness and conviviality into an entertainment that was "safe," morally unobjectionable, and affordable for a much larger family audience.

Wells often told colleagues that the vaudeville theater "should be many times cleaner than a home" to attract attendance. He censored the content of his shows and enforced his rules stringently. Wells' regional theatrical empire spread as he purchased the Granby Street Theater in Norfolk. Moving his base of operations down to Norfolk, he planned and built the beautiful Wells Theater there. His half-brother Otto Wells assumed control of day-to-day operations. Wells quickly assembled a circuit of theaters from Richmond to Norfolk to Atlanta (where at one point he controlled every theater but one in the city) to New Orleans to showcase his vaudeville acts. He became widely known as "the father of vaudeville in the Southeast."[9]

Jake Wells further emulated Keith by building a large, elegant theater in Richmond (which would be attractive to the middle class) in which to showcase his vaudeville acts. In 1905, the Bijou moved to a brand new theater building, located at 816-818 Broad Street, previously the site of the old Swan Tavern. The new Bijou featured repertory plays from the Bijou Musical Comedy Company and vaudeville bills in the off-season. Advertisements claimed that the Bijou offered "Always a Good Show – Sometimes a Great Show."[10] The old Bijou, renovated, became the (original) Colonial Theater, and 3-a-day family vaudeville was performed there. Soon, novelties such as motion pictures were added to the Colonial's program. His Richmond theatrical empire continued to spread as Wells took over management and theatrical booking of the Academy Theater in 1906. He acquired the booking management of the Lyric and installed "family vaudeville" shows there, while the original Colonial became a movie theater.

WEST END ELECTRIC PARK, *the Beverly St. (Idlewood) at Byrd Park, ca. 1905. A trolley waits in front of Idlewood Pavilion. This summer park featured vaudeville and early movies along with rides and carnival attractions.*

In addition to acquiring nearly all the theaters in Richmond and organizing vaudeville and musical comedy company circuits across the South, Wells also became interested in a new extension of the city's public amusement scene, open-air theaters at the new electric trolley parks, which power companies were building at the end of their lines to provide a pleasurable destination for city riders. Traditionally, regular theaters had closed during the hot summer months, for audiences found sitting in a closed, dark hall in July or August surrounded by hundreds of sweating theatergoers to be unpleasant and unhealthy. Managers continually hatched schemes to make their theaters cooler and more comfortable in hot weather. The Academy of Music promoted

the availability in the summer of their "water boys", who passed a tin rack holding six or eight glasses of ice water along the rows to keep patrons cooler.[11]

Richmond was the first city in the nation to put electric-powered trolleys into operation in 1880, replacing horse-drawn conveyances. The electric companies wanted to create a destination to draw patrons to ride out to the end of the line, so they built summer parks on suburban land at the edge of town. To lure patrons, they located near reservoirs or lakes, and they built picnic grounds. To make use of all the voltage they generated, they built amusement parks featuring electricity – the parks' towers, walkways, buildings and pavilions were studded with hundreds of light bulbs. A mass of electric lights was a

THEATER ROW, *800 block of E. Broad St., ca. 1914. A portion of the original Colonial Theater can be seen on the left. The Lubin Theater, a nickelodeon with vaudeville acts that featured an outlandish façade but a plain interior, and the Bijou vaudeville theater are on the right.*

novelty to most Americans; the bright lights brought out crowds like moths to the flame. Merry-go-rounds, rides, roller coasters, games of chance, novelty demonstrations, skating rinks and dancing pavilions all were popular attractions. The park owners, capitalizing on the popularity of theatrical entertainment and the closing of many downtown theaters in the summer heat, built open-air stages and offered a few vaudeville acts for free to lure in more patrons. Sometimes tickets to view the full show cost park visitors extra, or reserved seats were charged for, while standing was free.

By 1903, summer variety shows were being performed at the Broad Street Park, New Reservoir Park (which would become Byrd Park), Forest Hill Park, Westhampton Park, Main Street Park, and the Casino, the last a large and popular open-air theater south of

Cary on Beverly Street, which Jake Wells purchased. The Casino was open from 1903 until 1911. In 1905, the New Reservoir Park was revamped into Idlewood Park, another popular summer theater and amusement center. Wells purchased Idlewood in 1906. These open-air theaters expanded the amount of vaudeville being offered in Richmond, and they were also the sites of some of the city's first exhibitions of motion pictures. The electric parks, alas, had a short life span, and most were closed by 1912. The rising costs of operation, public fears of the spread of contagious diseases such as tuberculosis and polio, fierce competition from the legions of new nickelodeon theaters springing up on Broad and Hull streets, and the pressure from real estate developers to convert the land into new suburban neighborhoods spelled an end to these early amusement parks. [12]

The First Movies

In April 1896, the latest of Thomas Edison's many inventions, the Kinetoscope or motion picture projector, had its public debut at Koster and Bials' Music Hall, a New York City vaudeville theater. The machine projected light through photographs on a strip of film onto a screen to produce images with lifelike movement. The earliest "moving pictures" were 30-60 second-long scenes of waves crashing on the shore, trains steaming into stations, coronations and presidential inaugurations, and panoramas of far-away places. Audiences were fascinated with the "illusion of life" that these movies produced, and show business entrepreneurs immediately acquired projectors and films and brought these entertaining novelties to audiences across the nation. Each picture machine even had a different name, as the first film exhibitors attempted to make their programs unique.

Exactly when motion pictures were first exhibited in Richmond is a matter of some debate. Edith Lindeman placed the first motion pictures in Richmond as being "presented in 1898 at an open-air theater at Main and Vine Streets. These were quick newsreel shots of the Spanish-American War and were used to supplement a vaudeville program."[13] On January 7and 8, 1898, the Variscope film projector was featured at the Academy Theater, with an exhibition of all fourteen rounds of the recent Corbett-Fitzsimmons prizefight.

Harry Tucker recalled that his first experience seeing a motion picture "was in one of the big rooms in the Imperial Hotel at Governor and Franklin streets along about Spanish War times. A couple of good fellows showed up there with a little vest-pocket movie [projector] and one of Edison's phonographs. They gave nice little shows around among the fraternal groups and the Bible classes, and at night they'd gather with congenial spirits of the 'Horseshoe Club' in the bit room at the Imperial and show pictures on the wall."[14]

But perhaps the very earliest exhibitions of motion pictures took place at Richmond's most elite theater. Promoters of the Cineograph, which was exhibited at the Academy of Music May 1-3, 1897 at matinee and evening performances, billed their machine as "indisputably the greatest of all moving photographic inventions. Its views are larger, steadier, more graphic, and more interesting than those shown by similar inventions. The pictures shown by this machine are all new and entirely different from those shown on other machines, and include views of the inauguration of President McKinley, the inauguration parade, and an endless variety of beautiful and interesting views." The Vitascope machine (similar to the one that had been exhibited at Koster and Bial's Theater in New York) had performed at the Academy The-

ater two months previously, on March 2 and 3, 1897. Until other evidence surfaces, this Vitascope performance might perhaps be deemed the first movie show in Richmond.[15]

After their appearance at Richmond's best theater, motion pictures were soon on the bill at all the outdoor summer vaudeville theaters. Herbert Gibbs (who would work as projectionist for the Virginia Board of Film Censors for more than 30 years) got his start in the movie business by projecting early movies outdoors at Forest Hill Park. He recalled, "The movies were shown on a large wooden screen set up in the open...the power company sponsored free starlight movies so that Richmonders would ride out on the street cars to see them."[16] The Lumiere Company's Cinematograph projector was seen at the Broad Street Park Auditorium on October 9, 1898, in a show calculated to appeal to genteel Richmonders' interests. Reverend H.M. Wharton provided lecture and commentary while films of *The Passion Play* were shown on the screen. The Great American Vitagraph Company brought its motion pictures to the Bijou Theater on October 15, 1899; the patriotic, newsreel-like films showed the huge parades honoring Admiral Dewey that had recently been held in Washington, D.C. and New York City.[17]

Film producer Siegmund Lubin's films were shown at the Casino Theater on September 11, 1900. George Melies' magic films, brief comic chases, and Edwin Porter's early classics *Life of an American Fireman* (1902) and *The Great Train Robbery,* the biggest hit of 1903, were also popular. Richmonder Charles Hughes cherishes a story passed down through three generations, that when his grandmother (then a girl) and several companions attended a showing of *The Great Train Robbery,* they ran out of the theater in alarm because they thought the speeding train was going to leap off the screen and hit them. These brief films were also a staple of vaudeville shows as the final act on the bill; while some vaudevillians derisively called the films "chasers" (an act so bad that it would chase viewers from the theater, opening seats for the next audience to fill), movies continued to grow in popularity. Newspaper advertisements announced that movies would be shown outdoors every night at Idlewood, Forest Hill, and Main Street parks. Movies were a part of vaudeville bills at the Bijou and original Colonial off and on throughout the decade, by which time, in an ironic turnabout, vaudeville acts would become supplements to feature-length films.

In 1905, straight from its success at the St. Louis World's Fair, Hale's Tours came to Richmond, exhibiting movies in a "wagon car," or portable building made to resemble a railroad car, parked at the corner of Broad

FORMER SITE OF DIXIE THEATER, *8. W. Broad St, 1920s. Amanda Thorpe opened Richmond's first nickelodeon theater, The Dixie, in 1907 in a converted retail shop. Although by the 1920s, the former theater housed a grocery, its lasting impact on the neighborhood is seen in the Dixie Lunch, located two doors to the east.*

Street and 9th, next to the Bijou Theater. The interior was decorated like a passenger train car, and the structure was equipped with rollers to rock it back and forth. *Times Dispatch* readers recalled that when the pictures (travel films seen from the perspective of a train passenger) started playing, it felt as if one was riding on a train. The novelty theater, which operated for between six to nine months in Richmond, seated 30 or 40 patrons at a time. All this movie interest seemed to indicate that there was a market here for a new kind of theater devoted mainly to motion pictures. These first movie theaters were called "nickelodeons," a combination of the Greek word for theater, "Odeon," and the price of admission. Nickelodeons or "five cent theaters" were cropping up in converted shop buildings in cities and towns across the nation. [18]

Amanda Thorpe –Nickelodeon Pioneer

Richmond's first nickelodeon owner, and the city's first movie theater impresario, was Amanda Thorpe, a 45-year old widow from Norwalk, Ohio. For a woman to succeed in the world of business, when "respectable" women found few opportunities for working outside the home or practicing a profession, makes her achievements even more remarkable. How she ended up in Richmond running a nickelodeon, however, is not exactly clear, for information about her is scarce. The explanation that Thorpe herself liked to circulate was that she was traveling through Richmond in 1907 on her way home to Ohio from attending the Jamestown Exhibition, when she chanced to meet Jake Wells. She told him she was impressed with the city of Richmond, but she noted that she had not found a nickelodeon in town, and Wells ei-

RICHMOND BOYS' CHOIR OFFICES, *8. W. Broad St., 2001. The 100-year-old storefront building that once housed the Dixie Theater has been renovated and still serves the community today.*

ther bankrolled her first movie theater venture, or gave her advice and encouragement. Another version of the story, probably more accurate, says that Thorpe and her son Waldo had operated nickelodeons in Norwalk and Bucyrus, Ohio, and then one in Norfolk, which failed, before trying again in Richmond. A man named Jacobson had been exhibiting movies outdoors in an empty lot next door to the old Colonial Theater in 1906 and 1907. Amanda Thorpe purchased the rights to his show for $250 and opened the Dixie Theater, Richmond's first amusement hall dedicated to showing motion pictures, at 300 E. Broad Street, in December 1907. [19]

Thorpe's associate in this nickelodeon venture (and business partner for the next 15 years) was Walter J. Coulter, a 20-year old from Norwalk, Ohio, who had worked in Thorpe's Ohio theaters. Their Dixie Theater was an immediate success, perhaps too successful. It was jammed with patrons, and this drew the attention of the

Richmond city building inspectors. A March, 1908 *Times Dispatch* article, "Cheap Theaters Must Be Safer; Broad Street Moving Picture Establishments Required to Make Certain Improvements," reported, "It was learned last night that as a result of the theater inspection, the proprietor of the Dixie Moving Picture Show on Broad Street, near the old Bijou, has been directed within a certain time to seek other quarters as the board was of the opinion that that place should be closed. It was explained that there is no way by which the audience could leave in the event of a fire near the main entrance."[20] Thorpe relocated the Dixie Theater to a larger and safer space at 18 West Broad Street, and it continued to do excellent business, attracting many rival nickelodeons to open along the same street.

Despite the earlier adverse publicity the Dixie Theater had garnered, the *Times Dispatch* lauded Amanda Thorpe in November 1908 when she and Coulter opened

LUBIN AND BIJOU THEATERS, *800 Block E. Broad St., 1912. The Lubin's large and fanciful illuminated sign, and painted tinwork studded with incandescent light bulbs, drew in crowds of amusement seekers. Penny postcards touted Theater Row as one of the city's premiere attractions. Collection of Kathy Fuller-Seely.*

the spacious Rex Theater at Broad and 9th Streets. Thorpe and Coulter also marketed movies to the African-American community, transforming the Dixie into a nickelodeon for black patrons in 1912 and building the Hippodrome Theater on Second Street in Jackson Ward in 1914. Walter Coulter brought his younger brother Robert Coulter east from Ohio to work at the Dixie Theater. Robert had been working in nickelodeons since he was fourteen; his first job was to sit behind the screen and produce sound effects for the silent films by shooting off cap pistols and playing phonograph records. In 1917, Robert Coulter began a Richmond movie theater career that would last 65 years. [21]

The early nickelodeon theaters cropping up in Richmond and across the nation in 1907 were small store buildings converted into simple theaters. They did not cost much to equip, and the nickels poured into the owners' pockets by the thousand. Patrons sat on kitchen chairs placed on a level floor in a dark, sparsely decorated hall. At one end of the room was a metal projection booth, and at the other was a screen mounted on the wall, and

a piano to provide music. The motion pictures they exhibited had evolved from being 60 seconds in length to one reel long (lasting approximately 10-12 minutes). Five or six films were often exhibited in one program. Automatic player pianos (also called "nickelodeons" for patrons could insert a coin in the slot to hear music) were used by many of these little theaters to accompany the silent films and attract the curious in from the street. Some theaters had a tiny "orchestra pit" with room for a violin, piano and drum trio. As Edith Lindeman remembered the nickelodeons of her youth, "some were adequate playhouses, some were hastily remodeled store buildings, long, narrow, dark and redolent of human occupancy, salted peanuts and mints....The theaters were chilly in winter and hot in summer...but admission was only five cents, and you could stick around all day." [22]

If the nickelodeons' interior was plain, the exterior was often gaudy – with ornamental tinwork nailed over the storefront, painted bright colors and studded with glowing light bulbs. Brightly colored lithographed posters enticed passers-by with hints of the dramas and mys-

BYRD THEATER, *2905 W. Cary St., 2001. A glowing marquee at night still entices viewers to enter the theater.*

teries that would be shown on the screen. Phonographs and player pianos jangled and barkers urged folks on the sidewalk to come in and see the show. Nickelodeon programs included a variety of films, from Keystone Cop slapstick chases, John Bunny and Charlie Chaplin comedies, historical dramas, cowboy and Indian adventures, and melodramas featuring Mary Pickford or the Gish sisters. Also wildly popular were the *Perils of Pauline* cliffhanging serials, which sent children home breathless to wait for next week's installment, wondering if the heroine could escape the tiger, explosion or menacing saw blade.

Richmond's nickelodeon audiences, like those across the nation, were a mixture of people from the community — children, shoppers, mothers who parked their baby carriages outside the front door, businessmen and clerks on their lunch breaks, and many people who could not have afforded to regularly attend theatrical shows. At night, audiences included groups of young men and women, couples on dates hoping to kiss in the darkened back rows of the theater, whole families out for an inexpensive evening's entertainment, and window shoppers strolling past the lighted windows of the Broad Street stores. Audiences were often boisterous, chatting with

each other during the show, cheering on the heroes and hissing at the villains, and talking back to the screen, in an atmosphere reminiscent of theater behavior 100 years before. Herbert Gibbs remembered hearing of an amusing incident that occurred in a Broad Street nickelodeon: "It is said that a very irate woman stalked into that movie house one night and called out 'my husband is in here with another woman!' Every man in the place ran out the side door."[23]

In 1908, Richmond saw the opening of four additional small nickelodeons on Broad Street – the Gaiety, Majestic, the delightfully named Theato, and the Empire. Nickelodeon fever was catching, and even Jake Wells' original Colonial Theater began showing movies. In 1909, Thorpe's new Rex Theater and the five existing nickelodeons were joined by an astounding fourteen more: Belmar, Gem, Ideal, Idle Hour, Lubin, Orient, Royal, Virginia, Globe, Star, and across the river on Hull Street in Manchester, the Cozy Corner, Royal and Wonderland. Gaston Lichtenstein recalled the Virginia Theater's lady pianist, Bert Herman, who never seemed to tire: "She could have qualified for a marathon contest." Lichtenstein wrote that Miss Herman and another woman who relieved each other in shifts playing accom-

STRAND THEATER, *118 W. Broad St., 1928. The Empire Theater, built in 1911 as a playhouse where Lucille Laverne and John Bunny cavorted, in 1915 became a movie theater named for the grandest movie theater in New York City. In this photo, the Strand was closed after a fire in 1927.*

paniment to the silent films all day and night "prided themselves on furnishing continuous music. In the midst of a number, one would take up the melody [from the other] without losing a note."[24]

The Lubin Theater opened in December 1908 in a converted store building next to the Bijou Theater. It was a jewel in the chain of fifteen vaudeville-and-film theaters that film entrepreneur Siegmund Lubin was opening across the Mid-Atlantic region. Lubin invested more than $200,000 in these theaters. The Richmond Lubin reportedly cost $40,000 to build, but its box office returns proved to be phenomenal. As Lubin biographer Joseph Eckhardt writes, "A movie theater by itself could bring in anywhere from one hundred to fifteen hundred dollars net profit a month and some estimates even suggested that a profit of two thousand dollars a month was not unheard of. With [the addition of] vaudeville the profits were considerably greater."[25]

The Lubin Theater may only have been 37 feet wide and 132 feet deep, with fewer than 600 seats, but it called attention to itself with Richmond's most outlandish theater front, a façade which was covered with pressed-tin curlicues, medallions and furbelows, and a huge woman's head. Hundreds of white lights studded the painted plas-

ter and tinwork. The *Times Dispatch* reported at its opening, "The Lubin claims the distinction of being the most elaborately wired and the most brilliantly illuminated amusement house in the South. There are more than 1,100 incandescent lamps, the front having 424 lamps, with 706 in the interior." The writer enthused further about the decorative statuary around the stage. It boasted an orchestra of five musicians, and offered continuous performances from 2:00 until 11:00 pm of three vaudeville acts, plus illustrated songs and "the latest pictures of the world in motion from the Lubin workshops." The first week's program featured Miss Annie Abbott, "The Georgia Magnet," whose powers could levitate pool cues or render 300-pound men helpless just by laying her hands on their heads. Dandy Dan Anderson and Rollicksome Ruby Reymonds performed a comic singing act, Mr. and Mrs. Byron Spaun did a comedy sketch, and Miss Minerva Jaeger sang the latest Tin Pan Alley hits, while slides on screen illustrated the songs, and Lubin movies played, all for a dime.[26]

The Lubin's manager was Richmond optician Salo (Samuel) Galeski. Born in 1856 in Breslau, Germany, Galeski journeyed to America when he was 19. Philadelphia optician Siegmund Lubin trained him in the opti-

EMPIRE THEATER, *118 W. Broad St., 2001. After years as the Strand and Booker T. movie theaters, the old Empire has been restored as a playhouse; it is one the oldest theaters still in use in Virginia. It is home to the Theatre IV Company, the state's largest theatrical operation.*

cal business. Salo and his new bride Anna moved south in 1885 to expand the Lubin business empire. Washington, D.C. had been their destination until a couple on the train convinced them of the great opportunities in Richmond. Galeski built a thriving optical business here, and had a hand in numerous other ventures. At various times he was president of the Galeski Optical Company, a bank, an oil company, and a fraternal insurance organization. Galeski followed Lubin into show business and managed the Lubin Theater, which he purchased from Lubin in the summer of 1909 for at least $50,000. Galeski subsequently opened theaters in Norfolk, Roanoke and Washington, and an amusement park near the Boulevard. Galeski was a true entrepreneur who did much to further the spread of movies into middle class society. He sold his theater interests to Jake Wells in August 1915. In 1916, Wells re-christened the Lubin as the Isis Theater and advertised it as "Richmond's New Meeting Place." The Isis, minus the huge female head on the building's façade, but still displaying all the rest of its outlandish plaster, tin and electric decoration, amused moviegoers throughout the rest of the silent film era.

A shakeout among the nickelodeons occurred in 1910, as several Broad Street theaters closed — Gaiety,

Gem, Ideal and Idle Hour — and two more theaters opened on Hull Street, the Leader and the Pastime Picture Show. Entrepreneurs in Richmond's African –American community opened nickelodeons such as the Star, the Superior and the Pekin. Formidable new rivals arrived on the nickelodeon scene in 1911. Moses Hoffheimer built the Little Theater, a small house with 350 seats, as the first theater in Richmond to be constructed from the ground up especially to house movie shows. The Victoria Theater opened on Hull Street (it would later become the Ponton Theater). Herbert Gibbs, the Victoria's projectionist, operated hand-cranked projectors for eight hours a day. Films were rewound on a machine by hand, and each reel had to be rewound before it could be shown again. Being a projectionist took a lot of stamina in the days before electric motors operated the machines. Gibbs recalled that when no assistants were available in the projection booth, "the common practice was to crank the projector with one hand and to turn the rewinding machine with the other."[27]

In 1911 Hoffheimer also opened the 1,220-seat Empire Theater at 118 W. Broad Street, next door to the Little. If the Little was a nickelodeon, then the Empire was a playhouse, for it was more elegantly decorated,

ODEON THEATER, *211 N. Sixth St., 1926. Located between Thalhimer's and Miller & Rhoads, the Odeon was the perfect place for tired shoppers to rest their feet and watch a film. Built as the Superior Theater, a nickelodeon, the Odeon was torn down in the late 1920s during an expansion of Thalhimer's.*

had a sloped auditorium floor to allow its audiences to have better viewing, a larger stage and three times as many seats as the film theater next door. The Empire was built as a multi-purpose facility that could showcase vaudeville or stock company performances or films. Hoffheimer's inclusiveness of movie shows in his entertainment mix demonstrated that the movies had really achieved respectable standing, and a permanent footing in the Richmond entertainment community.

The 1,200 seat Lyric Theater at Broad and 9th streets, located across the road from the showplaces along Theater Row, also opened in 1911. The directors of the estate of local newspaper mogul Joseph Bryan financed its construction. The theater portion of the large office

building cost more than $150,000 to construct. The Lyric's auditorium was three stories high, and its lobby filled five stories. Edward Peples recalled, "In addition to the orchestra seats, there were two balconies; the front half of the first was comfortable but the rear half was dark and crowded." The second presented a real challenge – "the seats seemed to rise straight from the front railing, and one felt that the slightest misstep would plunge him headlong into the orchestra two floors below. Those in the higher rows hoped that the action would take place near the footlights because when the actors moved to the rear of the stage they vanished." Edith Lindeman described it as "a tight little theater with perfect acoustics." However for actors, "the situation was less than ideal. Dressing rooms were below stage and a heavy rainstorm could turn the floors from damp to puddly." The Lyric played family vaudeville with tickets costing 30-cents on the main floor and 10 cents for gallery perches; shows containing six or seven live acts plus a motion picture newsreel were performed three times a day.[28]

As the nickelodeon era of storefront theaters ended in 1914 change continued on the Richmond scene. Two of the city's oldest nickelodeons, the Globe and Leader, closed, but six new theaters opened – Albion, Hippodrome, Regent, Superior, Victor and Virginia. By 1915, Richmond's four vaudeville and legitimate stage theaters were flanked by approximately 15 movie theaters — the number was never exact, as the small show houses changed hands, names and opened and folded frequently.

Theatrical Stock Companies

For a century, Richmond's theaters had been home to resident stock companies. It was too expensive, tiring and difficult for actors to be on the road all the year, and some sought semi-permanent residence in a major city. When the Academy Theater of Music opened in 1886, it installed a resident stock company, which performed in Richmond for one to three months and then moved to other Southern cities for the balance of the year. The Giffen Company arrived in Richmond in 1900, and played at various times at the Academy and Bijou Theaters. The company's ingénue was blonde Grayce (pronounced Gracie) Scott, who was married to director Larry Giffen. The troupe's leading woman was Lucille LaVerne. Richard Bennett, who was father of movie stars Joan, Constance and Barbara, headed the company as handsome leading man in two summer stock seasons in 1905-1906. Leo Wise, manager of the Academy, recalled, "Dick used to come up from Barton Heights to the theater on 8th Street on his horse. The horse knew the way, but Dick never knew his part. En route he studied lines. Girls, rows of them, crowded around him as he went, but they never fazed him."[29]

Scores of Richmond's young women, swept up in the glamour and excitement of the actors and the stage, loitered at the back entrances of the Academy, Bijou, and Empire Theaters. A columnist for the *Times Dispatch* called them "stage door Maggies":

The "Johnnies" in Richmond...are largely outnumbered by those of the opposite sex, who have a propensity for haunting the neighborhood of the stage door. These matinee girls, or stage door Maggies, developed in Richmond when the Giffen Company was first organized here. To the credit of the girls, it must be said that most of them were attracted rather by a desire to see the ladies of the company [Scott and LaVerne], as they appeared in street attire, than by a wish to see the men, though, of course, they cast [furtive] glances at their idols, as the latter swaggered down the street. ...They are less noticeable after performances at the Academy than they are on matinee days at the Bijou. It is only after the appearance of some well-known actress, as for instance, Maxine Elliott, who always brings them out in full force, that the girls take up their position in front of the Academy. ...At the Bijou, it is a regular occurrence for the entrance in the alley on Eighth Street, leading to the stage door, to be crowded with females between the ages of fourteen and twenty. It is the "week stand" that leads to the desire to see what the players look like "off the stage."[30]

The Giffen Company folded in 1910, but both Grayce Scott and Lucille LaVerne continued to return to town annually with their own assemblies of actors. Grayce Scott was a petite, pretty woman with masses of blonde curls, blue eyes, and what an interviewer described as "the most exquisitely modulated voice – low, soft and magnetic." The young playgoers of Richmond admired her. The Grayce Scott troupe made a lasting impression on young female fans like Edith Lindeman, who had moved to Richmond in 1913 with her family. She recalled,

For a while, that group provided not merely entertainment, but a way of life for most of the city. They operated for long winter seasons at the [original] Colonial at Ninth and Broad and became so popular that the playhouse was renamed the 'Grayce Scott Bijou.'...The company played nine shows a week, Monday through Saturday nights with matinees on Tuesdays Thursday and Saturdays. Admission ran from 50 cents for the best orchestra seats to 10 cents in the rear of the balcony....There were nine of us high school girls who had A-row seats for every Saturday matinee and we were not unique. Groups of friends from all parts of town also had their regular nights, and if you couldn't discuss *The Fortune Hunter* or *Dorothy Vernon of Haddon Hall* over your hot-fudge sundaes, you just weren't with it.[31]

Lindeman continued, "The Company's popularity also was largely due to Grayce's tall, dark and handsome leading man, 26-year old Jack Warner. He had a Barrymore profile, a voice of brown velvet and a disarming (and highly commercial) habit of smiling over the footlights into the eyes of his idolaters in the front rows.

THE TIP

DeWITT NEWING — Editor

DEVOTED TO DOINGS OF THE GRAYCE SCOTT COMPANY
AT THE GRAYCE SCOTT BIJOU

VOL. III.   RICHMOND, VA., JANUARY 11, 1915   No. 2

An Interview With Mr. JOHN WARNER

Occupying the limelight, or rather the calcium, is by no means an easy task, though many of us may think differently. Many of us, indeed, look upon the men and women of the stage as a sort of sublimated set of creatures, quite apart from the normal variety of folk. There is unquestionably a glamour around the actors, and this glamour is intensified in the case of the stock actor, who is called upon week after week to portray different roles. The usual stock actor is more or less of a mystery man; he is learning and unlearning all of the time, and it is quite natural that we wonder at them. John Warner, or as he is more intimately and affectionately known, Jack Warner, is one of the few who are different, and it is probably this difference that has made him for this and all time the most popular leading man ever appearing with a stock company in Richmond. The following interview may prove illuminative of a different side of Mr. Warner's character.

IT WASN'T necessary for me to send my card in, because the interview had been arranged beforehand. To be very truthful, I had met Mr. Warner, Mr. John Warner, leading man of the Grayce Scott Players, if you please, and certainly one of the best liked and most popular leading men that Richmond has ever boasted, in a casual sort of way, and when I met him I carried a chip on my shoulder; I couldn't quite understand why this young man should be given the privilege of making love week after week to one of the most charming little ladies I have ever known. Of course I refer to Miss Grayce Scott. So, to get to his dressing room, while he was making up—I believe that's what they call the process—for Prince Florimond, in "Snow White and the Seven Dwarfs," I went back on the stage. I knocked at the door, and I am perfectly willing to confess that I was in much the same frame of mind that I am told certain ladies are in when they pay a perfunctory call, hoping all the time that the person called upon is not in.

In other words, I had a chip on my shoulder for this John Warner, this strapping fellow, who has won friends by the hundreds, and who forever and continually basks in the sunshine of popular approval. I didn't like him, and I didn't care who knew it; that is, I didn't care who knew it, so long as he didn't find it out, and I didn't much care if he found it out after I had interviewed him. As I believe I mentioned before, I rapped at his door, his dressing room, to be emphatic, and I waited for a reply. There was just a brief pause, and then a great robust voice, a little husky from a slight throat affection that the weather had brought about, rang out:

"Don't knock," bassed the voice, "don't knock; come right on in."

And before I knew it there I was, right in the presence of this youngster, this man of so many parts, this actor about whom I had heard so much and with whom I had traveled through almost every civilized country, because, though I confess to an unwarrantable antipathy to any man who can make love every day in the week to a pretty woman, I, nevertheless, have been quite keen for this John Warner, mayhap because he showed me various methods in the art of lovemaking that I felt I could use to advantage in days to come.

"He seemed so every inch a man
That I marvelled as I stood,
And mouthed a most expletive d—n
At harbored thoughts so rude."

I am not given to pretty speeches, certainly not pretty speeches concerning men, but let me announce right now that Mr. John Warner is just

(Continued on Second Page.)

COMING

"OLD HEIDLEBERG"

Richard Mansfield's Great Success.

A Sure-Fire Attraction.

THE TIP, *1915. Handsome actor Jack Warner was profiled in this publication of the Grayce Scott Theater Company. Warner's legion of young female fans eagerly read the interviews and news of upcoming stock company productions at the Bijou Theater.*

True, he played his love scenes with all the ardor of a stockbroker reciting the day's averages, but he never dropped a line nor missed a cue. He also walked the length of Monument Avenue each Sunday afternoon, and half the front porches were filled with giggling girls wating to see him stride past." Lindeman and her friends did their small part for the cause of feminism by throwing over Victorian restraints and frankly admiring their favorite male actors.

Richmond's teen-aged boys, on the other hand, were drawn to action dramas at the Bijou Theater. "She was glamour, adventure, enchantment and dreams," recalled a Bijou regular, who reminisced about "the voyages we once took with a 15-cent scrap of cardboard." No girls' sighing over leading men for them. They wanted the suspense and thrills of plays like *The Millionaire Detective* and performers like Thurston the Magician. A suave, tuxedoed gentleman, The Millionaire Detective had a crime-solving technique that riveted the boys' attention. Announcing that a murderer confronted with his victim would confess, "He would pronounce the ominous words, at the ritziest of dinner parties, and leaning over he would lift the cover from a large silver tureen placed directly in front of the hapless suspect. There, in the tureen, would be the grinning head of a dead man. Not only would the murderer leap to his feet but half the gallery as well." The Bijou fan recalled, "When something special came, such as *Across the Pacific*, which had a Gatling gun in the fifth act, or *The Boy Behind the Gun*, which had two, you couldn't afford to take chances with a 'rush' [upper balcony] seat. You saved your pennies, you did a few extra jobs, and got together all of 25 cents, two bits, that was, the exact price of one reserved seat in the second section of the first balcony."[32]

During the Grayce Scott Company's 1914 and 1915 seasons at the Bijou, the troupe published its own weekly newspaper, *The Tip*. Each four-to-eight page issue was filled with plot summaries of upcoming plays, details about the costumes of current productions, interviews with the players, profiles of the scene painters, box-office staff and backstage crew, Foster Studio photographs of the actors and actresses, and plugs for the firms that advertised in the paper. *Tip* editor DeWitt Newing (the theater manager, who also doubled in bit parts) had a column answering the queries of ardent fans (all female) about Miss Scott, the actors and plays. Readers voted on which plays they would like to see performed. Stamped "Please Exchange" on the cover to encourage readers to share it with their friends, during the several years of its publication, *The Tip* helped create and maintain a group of dedicated stock theater fans. Lindeman and her friends saved several of the earliest issues of *The Tip*, especially

ACTOR JACK WARNER, *1915.*

those that featured Jack Warner on the cover.

Farther up Broad Street, Lucille LaVerne assembled her own stock company at the Empire Theater. During the 1913 season, which stretched from April to July, the company played for ten weeks, gave 80 performances and sold 147,000 tickets.[33] Lindeman recalls that the Empire "was a popular theater with audiences, especially on Wednesday matinees, when each woman in attendance received a quarter-pound box of Huyler's chocolates and a dainty linen handkerchief to wipe her eyes during the sad scenes."[34]

At the start of her August 1914 season at the Empire, LaVerne engaged two guest stars, Mary Miles Minter and John Bunny, who brought the celebrity of Broadway and the movies to Richmond for a week. Former child star in the New York hit play *The Littlest Rebel*, (which had been written by Richmonder Edward Peple), Mary Miles Minter in her twenties was no longer a darling moppet, but she still specialized in played girlish roles. "Bouncing around in golden curls," Minter performed a one-act version of *Littlest Rebel* at the Empire. Within a

ACTRESS GRAYCE SCOTT, *1915. Miss Scott and all the members of her repertory theater company posed for publicity photographs at the Foster Studios.*

ACTOR JOHN BUNNY VISITS THE CONFEDERATE VETERANS HOME, CAMP LEE, *1914. Actress Lucille LaVerne took her guest star, then the most famous movie comedian in the world, on a tour of Richmond.*

ACTORS JOHN BUNNY AND LUCILLE LAVERNE, *At the Lee Monument, 1914.*

JOHN BUNNY, LUCILLE LAVERNE, JUSTICE CRUTCHFIELD, *Outside Richmond City Hall, 1914. Even Richmond magistrates cut up for the camera when the famous John Bunny was in town.*

few years, she would become a movie star rivaling Mary Pickford in popularity. (Incidentally, the sound film version of *The Littlest Rebel* in 1933 would bring stardom to a new curly-haired moppet, Shirley Temple. Temple's film co-stars would be Richmond's own Bill Robinson, and John Boles, a frequent visitor to Richmond who always stopped by retirement homes to visit the old ladies who remembered his many film roles as a Confederate officer.)

The real highlight of the special season-opening program at the Empire, however, was an appearance by 300-pound comic John Bunny, who was then the most popular movie star in the world. A moderately successful vaudeville comedian, Bunny had gambled on becoming a star in the upstart film business. His slapstick farces and domestic comedies co-starring spindly Flora Finch became huge hits the world over. Empire Theater owner Moses Hoffheimer's publicity machine went into high gear, and the newspapers were filled with stories and pictures of Bunny for several weeks before his arrival.

On August 15, 1914, John Bunny was given a royal reception in Richmond, taking an automobile tour of the city, visiting veterans at the Confederate Soldiers Home and being greeted on the steps of City Hall by Justice John J. Crutchfield, who presided over the city's Police Court. That evening, the Empire Theater was packed. In Bunny's act, a scene from one of his Vitagraph studio comedies was shown on screen, then he stepped from behind it onto the stage, to tremendous applause. He presented a monologue, "My Face – Its Cause and Cure," and then he and several supporting actors performed a comic pantomime, *The Honeymooners*. The reviewer said "Mr. Bunny again showed the audience why he is so celebrated a movie actor, for his miming is as precise as his expressions are droll. *Honeymooners* is a pleasant little comedy and it served to illustrate the genius of Mr. Bunny from his most solemn pomposity to his most funny sneeze." The show was pronounced "a great and glittering success," and matinee shows were added all week to accommodate the crowds. Tragically, Bunny would die of Bright's disease only eight months later at age 52, and the title of the world's most famous film comedian would pass to Charlie Chaplin, whose first films were shown in Richmond in autumn 1914. [35]

A number of LaVerne and Scott stock company performers went on to Broadway and Hollywood fame in later years, such as Margaret Illington, Gertrude Hoffman, Harrison Ford (the silent movie star) and Frank Morgan, the LaVerne Company's juvenile lead, who was known most famously for his performance as "The Wizard of Oz." Edward Arnold was the young, svelte leading man in the LaVerne Company in 1914-1915. His salary

ACTOR EDWARD ARNOLD, *1914. Juvenile leading man for the LaVerne Stock Company, a svelte Arnold modeled men's suits for a downtown retailer to earn extra money. He later gained fame as a character actor in the movies playing rotund, imposing businessmen and politicians.*

INTERIOR, EMPIRE THEATER, *118 W. Broad St., 2001. Audience members get to "meet and greet" actors from Theatre IV's production of* **Peter Pan***.*

was $50.00 per week. To earn extra money, Arnold posed in advertisements for Greentree's menswear store. He became a popular character actor in movies of the 1930s and 1940s, playing industrialists, judges, and politicians such as the rotund political boss in *Mr. Smith Goes to Washington*. Returning to Richmond to sell War Bonds in 1942, Arnold threw a party at the John Marshall Hotel with an open invitation to old friends who knew him when he played here in stock. Some 350 people joined him to celebrate his salad days at the Empire Theater.

The fortunes of stock companies in Richmond waned as motion pictures became the chief source of inexpensive entertainment. In an April 1915 article, a *News Leader* critic opined that all the big theatrical stars were in film now and that the movies were the biggest and best show in Richmond. The Empire was converted into a motion picture theater in December 1914, and it was re-christened the Strand Theater in honor of New York City's

first movie palace. Lucille LaVerne was forced to move her company to the Academy for the 1915 and 1916 seasons. Financial reverses plagued both stock companies, as ticket sales could not cover the salaries and expenses. In December 1915, Grayce Scott closed her company; she eked out three more seasons in Providence, Rhode Island before retiring. Soon afterwards, Lucille LaVerne gave up trying to make her company profitable in Richmond, and she moved to New York. She was back playing Richmond's Strand again in October 1917, but it was on film in Mae Marsh's *Polly of the Circus*. LaVerne appeared on Broadway and in several D.W. Griffith films, including *Orphans of the Storm* and *America* (which was partially filmed in Richmond). Moving to Hollywood when talkies arrived in 1927, she played many character roles. Today she is most remembered for providing the voice of the Wicked Queen and hag with the poisoned apple in Disney's first animated feature film *Snow White*

EMPIRE THEATER, 2001. *Cast members of **Peter Pan** sign autographs for the playgoers.*

(1937) and modeling the character for the animators to base their drawings on her movements.

Movies Rule in Richmond

By the mid-1910s, Richmond's entertainment scene was thoroughly dominated by the movies. With the stunningly rapid growth of this inexpensive entertainment came fears that what the movies were showing Richmond's women and children could be harmful. Film censorship became a public concern as some films began to flirt with sensational themes. In January 1914, Richmond police chief Werner stopped the exhibition of Theda Bara's racy film *The Vampire* at two Broad Street theaters after the president of the Richmond United Daughters of the Confederacy chapter complained that the film was "highly indecent." A committee of leading Richmond citizens joined Werner to view *Traffic in Souls*

and other new films that broached the topic of sexuality. A small number of movies were banned, others had scenes snipped out, and the storm temporarily blew over. (A state board of film censorship would be created in 1922.) Box offices may actually have benefited from all the publicity, which drew crowds of curious viewers to theaters to see what the fuss was all about.

The thorniest film controversy in Richmond history came in October 1915, when D.W. Griffith's movie *The Birth of a Nation* played for a week at the Academy Theater. One of the most persistently controversial films ever made, the movie used stirring cinematography and music to recount the Civil War and Reconstruction from a romantic white southern point of view that shockingly glorified the Ku Klux Klan and denigrated African Americans. Richmond's black community mounted a campaign to ban the movie, encouraged by the *Richmond*

ISIS AND BIJOU THEATERS, *800 E. Broad St, 1929. Broad Street shoppers bustled day and night along Broad Street, and Theater Row.*

Planet's coverage of NAACP protests against the film in Boston and New York.[36] A delegation of prominent professors from Virginia Union University, led by Dr. R. E. Jones, and including Dr. W.H. Hughes, Professors C. T. Russell and W.N. Colston and Rev. W. T. Johnson, plus five students presenting written petitions, met with Mayor George Ainslie. The group urged the mayor to prevent the film's showing in Richmond. Ainslie listened to their arguments, but he also polled mayors of other southern cities, and decided to allow the film to be shown.[37]

Many city officials attended the sold-out local premiere of the three-hour-long *Birth of a Nation* at the Academy Theater on October 25, 1915. Ladies of the UDC attended in crinolines and evening gowns, and a few ancient Confederate veterans were seated in a special section. Tickets for the film were $2, the price of a Broadway theatrical show. A symphony orchestra of 30 played a musical score written especially for the film, and stagehands created sound effects behind the screen. Review-

ers for the *News Leader* and *Times Dispatch* were ecstatic in their praise for the film's sophisticated photography, staging and evocative music. They noted that during the battle scenes, rebel yells nearly blew the roof off the theater.[38]

Richmonders were so movie-crazy in the mid-1910s that the city supported two locally published magazines devoted to motion pictures. *The Richmond Playgoer*, first published in 1907, eventually changed its name to *The Richmond Moving Picture Magazine*. It included a plentiful amount of photographs and featured information on upcoming films and articles about the actors appearing in them. An article in the December 1911 *Richmond Playgoer* debated whether the moving picture was helpful or detrimental to live theater and questioned how long the movies would exist. "As the *Playgoer* sees it," concluded the article, "the moving picture business is a permanent and valuable institution – perserverendum est! Let it persevere."[39]

Screenland – Richmond's own movie theater magazine,

LIBRARY OF VIRGINIA, *800 E. Broad Street, 2001. Today the Bijou block is the site of the state archives and library building.*

a five-cent weekly publication, was produced in 1916 and 1917 as a joint venture of the city's theaters and movie houses. Along with the magazine's player profiles and previews of upcoming feature films, the paper included advertisements for the city's theaters. The Albion touted that "*The Iron Claw* with Pearl White will grip you." Richmonders were urged not to miss a single episode of that spine-tingling serial. The Theato Five Cent Theater claimed to be "The Little House with the Great Big Value – Feature Days all the Time." The Little Theater showed a major film release for an entire week; the Bijou and Strand Theaters changed films twice a week. The Colonial, New and Odeon changed programs three times per week, and some nickelodeon-style theaters, such as the Albion, Isis, Rex, Theato and Victor, offered new programs every day. The Bijou Theater mounted a stage production of *The Little Girl God Forgot* and took pains in its advertising to remind a film-infatu-ated city in capital-lettered print that this was "NOT A MOVING PICTURE." [40]

The expansion of commercial entertainment in the first two decades of the new century – through vaudeville theaters, summer theaters at the trolley parks, repertory companies, nickelodeons, and feature-length films shown in more spacious, permanent movie theaters – had significantly altered how Richmonders spent their leisure hours. Inexpensive entertainments drew more people than ever into the popular culture audience. Live theater was beginning to decline in cities like Richmond, but the movies were in their ascendancy. All of these pre-World War I theaters, however, would be surpassed in the 1920s by a wave of new theaters. The Colonial, National, Capitol, Mosque, Loew's and Byrd theaters would bring a whole new atmosphere of picture palace splendor and luxury to movie-going.

CAPITOL SQUARE *and Theater Row, 1920s.*

CHAPTER 2

The Picture Palace Era
1920-1930

In the 1920s, the array of department stores, milliners and specialty shops on Broad and Grace streets, and the variety of theaters along Theater Row and on 2nd Street in Jackson Ward, made the city the shopping and entertainment capital of the Upper South. World War I had brought factory employment and prosperity to Richmond and its people. Due to annexation of surrounding communities and new jobs, the city's population grew by one-third between 1910 and 1920 to 172,000, and the surrounding metropolitan area had seen a 20 percent increase. The city drew in visitors and workers from across the region. Harry L. Seeley, Jr. recalls a saying, popular from the 1920s through the 1950s, that young people across rural Virginia, North Carolina and West Virginia learned the "Four R's – Readin', Ritin' and the Road to Richmond."

The wave of nickelodeon and vaudeville hall openings after 1900 was a prelude to the flood of new theaters that Richmond gained in the 1920s. As the new decade began, the venerable Academy of Music Theater, and vaudeville houses the Bijou and original Colonial, were joined by ten movie theaters: the, Dixie, Globe, Hippodrome, Isis, Rex, Star, Strand, Theato, Victor and Victoria. A boom in theater construction replaced the small nickelodeons (which had often been just shops converted into show halls) with silent film theaters that were spacious and comfortable – the Odeon, Bluebird and Broadway. Amanda Thorpe and Walter Coulter's greatest achievement to date, the Bluebird Theater radiated happiness not only though its name, but also at night through its large illuminated electric sign over the mar-

quee, in which blinking lights made a bird fashioned out of blue and white light bulbs seem to flap its wings.[1] The Broadway Theater featured a ten-piece orchestra to provide music for its silent films. The first neighborhood theaters, the Brookland on the city's northside, and the Venus, on Hull Street in Manchester, opened by the mid-1920s to provide convenient entertainment for the families and children who lived further away from the downtown theaters. Theater building continued with increasing intensity in the later 1920s, as entrepreneurs in Richmond and across the nation learned of the profits to be made in the huge, fantastical theaters — picture palaces — that were opening with great success in big cities such as New York and Chicago. By 1928, Richmond, too, would have three new picture palaces, plus two Broadway-style legitimate theaters and a mammoth new auditorium. The way Richmonders went to the movies and theater would again be significantly changed.

While the 1920s in Richmond and across the nation was a time of enormous expansion for the movies and their theaters, it was a much more difficult era for theatrical and vaudeville shows. The system of theater companies touring the nation with major stars, which had been the staple of Richmond's entertainment scene since the 1870s, collapsed during the 1920s. The tremendous popularity of motion pictures had lured away the steady patrons of touring shows; the creaky old plays returning to town every year had lessening appeal for audiences. The spiraling cost of transporting actors, costumes and stage equipment from town to town doing one-night stands bankrupted the touring companies. Three hun-

ACADEMY OF MUSIC BURNS, *100 N. Ninth St., 1927. The Academy was destroyed by fire on February 19, 1927. Scenery blowing into the gaslights purportedly touched off the blaze.*

AFTER THE FIRE, *1927. Two stories of the historic 41-year old theater were lost. The building was soon torn down to make was for the Federal Reserve Bank.*

BLUEBIRD THEATER,
*620 E. Broad St., 1927. Amanda
Thorpe and Walter Coulter opened
this movie house on the eastern edge
of Theater Row. The building's
façade was adorned with an illuminated electric sign of a bluebird with
flapping wings, made of blue light
bulbs, which could be seen at night
all along Broad Street.*

dred companies active in the 1910s were reduced to less
than 70 in the 1920s. Fewer stars came to the Academy
Theater each year, although a notable exception was Al
Jolson, top entertainer of the decade, who starred in several musicals that made stops in Richmond. The Academy and Lyric theaters, now so often dark, limped along
by booking motion pictures in between stage shows to
try to make ends meet.

The 40-year old Academy of Music Theater met an
ignominious end when it burned on February 19, 1927.
The theater's last play was *Alias the Deacon*, performed
by the Academy Company stock troupe. The fire started
after a performance when wind from an open window
blew a piece of scenery into a gas light still turned on
backstage. No one was injured, but the building was destroyed. After the Academy blaze, its play bookings were
transferred to the Lyric Theater, and the valuable land
on Franklin and 8th streets became the site of the Federal Reserve Bank.

BROADWAY THEATER, *712 E. Broad St., 1927. When
the Broadway opened, World War I had just ended, and
war-themed films were popular. Those films made a come-
back in the late 1920s and were promoted with great fanfare.*

COLONIAL THEATER, *714 E. Broad St., 1921. One of the jewel's of Jake Wells' theatrical empire, which opened in 1921. Wells touted it as "the finest motion picture theater in the South."*

The Colonial and National Theaters

While legitimate theater was struggling, Broad Street's Theater Row flourished. In 1920, Jake Wells demolished the original Colonial Theater on the 700 block of Broad Street. The old structure, built in the 1870s, had been remodeled by Wells into his original Bijou in 1899, and was rechristened the Colonial when a new Bijou was built on the next block. In the late 1910s, the original Colonial had been condemned by the city. In its place, Wells built a beautiful new 1,900-seat Colonial Theater, which he claimed was the largest movie house south of Washington, D.C. It had an elegant beige marble façade. The lobby contained marble steps, a sunken lounge filled with couches, and walls decorated with mahogany wood accents and plaster ornamentation created by Richmond sculptor Ferrucio Legnaioli. The auditorium featured the novelty of tiered rows of seats, which eliminated the need for balconies and the steep staircases that led to them. Colored lights moving across the

ivory and gold-hued wall decorations made the interior colors shift from rose to purple to blue. The Colonial was equipped with an orchestra pit for 14 musicians, and an organ that cost $21,000.[2] Despite its elegance, some thought that the Colonial's interior was dreary, and the restrooms were inconveniently located all the way down in the basement. Bob Burchette recalls that entering the Colonial was like walking into a dark, dank castle. Plants could not live long in the lobby or mezzanine with their low ceilings and windowless walls.[3] The Colonial opened October 12, 1921, with Thomas Meighan starring in *Cappy Ricks* and a Harold Lloyd comedy. The Colonial would bill itself as an upscale movie house (an illuminated sign on the roof proclaimed it a "photoplay theater") that hosted occasional live events and shows on stage.[4]

In 1922, a group of businessmen purchased Amanda Thorpe's Rex Theater (opened in 1909) and demolished it to construct an elegant half-million dollar auditorium

THEATER ROW BUILDING, *700 Block E. Broad St., 2001. The Colonial Theater's lovely façade was saved to add historic architectural interest to the Theater Row office building, which was constructed by the City of Richmond.*

on the same block as the Colonial Theater. Owners John Pryor and Frank Ferrandini, business partner of Ferruccio Legnaioli, formed the First National Amusement Company, allying them with a nationwide group of film exhibitors in the First National circuit. In a novel publicity stunt, the National's backers posted signs at the construction site urging Richmonders to vote for what kinds of entertainment they wished to have at the new theater. While the owners reported that Richmonders voted to have the National feature silent movie shows with a large orchestra to accompany them, the builders covered all the bases.[5] The National was large and adaptable enough to accommodate theatrical, vaudeville and musical comedy companies, as well as movie shows. Theater critic Roy Proctor has described the National as the closest thing Richmond has ever had to a Broadway-style playhouse. Theater architect C.W. Howell, known for his buildings across the South, designed the four-story building. It cost $470,000, a significant investment in the city's

entertainment and in its future.

The National was opulent throughout; it had an Italian Renaissance-style façade of sandstone-colored brick and stone with terra cotta ornamentation, including what one commentator noted as "a frieze of full size classical [unclothed] male figures dancing among garlands of flowers with one figure playing the lyre and another unfurling a reel of film." The lobby boasted a large marble staircase, elegant "Adamseque" architectural decorations and a large illuminated ceiling dome, all created by renowned local marble and plaster sculptor Ferruccio Legnaioli. One of Richmond's most prominent artists, Legnaioli was a graduate of the Academy of Fine Arts in Florence, Italy. Immigrating to the United States, he settled in Richmond and became a partner in a design firm that sculpted architectural and decorative ornamentation in plaster, bronze, marble and cement. He created the statue of Columbus that stands in Byrd Park, and would sculpt plasterwork decorations for the Lyric,

Empire, Colonial, National, Capitol and Byrd Theaters. His work is visible in business buildings and homes throughout Richmond, for he crafted hundreds of plaster ceilings, tiled porches and interior and exterior decorations.[6] "Legnaioli is a sculptor and modeler of recognized ability, and critics throughout the country praise the excellence of his work," a *Times Dispatch* profile noted. Reporters covering the National Theater's opening described some of the intricacy that went into Legnaioli's work:

> Delicate, lilting frescoes adorn the interior of the National Theatre, tinted with pastel shades of yellow and green, classical, yet with more than a hint of modernity.... The scope of the work is tremendous, for it covers practically the whole interior of the amusement house. But it is entirely composed of small blocks, each worked out with consummate skill and taste, and moulded separately. ...Following the plans of the architect, these sculptors made careful reproductions of each varying design, and from these originals took casts, or forms, in hardened glue. Into these was the plaster poured and exact replicas, nearly impossible to make by any other means, were thus secured. With the hardening of the relief, a special gloss tint was applied, outlining the figures or coloring them according to the decorative scheme, and all that remained was to place them in their proper position on the wall.[7]

On the National's opening night, November 11, 1923, Governor Lee Trinkle and Mayor George Anslie joined the more than 2,000 eager patrons who jammed the 1,300-seat theater to see the Thomas Ince film *Her Reputation*, starring May McAvoy. A *Times Dispatch* reporter deemed the building "handsome, stately, adorned but not ornate, spacious, comfortable, but one word will do it – it is beautiful." The four story building contained a stage 26 feet deep, eight dressing rooms, an opulent two story lobby painted in yellow, white and Wedgwood blue, and a grand marble staircase leading to the auditorium. Seating on the main floor of the theater was augmented by four boxes along the sides and a balcony. The orchestra pit seated 24 musicians and was touted as the largest in Virginia. Twelve thousand square feet of office space was incorporated into the building; there was a spacious billiard parlor in the basement, theatrical booking offices on the second floor, and a restaurant and retail space on the ground floor. A children's nursery room with a lovely mural painted on its walls was provided on the second floor, along with a ladies' retiring room, where tea was served every afternoon from 3:00

COLONIAL THEATER PROGRAM, *1923. This movie playbill features an illustration of the Colonial's tiered auditorium, a new feature that removed the necessity of supporting structural columns that obstructed viewer sight lines.*

to 5:00 p.m. The National Theater building epitomized elegance and "high class" entertainment, with enough dignity in appearance to lure the most conservative middle class patron of the arts to the north side of Broad Street. It offered every viewer a truly fine social event for its 40 cents admission price.

Tradition holds that a ghost haunts the National Theater. Richard McCann noted in 1974 that "a vaudeville performer who hung himself from the rafters in 1928 unscrews the light bulbs backstage as quickly as they're put in. A number of workers have seen him – only a few weeks ago an usher went backstage and cut off the lights. Before he was halfway back down the aisle they shot back on. One usher, after seeing the ghost, tore out and never came back, even for his check."[8] Rumor is that the ghost is still in residence at the National today.

The National's original owners, Pryor and Ferrandini, reaped perhaps the largest profit in Richmond theatrical history when they sold the building in 1925 to Wilmer and Vincent, who purchased the National plus the Strand (old Empire) Theater for $1,000,000. The National Theater, which often showed movies during the week, adding vaudeville or musical revues on the weekends, was a great success. It joined the Broadway (built 1919), Bluebird (1917), Colonial (1921), Isis (1908) and Bijou Theater (1899) to become the centerpiece of Richmond's famous Theater Row. In 1924 Jake Wells had sold his interests in Richmond theaters to his long-time partners Wilmer and Vincent, who thus owned or controlled bookings at most of the major theaters in Richmond — the Colonial, the new National, Bijou, Isis, Odeon, Strand and Academy. Unfortunately for the new owners, fire swept through the Strand in 1926, causing $30,000 in damages. The theater remained closed until 1934, when it was sold and reopened as the Booker T. Theater.

Older Richmonders today fondly remember going to see the silent movies at these Broad Street theaters when they were small children. At ten years old, Lucille Borden traveled downtown frequently by herself on the streetcar from her home in the West End to attend the Theater Row picture shows. One of her favorite theaters she knew as the "Izz Izz;" her mother was very concerned and confused about where her child had been all day (the Izz Izz?) until she finally figured out that Lucille had meant she had been at the Isis Theater. Dr. Randolph Trice recalls attending the silent movies as a little boy in the company of his father; his dad would have to read the subtitles aloud to his young son. Trice mostly remembers the ire of patrons in front of them, turning around to stare and shush those who dared disturb their concentration on the art of silent cinema. "But that didn't bother my father. He kept reading the titles to me, anyway," Trice laughs.

Movie stars made the occasional personal appearance in Richmond. Handsome leading man Thomas Meighan came to the Lyric Theater in 1920 to promote his latest film, and was met by throngs of "stage door Maggies" that dwarfed anything the Grayce Scott Company's Jack Warner ever saw. In 1922, actress Viola Dana, who appeared in everything from daredevil serials to flapper comedies, appeared at the state capitol to speak on behalf of an American Legion membership drive. She met Governor Lee Trinkle, and hundreds of people mobbing the Capitol steps nearly stampeded in their zeal to see a real Hollywood celebrity. Miss Dana

supposedly had a bad cold and could not talk loudly enough on a chilly day, or perhaps intimidated by the mass of adoring fans, she merely shook Trinkle's hand and waved at the crowds.[9]

Richmond even had a brush with the production of a major silent film. In October 1923, director D.W. Griffith came to Richmond to shoot scenes for his newest epic, *America,* a drama about family and community conflict set during the American Revolutionary War. He and his large crew and cast (which included Lucille LaVerne) lodged at the Jefferson Hotel, and shot scenes for several days at the Westover mansion. Griffith borrowed silver from Schwarzchild's Jewelers to dress the set of the wealthy colonial family's home. Schwarzchild's was so proud to have been involved that they lent the items for free, and afterwards they took the rather unusual step of purchasing a quarter page ad in the *News Leader* titled "An Interesting Tribute," in which they reproduced Griffith's signed thank you note. Connections to the glamour of the movies (no matter how small) have always been a thrill.[10]

Richmond's silent movie theaters held special events to keep themselves in the public eye. A couple was once married on the Bijou stage, and amateur contests brought audience participation to several theaters' programs. The Colonial Theater and *News Leader* sponsored a Charleston contest on stage in March 1926. "Nobody in Richmond ever had seen the Charleston executed half so well. The contestants had all of the technique, but were infinitely better than professionals, because they were young, enthusiastic and keyed up to the utmost pitch," the *News Leader* reported. Judge Harry Schwarzchild solicited audience applause to choose the winners. Waverly Jones won first place when "the house roared like a Cape Cod gale." Ellen Lawrence took second place. Twelve-year-old Sidney Horwitz defeated all the female contestants to win the award for best juvenile dancer. The gawky boy was transformed as "The Footwarmers' music got into his overgrown feet and made an artist out of him." Virginia Myers, age six and Marjorie Seay, who was only four, were the other winners. The night of the finals was an event all of Richmond wanted to see. As the paper reported, "A line a hundred yards long and four abreast had formed at the door an hour before the dance...At 9:30 when the finals began, the line at the doors was even longer. Upward of 3,000 people were disappointed." The contestants gave a late night exhibition at 11:00 p.m. for the overflow crowd, and followed up with two more shows on Saturday.[11]

The Picture Palaces

During the 1920s, nearly 4,000 picture palaces – huge, fantastical, gaudy, sumptuous theaters – sprang

NATIONAL THEATER, *704 E. Broad St., 1929. Opened in 1924, the elegant National was the closest approximation of a Broadway-style theater in Richmond. Stylishly dressed flappers included the shows at the National, Broadway, Colonial, Isis and Bijou into their downtown shopping excursions.*

up in cities across the nation, raising the practice of film exhibition to a crazy art form where the environment contributed as much to the pleasures of movie going as did the films on screen. These opulent theaters were not reserved for the wealthy elite, however, as theater industry spokesman Harold Rambusch explained in 1929: "In big modern movie palaces, there are collected the most gorgeous rugs, furniture and fixtures that money can produce. No kings or emperors have wandered through more luxurious surroundings. In a sense, these theatres are social safety valves in that the public can partake of the same luxuries as the rich and use them to the same full extent." The picture palace idea was fully developed in Richmond, as a *Times Dispatch* reporter, reviewing the new Loew's Theater, commented: "It has always been suspected that the theater to most persons is a refuge from reality; but until recently the illusion was confined to the entertainment presented there. Now the purpose

is to surround the patron with this illusion, to swaddle him with luxury...[the theater has changed] from a place to go see to a place to go."[12]

How did the picture palaces come about? One factor was that New York executives of the Loew's, Paramount, Warner Brothers and Fox film corporations (who controlled the distribution of films to America's theaters) realized in the late 1910s that the best way to showcase their studio's film products, and to reap the largest profits from them, was to build their own theaters, instead of merely renting out the films to theaters owned by others. These corporately controlled theaters could have the exclusive rights to show a new film when it was first released, when moviegoers would pay the highest prices to see it. Executives found that large, elegant theaters drew thousands of patrons, were the pride of their communities, and were quite profitable. So, as happened in cities across the United States by the mid-1920s, a sometimes-

NATIONAL THEATER, *2001.*

fierce competition emerged in Richmond between film corporations (like Loew's), national theater chains (like First National, which financed Richmond's National Theater), existing independent film exhibitors (including Walter Coulter), and other entrepreneurs entering the lucrative movie theater market (such as Morton Thalhimer, and the Acca Temple Shriners). In the 1920s, the competitors vied to build ever-more elaborate and splendid picture palaces – cathedrals of the movies – to capture the largest share of Richmond movie patrons' entertainment dollars.

Photographer Anthony L. Dementi covered the opening of the picture palaces and growth of Richmond's theater chains through the golden age of moviegoing. Dementi, who started work with the Foster Studio in 1917, formed his own photography studio with William Faris in the early 1920s. Over the years, Dementi Studio clients included the Loew's, Neighborhood Theaters, Wilmer and Vincent theater chains, and Dementi also took many photographs of theatrical events for the *News*

Leader. The studio's beautiful photographs provide us with rare, richly detailed documentation of these theaters, their audiences, and the time period, and they help us see more clearly how theater- and moviegoing became thoroughly integrated into Richmond's popular culture.

The Capitol Theater and the Coming of "Talkies"

In 1926, real estate developer Morton G. Thalhimer found himself unexpectedly entering Richmond's movie theater scene. When a business deal fell through, Thalhimer was left holding a half-built theater located a mile away from the downtown theatrical center. Thalhimer decided to take over the project, at 2424 West Broad Street, across from the train station, and complete the Capitol Theater. The Capitol opened soon after the Brookland Theater, creating a second residential entertainment center on the outskirts of Richmond, and affirming that movies had become a regular, weekly part of family amusements. The Capitol's patrons would be a little different from the Theater Row crowds — families

INTERIOR, NATIONAL THEATER, *1920s. The "Adamsesque" lobby dome and auditorium walls of the National were adorned with the intricate plasterwork decorations of Richmond sculptor Ferruchio Lengolioli.*

in the West End and Fan neighborhoods, plus train travelers and guests staying at the William Byrd Hotel next door. The Capitol Theater's success launched Thalhimer permanently into the film exhibition business; he subsequently established Neighborhood Theaters Incorporated, which would grow into a powerful regional chain of theaters.

The Capitol Theater opened November 8, 1926 with much newspaper hoopla; its first film was a silent MGM feature, *The Waning Sex*, starring Norma Shearer. In many ways, the Capitol was Richmond's first picture palace, even if it contained only 666 seats. Its architects were Carneal and Johnson, who had previously built the Colonial Theater. The Capitol Theater's elaborate interior

was designed to look like a Spanish garden, with iron gates, potted plants, and sculpture-filled niches created by Ferruccio Legnaioli. It was also Richmond's first "atmospheric" theater (a fanciful style that seated audiences in an environment rather than an imposing marble auditorium, and one which would reach its zenith locally in Loew's Theater). The Capitol featured family-friendly amenities, such as a nursery and playroom for children, and a ladies retiring room complete with a writing desk and complimentary stationery.[13]

The Capitol opened as a silent movie theater, but Thalhimer leapt at the chance to acquire the expensive new sound film equipment that was generating tremendous interest all around the nation. The Capitol was the

CAPITOL THEATER, *2525 W. Broad St., 1926. Shown here at its opening as a silent movie theater, the Capitol soon had the distinction of showing the first "talkies" in Virginia.*

first theater in Virginia to show "talkies," in September 1927. Its first sound film, the Warner Brothers feature *When a Man Loves*, starring John Barrymore, used the Vitaphone system, in which sound was recorded on large records which were mechanically synchronized with the film. This first "talkie" feature had no talk. It was essentially a silent film that had accompanying music recorded by a film studio orchestra. In November 1927, Thalhimer also acquired one of the new Fox Movietone sound systems, which united sound with film by recording it directly onto the film in an optically printed soundtrack. The Capitol had the first Movietone system installed in Virginia, and only the sixth in the nation. Its first Movietone feature, *What Price Glory?* was still a silent film with recorded musical soundtrack. This was perhaps a blessing, for the hit movie was based on a famous Broadway wartime drama whose dialogue was notoriously salty. Lt. Flagg and Sgt. Quirt silently mouthed their epithets to each other while orchestra music played, to the shock of those Capitol Theater viewers who could read lips.

CAPITOL THEATER INTERIOR, *1926. This neighborhood theater, located near the Broad Street train station and West End suburbs, claimed to be the first "atmospheric" theater in Richmond. Its auditorium resembled a Mediterranean garden with murals, urns and foliage along the walls.*

The first spoken dialog "talkie" at the Capitol came with a Fox Movietone newsreel showing Charles Lindbergh's takeoff for Paris. Another early "talkie" newsreel, which Senator Harry Byrd stopped by to see, depicted Admiral Richard Byrd's attempt to fly the Atlantic. Early sound

AERIAL VIEW OF THE MOSQUE AND FAN DISTRICT, *Laurel St at Monroe Park, 1927.*

film projecting equipment caused theater managers many headaches (as is shown hilariously in the film *Singin' In the Rain*.) Neighborhood Theaters executive Sam Bendheim Jr. recalled how grateful the Capitol staff was to get the Movietone sound-on-film system. "Before, the custom had been to buy a film and a separate record supposedly keyed to the movie. Sometimes, you'd find yourself with a horse singing grand opera."[14]

The Capitol scored its breakthrough talkie hit in January 1928 with its presentation of *The Jazz Singer*. The Vitaphone film was a none-too-original melodrama whose silent scenes were interspersed with musical numbers in which Al Jolson actually sang and spoke a few lines to the audience. It was an astoundingly popular film, and it played for weeks at the Capitol. It was also the first talkie most older Richmonders remember seeing when they were children. They recall Jolson singing *April Showers* and *Mammy* and calling out "You ain't heard nothing yet!" Thrilled audiences clamored for more talkies.

While the balky sound machines may have given theater managers fits, the new technology brought thousands of dollars into the box office, and silent films appeared to be on their way out. This alarmed the scores of musicians who had earned good money for fifteen years playing in theater orchestras and accompanying movies on the organ and piano. In August 1928, the Richmond Musicians Association (the local union) wrote to the *News Leader* expressing its fears that "synchronized mechanical music" would take away their jobs. They argued that experiencing "genuine" live performances was essential to keeping the public musically educated and that "canned music" was only a counterfeit of the real thing.[15] The musicians could not stem the tide of technological advancement, however, and theater owners were happy to trim their payrolls, especially when they felt the Depression's pinch. Within a year, orchestras were only found at the National Theater, and sometimes at Loew's. The silent movie accompanists lost their jobs. Only the

AERIAL VIEW OF RICHMOND'S LANDMARK THEATER, *VCU and Fan district, 2001.*

organists, masters of the "Mighty Wurlitzers" at the Byrd, Loew's and National, remained. Other local theaters removed their organs, or just boarded over and forgot them in the wake of the talkie revolution.

In August 1929, A *News Leader* editorial rejoiced (with tongue in cheek) that the coming of talkies had meant an end to the pest who insisted upon mumbling the subtitles aloud "in spite of the quips and comic strip threats made at him." But the writer feared that a worse menace was loose – amateur singers in the audience who warbled the film's theme song along with the actors. The *News Leader* suggested, "perhaps, after all, it is better to return to the silent drama before more evils arise."[16]

The Mosque

Fraternal societies were at their peak membership throughout the United States in the 1920s. Members of Richmond's Acca Temple Shrine broke ground in January 1926 for a large multi-purpose facility that would house their many activities, meetings, formal functions and entertainments. The Richmond Shriners ambitiously planned an auditorium that could seat nearly 5,000 people. Like many other Shriner groups during the 1920s, they drew on then-popular Middle Eastern names and decorating schemes for their building, which they christened the Mosque (today known as Richmond's Landmark Theater). The Acca Temple located their building at the corner of Laurel and Main streets, on the edge of Monroe Park. The Mosque cost $1.75 million dollars to construct, handing the Shriners a huge mortgage payment that they nevertheless assumed would be easily met. With civic pride and boosterish spirit, backers assumed that the theater could pay for itself from the revenues gained when the city rented the auditorium for important school and civic functions, and from engagements by to local opera, symphony, theater, and concert promoters.

Previous to the Mosque's opening, concerts had been held at the City Municipal Auditorium, a former meat market on West Cary Street that the city had renovated into a large hall for musical entertainments and conventions. The brick building that Edith Lindeman termed "a huge barn of a place" had 3,000 seats set on a flat floor, above which was a low balcony which ringed three

THE MOSQUE, *1930s. After 75 years, remarkably little has changed about the exterior of the Mosque, built by the Acca Temple Shriners in 1927. Purchased by the city in 1940, renovated and renamed in 1995, it remains Richmond's largest theater and concert hall.*

MOSQUE AUDITORIUM, *1927. The theater's richly decorated, enormous auditorium held 3,600 patrons, as many as New York City's famous Paramount Theater.*

RICHMOND'S LANDMARK THEATER, *Laurel St. At Monroe Park, 2001.*

sides of the building. The auditorium was alternately drafty or hot, and opening windows set high on the walls controlled temperatures. Notwithstanding its humble beginnings and lack of elegance, the City Auditorium had seen such stars of the opera and concert hall as Alma Gluck, Efram Zimbalist, Rosa Ponselle, John McCormick, Lawrence Tibbett and Ignace Jan Padewerski. Statuesque opera singer Geraldine Farrar performed there in a sequined, strapless gown that created quite a sensation in conservative Richmond social circles. Edith Lindeman reported, "an account of the concert noted, in effect, that the beauteous Farrar was 'all glittering singer below the waist and all gleaming singer above.'"[17] Richmond's opera and symphony supporters were delighted to learn that the Shriners intended to build a more comfortable and suitable venue for their concerts.

The Mosque was massive, a Shriners' castle decorated in Moorish oriental style. The main portion of the building was five stories tall, and the front had two tall minarets, which added five more stories to the building's height. Newspaper publicity at the opening touted the building's impressive statistics, including news that 75,000 square feet of 22-carat gold leaf was applied to the dome. The Mosque's auditorium seated 4,763, with 1,931 seats in the orchestra and 2,832 more in the balconies. As a *News Leader* reporter wrote at the time, "The stage draperies were supposed to represent the hangings of a rich

sultan's tent in ancient Arabia. They were studded with artificial rubies, emeralds and diamonds, and gold cords, tassels and fringe were in abundance. When the curtain moved, all the imbedded jewels reflected the colored lights which was dazzling."[18] Designed by Richmond architects Marcellus Wright Sr. and Charles M. Robinson, the 176,000 square foot structure had six levels of lobbies, a vast auditorium, a huge stage, several stories of dressing rooms, a ballroom large enough to hold 3,500 dancers, a bowling alley, four large meeting rooms, a banquet hall that seated 1,500, an 18 by 80 foot swimming pool in the basement, and 42 hotel rooms for visiting Shriners. The auditorium also featured a huge Wurlitzer organ with 17 ranks of pipes.

The opening program at the Mosque on October 28, 1927 featured a performance by Metropolitan Opera contralto Ernestine Schumann-Heink, who at age 66 was on her farewell tour. The auditorium was packed with more than 4,500 attendees. The second night featured a combined bill of film and vaudeville acts. A week of Grand Opera with the San Carlo Company of New York followed in January. In 1928, the privately owned building saw 50 public performances. The Metropolitan Opera Company appeared at the Mosque for three nights in 1929. Ponselle and Martinelli performing the opera "Aida" established a box office record with ticket sales of $23,500. In 1930, however, the Mosque only hosted

AUDIENCE AT MOSQUE, *Late 1920s. A stylishly dressed crowd of Richmond women fills the Mosque's capacious auditorium.*

26 public performances. Because the auditorium was so very large, it proved to be nearly impossible for Shriners or concert promoters to fill it on a weekly basis, and the huge costs of operating the building outweighed the revenues. The managers tried to put on movie shows at the Mosque, but the massive auditorium overwhelmed the films. After all, the Mosque seated more people than the huge Paramount Theater in New York City. The Shriners could not afford their huge building during the Depression, and the Acca Temple turned over the mort-gage to the New York Life Insurance Company. After much local political debate, the city of Richmond would purchase the facility for $200,000 in 1940 (a large amount in Depression times, but still, quite a bargain). The city used the Mosque for school functions, concerts and meetings. Despite its financial woes, the building was of vital importance to Richmond's cultural life. A reporter later remarked, "It would be hard to imagine Richmond without the Mosque, for it is the only adequate public auditorium in the city."[19]

Loew's

Marcus Loew and other representatives of the Loew's Theaters/ MGM film corporation scouted Richmond as a location to build a movie palace in 1926. They were expanding their theater holdings in the Southeast, and Richmond looked like a promising site, although apparently there was not any prime space available for sale on Broad Street. Instead, they acquired a tract on Grace Street, one block south of Theater Row. They broke ground for a new theater in January 1927. Although it was not on the main thoroughfare of the entertainment district, it was nestled between Richmond's two largest department stores on a street of exclusive shops. Locating on Grace Street would seal the Loew's Theater's reputation as a "high class" theater, earning respect and business from the most status-conscious middle class and wealthy patrons, especially the women who shopped at Thalhimer's and Miller & Rhoads and lunched in the Tea Room. But the splendors of Richmond's fanciest picture palace were also open to children and teenagers, young dating couples, families out for a night on the town, businesspeople, shop girls and rural visitors in town to see the Big City. African-Americans, however, were not admitted, an exclusion that would only be rectified during the Civil Rights movement in the 1960s.

The Loew's held a pre-opening special event on March 10, 1928, during which time anyone could tour the theater for free; 12,000 Richmonders walked through the building. Even more than the MGM films it would be showing, the Loew's Theater itself was the star attraction. The fanciful building, in the trademark atmospheric theater style of architect John Eberson, cost $1,250,000 to construct. "The exterior in red-brown brick has an ornate curved wall," wrote Annette Burr. "This five story tall façade rises in a brickwork diamond pattern to a false peak curved like a Spanish Mission church front. The façade is decorated with Spanish-Moorish elements such as shells, leaves, urns and cornucopias. Blue terra cotta jewels decorate the font." Blue terracotta columns separated the arches between the seven shop spaces that lined the street level of the theater. From the large, low-ceiled lobby (which could comfortably hold 1,500 patrons waiting in line to see the next show), movie-goers walked up the staircases to the balconies, moving through a series of rooms decorated in Spanish-Moorish theme with stained glass panels, ornate plaster terracotta wall ornamentation, statues and coordinating carved wood furniture, towards the auditorium.

The auditorium, which seated 2,000 people, resembled the interior of a moonlit Spanish patio and garden. The fantasy-inspired design was in the "atmospheric" style developed by the Austrian-born theater architect John Eberson. Eberson began his career with Michelangelo Studios in Chicago and New York. He trained painters and architects how to create the opulence he wanted for his movie palaces. Many of the decorative objects such as statuary, urns, and furniture at Loew's were not mass-produced, but were hand picked by Eberson himself from various antique shops, or were hand made by his artists. Six parrots in cages (four stuffed, two live) were scattered through the theater's lobbies, a Loew's chain trademark. Mechanical doves popped in and out of side balcony coves hidden along the auditorium's Spanish garden walls.

Eberson described his atmospheric auditorium as "a magnificent amphitheater under a glorious moonlit sky...an Italian garden, a Persian Court, a Spanish patio or a mystic Egyptian templeyard...where friendly stars twinkled and wisps of clouds drifted."[20] The illusion was very popular with the public. Guy Friddell recalled watching the "moon, clouds and stars – wheeling across the ceiling while we sat below, heads back, mouths agape. It was a week before anybody knew what was even playing on the screen. Let's go down to the Loew's and look at the stars, we used to say."

The Loew's starlit ceiling, while magical and playful, was actually also an innovative cost-cutting measure. Theaters full of marble, brass, gilding and crystal chandeliers were increasingly expensive to build. The Loew's rainbow-shaped roof made for good acoustics, and the sky was a simple coat of paint. The stars were created with small light bulbs wired into the ceiling. The clouds were silk-screened onto large fabric panels that waved back and forth under spotlights to make wispy movements across the "sky." Atmospheric theaters cost only one-quarter as much as traditional marble-encrusted theaters did to build. The "cloud machine" cost only $290.00.

As the Loew's opening night neared, Tony Dementi captured Eberson on film pointing out details of the new building's exterior to Colonel John Schiller, vice-president of the Loew's theatrical circuit (this house would be the 350th theater in the chain). Eberson, the perfectionist, worked his staff up to the last minute to make everything just right for the inaugural show. In fact, legend says "Earlier that day Richmond stagehands experienced [a] Loew's thunderstorm when the clouds drifted by a bit too swiftly for Eberson's exacting taste."[21]

On the gala opening night, April 9, 1928, 2,200 patrons waited in line outside in the cold and rain, anxious to bask in the warm glow of the Mediterranean gardens inside. The first person in line to purchase a ticket was a fifteen-year old newspaper boy, Armand Doyle. He had walked all the way from his home on Church Hill, leaving at 6:00 am in hopes of being first at the door. Such

LOBBY, LOEW'S THEATER,
1928. The richly textured stucco walls, antique furniture and tapestries, fine carpets, caged parrots and uniformed ushers made the Loew's resemble a fairytale castle to the patrons who waited in the lobby for entrance to the auditorium.

was Doyle's affection for the theater that, even though he had long since moved to Chicago, he returned to Richmond in 1978 to take part in the Loew's Theater 50th anniversary celebration. To accompany the silent films at Loew's, there were 12 musicians in the pit and an orchestra leader, and a magnificent 13-rank Wurlitzer organ. The Loew's first organist was Lloyd Oscar, billed as "Wild Oscar." An opening night reviewer called him "a deft exponent of syncopation, a nimble musical trickster and a singer of pleasant and agreeable voice." A corps of 19 uniformed ushers showed patrons to their seats. The new theater offered continuous performances from 11 am to 11 pm, and tickets cost 25, 35 and 50 cents. Although it opened as a silent film theater, the Loew's was wired for sound five months later, in September 1928. Its first "talkie" was *The Patriot* with noted actor Emil Jannings.

The inaugural feature film at the Loew's was *West Point*, a silent MGM romantic drama starring up-and-coming young movie actor William Haines, and starlet Joan Crawford. Born in Lexington, Haines was a Virginian who as a teen, had lived with his family in Richmond for several years working as a store clerk. Newspaper advertisements proudly identified him as "Richmond's Own and Only Movie Star."[22] His parents, Mr. and Mrs.

PLAYBILL, LOEW'S THEATER, *1928. Richmond's "own and only movie star," William Haines, starred with Joan Crawford in the inaugural film at Loew's, **West Point**.*

LOEW'S AUDITORIUM, *1928. Decorated in John Eberson's famous "atmospheric" style, the Loew's fantasy-inspired auditorium resembled a Spanish garden at night. Impressed moviegoers craned their necks to see stars twinkling in the deep-blue ceiling's "sky," and watch clouds and moon drift overhead.*

George Haines still lived in town and were honored guests at the premiere (Haines himself could not attend). William Haines had become a popular young leading man in MGM silent films in the mid-1920s with appearances in Mary Pickford's film *Little Annie Rooney*, the popular comedy *Sally, Irene and Mary*, and the college football film *Brown of Harvard*. He played the fresh-faced, athletic young hero to perfection. Haines subsequently started in MGM's silent films *Tell it to the Marines* with Lon Chaney, the marvelous Hollywood satire *Show People* with Marion Davies, and his best role as the young gangster in *Alias Jimmy Valentine*. Richmond's brush with Hollywood fame was brief, as Haines did not last long in the talkies; nevertheless he did reinvent himself in a new career as one of Hollywood's most successful and expensive interior decorators.[23]

JOHN EBERSON AND LOEW'S PRESIDENT JOHN SCHILLER INSPECT THE NEW THEATER, *1928. Legend has it that architect Eberson created a thunderstorm of his own backstage when the projected clouds drifted too quickly across the auditorium's ceiling on opening day.*

BYRD THEATER, *2905 W. Cary St., 1946. Built by Walter Coulter and Charles Somma in 1928, the Byrd has been Richmond's homegrown picture palace for 75 years, and is on the National Register of Historic Places.*

The Byrd Theater

Film exhibitor Walter Coulter had done much to make the movies respectable entertainment for white and black patrons in Richmond at theaters like the Rex, Hippodrome, and Bluebird opened with his original business partner Amanda Thorpe. Coulter continued to be a major player in the movie theater-building boom of the 1920s. In 1925, Coulter branched out to stake a claim in the suburban theater market by building the Brookland Theater on the city's North Side. Critics said a theater far from downtown would surely fail, but the Brookland was a great success. Coulter also built the Bluebird Theater in Petersburg. In 1927, Coulter and new his business partner Charles Somma began planning for the construction of their own elegant movie palace, to be called the William Byrd Theater (soon shortened to "The Byrd"). Somma made his start in the Richmond theater business by purchasing the Dixie and Hippodrome the-

aters from Coulter and Thorpe. Somma subsequently acquired the Globe and Rayo movie houses, making him the leading owner of black movie theaters in the city. In the early 1920s, Somma became Coulter's partner in the Bluebird Theaters in Richmond and Petersburg, and together they built the Brookland.[24]

Coulter and Somma's decision to build their new theater on Cary Street (then called Westhampton Avenue) also raised some skeptical eyebrows. Westhampton was a mixed residential and retail street, in the West End suburbs several miles from Theater Row. Coulter and Somma gambled that neighborhood patronage and Richmonders' increasing use of automobiles would mean that the city would find its way to the Byrd's door.

The Byrd Theater opened Christmas Eve 1928, with a First National studios film entitled *Waterfront*, starring Dorothy Mackaill and Jack Mulhall. George Stitzer (a Byrd employee for 55 years who was doorman on opening

BYRD THEATER, *2905 W. Cary St., 2001.*

night) recalled that the film was a half-silent, half-talkie melodrama whose plot concerned a young girl who worked at a newsstand near the docks and who fell in love with a handsome sailor. The film had Vitaphone musical accompaniment, and manager Robert Coulter (Walter's younger brother) later recalled that "the sound was on 16-inch records and we had to be very careful to get sound and action synchronized."[25] Also on the program were Mack Sennett's first all-talkie comedy, *The Lion's Roar,* and Fox Movietone newsreels.

The Byrd's décor featured rose and gold curtains, draperies and fringe, marble walls, a gilded ceiling with plasterwork by Legnaioli, French Empire-style furniture on the mezzanine, a rococo 20 by 8-foot fish pool and fountain in the lobby, pastoral murals set into windows along the walls, turns filled with green foliage. A harp and piano (that magically played by themselves!) were ensconced in niches at the sides of the stage, and the

magnificent Wurlitzer organ rose out of the pit. A focal point was the huge, glittering two-ton crystal chandelier (of which the management has always been so proud) hanging in the auditorium which featured 5,000 Czecho-slovakian crystals, and which was lit by 400 light bulbs in red, blue, green and gold. An opening night reviewer enthused, "From the moment of entering the lobby, wainscoted with Grecian marble in tones of brown and buff, with its bronze doors and stair railings, its unusually well executed frescoes and its beautiful crystal fixtures, one is impressed with the feeling of luxury the promoters of this enterprise have tried to provide – not costliness merely, but beauty, comfort and refinement."[26]

The theater's facade was of red tapestry brick with terracotta trim. Its original neon sign was 45 feet tall and was described as "one of the most massive electrical effects of the kind to be seen in the South." Building costs were estimated to be between $800,000 and $960,000.

BYRD THEATER INTERIOR, *1928. The Byrd's auditorium is decorated in a red and gold French Empire-period style. The famous chandelier contains over 5,000 crystals. Manager Robert Coulter trusted no one but himself to clean and dust the fixture for 47 years.*

The Byrd's auditorium originally seated 800 patrons downstairs in the orchestra, and 596 in the balcony, but was reconfigured several years later to seat 900 on the main floor and 480 upstairs. The Byrd also featured a huge Wurlitzer with 17 ranks of pipes, the largest and most impressive organ in Richmond. Carl Rond, a Dutch immigrant, educated at the Royal Conservatory in Amsterdam, was in charge of music at the Byrd. He had previously been organist at Coulter and Somma's Brookland Theater for four years.[27]

Richmonders probably made constant comparisons between the Loew's Theater and it's rival the new Byrd, but in many ways the two picture palaces complemented each other. While the Loew's atmosphere was all Spanish garden-fantasy, architect Fred Bishop designed the

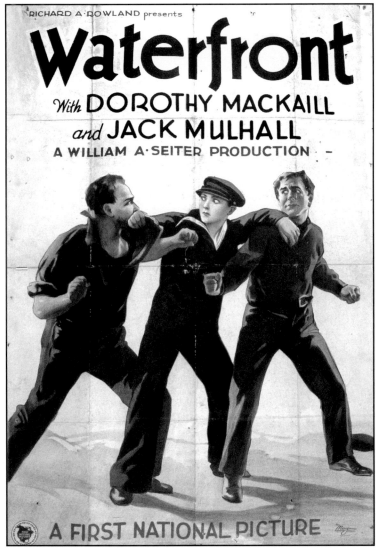

WATERFRONT POSTER, 1928. *This half-silent, half-talkie film was the inaugural show at the Byrd Theater, Collection of Kathy Fuller-Seeley.*

Byrd to recreate the environment of a French royal palace of the Empire period. The Loew's had nearly twice as many seats as the Byrd (2,200 vs. 1,400). The Loew's was a flagship theater exclusively showing MGM films weeks before they could be found at any other theater. The Byrd showed a pastiche of Fox, Warner Brothers, and RKO films, but it also had local control of United Artists and later, Disney films. The Loew's was in many ways a house corporately-controlled out of New York, with a number of managers coming through town (although George Peters, who arrived in the early 1940s, would remain manager for 20 years). The Byrd was very much a Richmond, homegrown institution. Its manager,

Robert Coulter, held tenure for 47 years.

In 1929, Richmond found itself with a rich variety of lovely theaters – the Colonial, National, Mosque, Loew's and Byrd, plus the Lyric, as well as suburban theaters like the Brookland and Venus, and the dozen older movie and vaudeville theaters lining the Broad Street and Hull Street corridors. Movie attendance skyrocketed in Richmond, and across the nation (national figures rose from 50 million tickets sold per year in 1925 to 90 million in 1929), spurred by the novelty of talkies, and the opulent new theaters in which to view them. It was a time of movie-going bounty, but a shakeout was soon to occur.

RICHMOND SKYLINE, *1930s.*

CHAPTER 3

Richmond Theater
1930-1940

The stock market crash of October 1929 marked the beginning of the greatest economic downturn the United States ever experienced. A quarter of the country's workers lost their jobs, and another 25 percent found only part-time employment. Production plummeted, banks failed, businesses closed, and droughts destroyed farms. While Richmond and Virginia did not suffer as severely during the Depression as did the industrial North and agricultural Midwest, times were hard for many. Salaries for teachers and city workers were slashed, farmers' crops were ruined, and African Americans especially found, poor living conditions and low wages. Some other Richmond workers, managers and investors prospered, however, buoyed by the expanding production of cigarettes, rayon, cellophane and other goods in local factories. Many of Richmond's finer stores and the larger theaters, like Loew's, Byrd and National, continued to do good business. However, most of the city's older (and smaller) silent movie theaters were affected. In times of unemployment and belt-tightening, many workers and their families, the usual patrons of the small theaters, could not afford to go to the movies as often as they had. Wiring an older theater for sound was expensive, and the smaller exhibitors could not afford it when box office revenues were dropping. Along Broad Street, the Isis, Theato, Bluebird, Broadway and Bijou Theaters closed, and the Odeon was torn down to make way for expansion of the Thalhimer's department store building. Across the state, 100 of Virginia's 300 movie theaters were shuttered. The dire situation for the film exhibition industry eventually improved, but it did

so more quickly in the state's cities than in its small towns. Richmond's closed movie houses were eventually sold to theater chains including Morton Thalhimer's growing Neighborhood Theaters, Inc. (NTI). They were wired for sound, their exteriors were refurbished, their interiors were redecorated in Art Deco style, and they became second- or third-run theaters.

The closed Bluebird Theater reopened three years after its 1930 closing. The Grand Theater, as it was renamed, became what the film industry called a "grind house" or "action house." The Grand showed a steady stream of grade B westerns, horror shows, adventure specials, and serials starring Tom Mix, Tarzan, and the Green Hornet. Such films were the favorites of children, teens, workers and shop clerks on their lunch hours. The Broadway was remade into the State Theater. The old Isis/Lubin Theater building, closed for nine years, was finally wired for sound and reopened as the Park Theater in 1938. The Bijou Theater (built in 1899) was redecorated with new carpet and paint, and its lobby and façade were given an Art Deco makeover with glass panels and aluminum trim. It was renamed the Strand, and reopened in October 1933 with the movie *The Gold Diggers of Broadway*. The venerable old house lasted five more years before it was remodeled into a bowling alley in 1938. The building was later torn down to make way for a Trailways bus station. In the 1990s it became the site of the Library of Virginia.

The Spring of 1930 saw the last season of regular full-time vaudeville shows at the National and Lyric theaters. On the bill at the National were Cole and Snyder, Eliza-

(Above) **STRAND THEATER**, *810 E. Broad St, 1936. The 30-year old Bijou Theater was renovated and renamed the Strand in 1933. It showed western and action films, a favorite with young boys during the Depression. The Strand closed in 1938, and became a bowling alley, then was demolished to make way for a Trailways bus terminal.*

(Left) **GRAND THEATER**, *620 E. Broad Street, 1934. Renovated in 1933 with a new façade replacing that of the old Bluebird Theater, the Grand Theater also showed cowboy and action films. Shirley Temple was the top box office attraction of the 1930s.*

beth Brice, Happy Harrison's Circus, and the Betty Jane Cooper Revue. While occasional headliners like Eddie Cantor and George Jessel, or fan dancer Sally Rand and her "All Star Broadway Revue", made special appearances at the Mosque during the decade, the nation's vaudeville circuit was all but dead. Vaudeville had been done in by a combination of the huge success of the "talkies," the rising costs of transportation for live acts, and the ravages of the Depression. The National Theater played movies during the week, accompanied by a live act or two on stage, with the addition of Jack Kaminsky's orchestra and the Hal Sands dancing girls on the weekends.[1]

Touring theatrical troupes' visits to Richmond were

even fewer during the 1930s, but there were some memorable performances. For two seasons, the *News Leader* sponsored appearances of the New York Theater Guild at the Lyric Theater.[2] Edward Peples recalled the Theater Guild production of Eugene O'Neill's *Strange Interlude* in February 1930, which took five hours to perform. The first act started at 5:30 p.m., there was an hour break for dinner at 8:00, then the play continued until 11:30 that night. Peples wrote, "In an orchestra seat one felt more than a little cramped after five hours of watching, but those of us in the last rows of the second balcony were almost afraid to try the perilous flight of steps to the ground – our knee joints didn't want to bend in the right

COLONIAL THEATER AUDIENCE, *1930s. Saturday movie shows were the delight of children across the city.*

direction. Although I cannot clearly recall what most of the actors' faces looked like, I can still describe the tops of their heads and the way they combed their hair."[3]

Richmond theatrical highlights of the 1930s included Alfred Lunt and Lynn Fontanne performing at the Lyric in *There Shall Be No Night*; Katharine Hepburn appearing in *The Philadelphia Story*, Victor Borge's first American tour, and Boris Karloff playing in the original Broadway company of *Arsenic and Old Lace*. Katharine Cornell and Basil Rathbone brought *The Barretts of Wimpole Street* and *Candida* to the National Theater in May 1934; a 19-year old Orson Welles was a cast member in the company. The Mosque, although in severe financial trouble, was still home to many of the biggest concerts and musical shows in Richmond. During the 1930s, it hosted the first (short-lived) Richmond Symphony. The Metropolitan and American Opera companies performed there, and stars Ezio Pinza, Lily Pons, Marian Anderson and Grace Moore appeared on the Mosque stage. Richmond-born tap dancer Bill Robinson, star of Broadway and Harlem musical reviews, returned to town in June 1931, performing at the Mosque with Eubie Blake's orchestra in the show *Brown Buddies*. Robinson returned again in 1932 with the show *Going to Town*. George Gershwin gave a concert at the Mosque in March 1934. Eubie Blake brought his hit musical *Shuffle Along* to the National in April 1934, for one midnight performance. The ballroom in the basement of the Mosque hosted all of the best-known big bands of the era, including a performance by Ella Fitzgerald and her Orchestra in September 1940. The National Theater held concerts by Paul Whiteman, Fred Waring and his Pennsylvanians, and other popular bands. The largest-grossing show of the decade at the Mosque took place on March 21, 1939, when singing movie star Nelson Eddy gave a concert. His performance completely packed the huge 4,700-seat theater, and the management also squeezed a further 300 attendees into seats placed behind the performer on the stage.[4]

RICHMOND SCREENLAND, *1933. A local publication of Richmond movie theaters kept fans up to date on new films and stars, and urged them to come out to a show.*

At The Byrd – The Mickey Mouse Club, Sunday Shows and Air Conditioning

Richmonders who grew up in the 1930s, 1940s and 1950s have fond memories of attending the Saturday morning children's shows at the Byrd Theater. In the early 1930s, the Saturday morning affairs were called "The Mickey Mouse Club." In a promotion sponsored by the Walt Disney Company (which predated their televised *Mickey Mouse Club* shows by 25 years), Disney supplied exhibitors with cartoon films, membership badges for the children, and ideas for souvenir giveaways, talent shows, and holiday-related activities to be held at participating theaters. The Club program stressed that moviegoing was a healthy, positive experience for children, and the films and activities strove to teach lessons in good character and citizenship. Disney also supplied theaters

with advertising slides to show on the screen in between films, that featured pictures of the new Mickey Mouse merchandise (books, toys, house wares, and wristwatches) that was available at local stores – a precursor to today's promotional tie-in schemes.

The educational and business aspects of Disney's clever merchandizing did not matter to the children, however – they just wanted to watch cartoons. The Mickey Mouse Club programs at the Byrd started at 10:00 a.m. and continued until 12:30 p.m., leaving ushers just time enough to clear the house before the first afternoon matinee began at 1:00 p.m. The shows were also held at the Brookland Theater. Children received two-and-a-half hours of entertainment for ten cents. Bill Jordan remembers being a part of those Mickey Mouse Club shows, when kids were lined up outside the theater along Westhampton (Cary) Street all the way around to Sheppard Street, clutching dimes and waiting impatiently to get inside. During the show, children saw two cartoons, a western or a comedy, and a cliffhanger serial. Dr. Randolph Trice recalls, "The heroine would be stretched out on the railroad track with the train coming, and then this sign would appear 'to be continued.' And so you had to come back the next Saturday to see what happened to the poor girl." Slapstick comedies were also popular with children, he says. "We'd see the same Laurel and Hardy movie over and over again and just wait for the scene we knew was coming up, and for some reason it was funnier the second, third and fourth time than it was the first." Trice admits that despite its many appeals, his interest in the Mickey Mouse Club's shows waned as he grew up and learned about girls.

Byrd Theater manager Robert Coulter kept a firm but friendly eye on the children. Parents all over town knew that it was safe to send their children walking to the Byrd, or parents could drop their kids off by car at the theater's front door. "Bob Coulter had quite a reputation," Trice remembers, "he was sort of the babysitter for hundreds of families in Richmond. They would take their children up to the theater and Mr. Coulter said, 'I'll look out for them.'" Coulter's Saturday morning shows were a tradition for several generations of Richmonders. "When I was a parent and leaving my own children off there with Mr. Coulter," Trice recalls, "I could come back later and he would say, 'Oh, Wilson [my son] is right down here.' He knew the names of all these children and where they were sitting. A remarkable man." Coulter also kept children from being too rowdy inside his theater (unlike at other children's shows, which had the reputation of being madhouses on Saturday). Jordan remembers that the Carillon Theater, just up the next block from the Byrd, had its own Saturday morning show, but the Carillon would only have perhaps 10 children in attendance, while the Byrd's seats were always filled.

Robert Coulter's grandson Bob Coulter recalls a happy childhood spent with his grandfather at the Byrd's Saturday morning shows, which dropped the Mickey Mouse Club name by the late 1930s, but which continued for 30 more years. Mr. Coulter would give Bob a quarter to go buy a sandwich next door at the New York Deli. If the afternoon's regular feature was suitable for young viewers, and Bob had behaved well, he was allowed to stay and watch it, too. Bob recalls exploring all of the Byrd's hidden nooks and crannies, many shown to him by Byrd ushers. On one occasion, however, his explorations went a bit too far. One Saturday afternoon, as the ushers were cleaning the theater for the matinee after the children's show, Mr. Coulter was shocked to see the Mighty Wurlitzer emerging from its hidden depths, ascending from the pit in the floor, while a chagrinned young boy held on to the rising organ bench for dear life. Young Bob got in big trouble with his grandfather that day.

Stores, banks, theaters and other amusements had traditionally been closed on Sundays, in accordance with "blue laws" that dated back to Colonial times. Increasingly in the 1930s, more people were laboring long workweeks and sought opportunities for relaxation and necessary shopping during their precious weekend hours. Pressures built to allow stores and movie shows to be open on Sundays, and a long struggle ensued between religious conservatives and business entrepreneurs. Virginia's restrictions on boxing and Sunday baseball games were liberalized in 1934, at the end of Prohibition, as a way to boost business during the Depression.[5] In Richmond, negotiations to allow Sunday movie shows began in December 1934, but took 18 months to resolve. Theater managers got themselves arrested frequently as they tried to overturn the laws. On one Sunday in 1934, Robert Coulter and six Byrd Theater employees volunteered to put on a show to benefit the Crippled Children's Hospital. More than 8,000 people crowded into five showings that day. Coulter, the projectionist and ushers were served with warrants, but it proved how popular such shows could be.

Virginia first allowed Sunday movies on May 25, 1936. "The opening of the theaters is a result of the acquittal of Charles A. Somma, general manager of the Byrd, on a charge of operating the theater on Sunday April 19, in violation of the state blue law," reported the *News Leader*. "A hustings court jury held Monday that the moving pictures were a necessity and therefore legal." The jury ruled that Sunday movies "improved the moral and physical welfare of the people." Richmond film ex-

hibitors were jubilant. "Theater Signs Flash Welcome of Big Sunday Crowds Here," the *Times Dispatch* announced. Exhibitors were careful not to offend the conservative elements in town, however – Sunday movie shows would only begin at 2:00 pm. "Movies Not to Rival Churches," another headline read. Loew's manager assured critics that ending the ban would put more men to work in the movie houses, and thus end the Depression.[6]

Another of the main draws of Richmond's movie theaters, especially during long, hot summers, was the chance to escape from the boiling heat of the streets, or a cramped apartment after supper. Air conditioning previously had been used for commercial purposes only, such as meat refrigeration. By the mid-1920s, however, the cost of cooling equipment had become more reasonable, and theater owners began installing it to overcome that age-old problem of having to close up in the hot months. Their innovative use of large cooling systems in their picture palaces not only improved human comfort, but also drew tremendous crowds to the box office. Movie houses are credited with putting air conditioning into the main stream of southern life.[7] Dr. Trice recalls that the Byrd was one of Richmond's first theaters to be outfitted with it. The theater held a grand re-opening ceremony afterwards with a big sign in front that announced, "Cooled by Carrier." "It sold a lot of movie tickets," he recalls, "when it was a hot summer day in Richmond, you'd go to the Byrd to cool off." Edith Lindeman recalled that most movie theaters in Richmond were not air conditioned when she started working for the *News Leader* in 1933, but as soon as they could, other theaters followed the Byrd, often before local department stores, banks and other public buildings were fitted with the equipment. Movie theater marquees and newspaper advertisements in the summer would feature enticing little icicles in the corner, luring in patrons with the promise that it was "twenty degrees cooler inside!" It would be until the 1950s before many homes began to sprout window AC units. There was a great sigh of relief among families wilting through graduation ceremonies when the city-owned Mosque was finally retrofitted for air conditioning in the 1960s.[8]

Eddie Weaver and Richmond's Theater Organs

The "Mighty Wurlitzers" at the Byrd, Loew's and Mosque have been renowned from the time that they were installed in 1927 and 1928 to provide accompaniment for silent movies. Organs had not been widely associated with non-secular entertainment before the rise of elaborate motion picture theaters. Before the 1910s, pipe organs had been chiefly used in large churches and cathedrals. Playhouses had primarily used orchestras of

BYRD THEATER, *1935. Dressed up to attend an evening performance, Richmonders continued to flock to the movies. Despite the Depression's hard times, moviegoing was America's most popular form of entertainment.*

from three to 30 musicians. Nickelodeon theater managers wishing to provide inexpensive musical accompaniment to silent films employed three-piece groups and pianists, providing many a small town musician with welcome employment. By the early 1910s, movie theater owners began to turn to a new generation of multi-function organs to provide the music. The Rudolph Wurlitzer Company of North Tonawanda, New York, perfected the complex "unit orchestra" invented by Englishman Robert Hope-Jones, and Wurlitzer quickly became the preeminent builder of large, elaborate and powerful pipe organs. They became featured centers of musical entertainment in clubs, restaurants, and department stores as well. The Wurlitzer Company's new instruments were also capable of producing other sounds — drums, piano, xylophones, cymbals, and special effects (such as train whistles, thunderclaps, or rain storms). All actions were controlled through a central console. Wires, electro-mag-

nets and forced air sent through tubes propelled the drumsticks, pushed the hammers on piano keys, and operated the woodwind stops. The pipe organ's interior workings were housed in large boxes or chambers under, over or behind the stage, while the organ console itself became ever larger and more theatrical.

The organist who operated this huge musical machine became increasingly important. He or she became a star, dressed formally in tuxedo or gown, arising from underneath the stage seated on a bench attached to the magnificent, gleaming console. The organist was seemingly always in motion, hands playing melodies along five or six ranks of keyboards, fingers darting to push and pull the special stop keys that made the other instruments play, and feet pumping the various floor pedals in a crazy dance.

The organist often made a dramatic entrance, rising from the orchestra pit on the console, and played an

BYRD THEATER, *2001. The dress code for going to the movies has loosened, but Friday and Saturday nights still mean going out to the movies for many couples and groups of friends.*

overture to warm up the crowd for the show. Sometimes there would be a sing-along portion, when words to a Tin Pan Alley favorite were shown on the screen, and a bouncing ball guided the audience in warbling enthusiastically along with the organ. In the days of silent movies, the organist would provide musical accompaniment for the comedies, newsreels and features. Often times he or she adapted popular tunes to fit the mood (such as frantic chase, tender romance, or slapstick pratfall). Usually the big feature films came with a pre-arranged or suggested score to follow.

The magnificent Wurlitzer organ at the Byrd Theater featured 1,229 different pipes that were housed in four chambers above the auditorium ceiling. From the mass of instruments, air tubes, and machinery hidden in the attic over the stage, it could produce the following sounds: quintadena, celeste, viol d'orchestra, strings, flute, tibia, tuba, trumpet, oboe, saxophone, clarinet, 88-

note grand piano, xylophone, marimba, bells, steel harp, snare drum, bass drum, kettle drum, tom-toms, tambourine, castanets, Chinese blocks, cymbals and the sound effects of trains, aeroplanes, crashing surf, horse's hooves, roaring flames, fire gong, bird chirps, and a steamboat whistle.[9]

Eddie Weaver was Richmond's most famous theater organist by far, and one of the city's biggest local stars. James Edward Weaver was born in Catasauqua, Pennsylvania, in 1908 and grew up in Allentown, where he received his early musical training in piano and organ from his mother, a piano teacher, and his father, a choir instructor. He attended the Eastman School of Music in Rochester, New York, to study the church organ, but soon changed his mind. He found the movies entrancing, recalling, "I wanted in the worst way to accompany silent pictures." He switched majors to theater organ. Unfortunately, soon after he got out of school, the talkies came

EDDIE WEAVER, *1950s. Richmond's premiere movie theater organist, Weaver made audiences smile and sing along with his Wurlitzer at the Loew's and Byrd theaters for nearly 50 years.*

in, but the larger theaters kept their organists to perform between shows, so the talented Weaver thrived. He worked at theaters in Batavia and Buffalo, New York; Coral Gables and Tampa, Florida; and Washington D.C. He worked in New Haven, Connecticut, for ten years as theater organist (with very rowdy Yale University students in the audience) and as bandleader at the Taft Hotel.[10] When the band split up in 1937, Weaver, now married with a young daughter, sought a more settled position, and he interviewed with Loew's executives in New York for a position in Richmond.

When Eddie Weaver first started working at the Loew's Theater, he played four shows a day, six days a week, and earned $100 a week, a good salary in those days.[11] After doing a stint in the Army during World War II in the Special Services unit, performing at McGuire Army Hospital, Weaver returned to Loew's in

1944. An indefatigable performer, he played church functions, community charity drives, and conventions. He played programs for WRNL and WRVA radio in the mornings, and in the afternoons he performed at the Miller & Rhoads Tea Room. As Carol Keenan remembers, "Young girls were allowed to have Saturday lunch at the Miller & Rhoads Tea Room and attend the feature at Loew's. When Eddie Weaver prepared to leave his organ and M&R, we knew it was feature time and we would hurry to pay our checks so that we would be in time for his sing-along before the showing."[12] Organists such as Weaver were also expected to accompany the singers, dancers and comedians who occasionally performed live on stage before the movie show. His daughter Jody W. Wampler said, "He was proud of having worked with a lot of stars – Bing Crosby, [George] Burns and [Gracie] Allen, Ray Bolger, Red Skelton – in those

BYRD THEATER WURLITZER ORGAN, *2001. Bob Gulledge, a former student of well-known Richmond organist Eddie Weaver, plays the famous Byrd Wurlitzer organ on Saturday nights, and helps maintain the fragile instrument.*

segments and sketches."

One of Weaver's favorite stories was this: "The only exciting thing that happened to me at Loew's was the one night...the safety stop on the organ elevator broke, and the organ went up several feet farther than usual. I turned around to say something to the audience, and was looking into the balcony! I was scared to death!" Weaver recalled in an interview, "I didn't know whether to play *How High the Moon* or *Nearer My God to Thee*! It took them eight hours to crank it down by hand."[13]

Dr. Randolph Trice recalls, "One of Eddie Weaver's tricks was to play one tune with his right hand, a different tune with his left, yet another tune with his feet and get them all synchronized – that was a feat. He could keep *There's a Long, Long Trail a' Winding, Keep the Home Fires Burning* and *Love's Old Sweet Song* going simultaneously, to the crowd's delight." "Small boys could always be counted upon to rush to the first rows whenever the [spot] lights went down around Eddie's feet," Edith Lindeman noted.[14]

Among Weaver's specialties was the audience sing-a-long. Weaver once estimated that he had played more than 3,600 songs for Loew's crowds, ranging from the day's popular tunes, to old fashioned favorites, to tongue-twisters guaranteed to warm up a quiet house, to birthday greetings to youngsters in the audience, to parody songs on local subjects, which he wrote himself. Humorous takes on city, state and presidential politics always went over well, as did a ditty he wrote which was sung to the tune of *Clang, Clang, Clang Goes the Trolley* when Richmond streetcars were replaced by buses. Guy Friddell recalled of his many happy evenings at the Loew's spent listening to Eddie Weaver, "The song I liked best was *Springtime in the Rockies* with a little white moth ball bouncing along on the words on the screen for the squares – drips, they were then – in the audience."[15]

Different types of films and audiences called for different music, Weaver felt. Slapstick Abbott and Costello comedies and children's matinees were the time for fast music, novelties, tongue twisters and Woody Woodpecker. Romantic films and weepy melodramas brought out women and teen couples on dates. For them, Eddie prescribed love songs, answer songs with parts for girls

BYRD THEATER, ORGAN WORKS, *2001. Above the auditorium ceiling, dozens of instruments and a maze of tubing and wires attached to the mighty Wurlitzer organ provide a symphony of musical sounds and special effects.*

and boys to sing separately, and novelty or "cute" songs. Women were the most enthusiastic singers in his audiences, Eddie believed, and their husbands the least willing to give it a try. "They hardly ever sing at the afternoon shows. The guys who watch westerns don't sing much either. They just sit, but I think they really enjoy the music. Girls are quicker to sing than boys."

Nevertheless, Eddie Weaver always made hard work look easy – he memorized all his songs and never "faked" his way through a performance. He carefully arranged his songs in keys which would be comfortable for his audiences to sing, and he was a good time manager — for a musical program that was too long or short, or included just one chorus too many, threw off the timing of the entire movie show schedule. "That's the part that drives you nuts," he admitted. Finishing his set, Eddie and the organ would descend again as the film started, and a trick of the lights might turn him into a skeletal "Phan-

tom of the Opera" with bony arms flying around the keyboards.

In 1960, when he retired from Loew's Theater after 23 years, Eddie Weaver and the organist at Radio City Music Hall were the only remaining full time movie theater organists. Although he kept the Miller & Rhoads Tea Room job, he was feeling underutilized, so he moved over to the Byrd Theater, playing twelve shows a week for nearly 20 more years, during which time he was the *only* full time theater organist in the nation. In 1982 he cut back to Friday and Saturday nights. He retired from the Byrd in May 1983, but he continued to make personal appearances. His last public performance was at a concert celebrating the restoration of the Loew's Wurlitzer Organ at the Carpenter Center in 1992. The grand master organist continued to play until close to his death at age 92, in January 2001. Eddie Weaver and those marvelous theater organs will always be Richmond traditions.[16]

OUTSIDE LOEW'S THEATER, *600 E. Grace St., 1934. Lines of eager moviegoers queued up along Grace Street to purchase tickets to enter Richmond's most elegant movie palace.*

Theaters in Richmond's Neighborhoods

After the opening of the picture palaces in the late 1920s, there was little new movie theater construction in downtown Richmond. The city's residential suburbs, however, looked like favorable areas for theater expansion. Walter Coulter had led the way in 1925 by building the Brookland Theater north of the city in the Barton Heights neighborhood. The Brookland's goal was not to drain patronage away from the downtown movie houses, but to provide a nearby, comfortable, affordable theater that neighborhood children, women and families could patronize frequently. The Brookland's audiences did not have to dress up, or take a long trolley ride, or pay a high price for their tickets to see a good movie show. They could attend a neighborhood theater once or twice a week and still go downtown to the Loew's on a Saturday or Sunday evening as their major weekly social event. In an era before television brought entertainment and news into the home, the average American went out to the movies two or three times per week. Having a movie theater in the neighborhood was a convenience and a treat. The Brookland's success helped to spur the opening of the Capitol and Byrd theaters, located several miles from Broad Street's Theater Row. But the financial pinch of the Depression and the abundance of movie seats in the new palaces made it difficult for film exhibitors to expand further into the city's residential areas until the economy improved. But when that happened, the race was on.

Competition between theater owners to dominate Richmond's suburban market began as soon as economic indicators began to brighten in 1934. The Wilmer and Vincent movie theater chain (which had taken over Jake Wells' empire in Richmond) mounted a challenge against

BELLEVUE THEATER, *4026 Rappahannock Ave., 1937. Located in the Bellvue neighborhood on Richmond's north side, the Art Deco-styled Bellevue Theater offered inexpensive, second run movies and a saturday morning show full of excitement to local residents. Today the building has been adapted for use as the Samis Grotto Temple Shrine meeting hall.*

Morton G. Thalhimer's Neighborhood Theaters, Inc. (NTI) chain, announcing plans to build numerous theaters in the Richmond suburbs located right next door to each of the movie houses NTI planned to open. In May 1934, Wilmer and Vincent remodeled an existing brick building and opened the Carillon Theater on Cary Street, two doors down from the Byrd Theater. It was a medium-sized theater with 600 seats. Its first film was *Dancing Lady* with Joan Crawford.

Art Deco styling was prominent in the theaters built in Richmond and across the nation in the 1930s. New movie houses like the Henrico, Bellevue, and Bill Robinson theaters were constructed with sleek, unadorned, streamlined exteriors, with interiors to match. They had no plaster curlicues on the walls or across the stage's proscenium arch, no crystal chandeliers, no stars in the ceiling. They were also significantly less expensive to build, decorate and maintain than were the fancier downtown theaters, an important consideration in the Depression. The Capitol Theater was redecorated in streamlined fashion in 1936, ten years after its opening. The renovation was beneficial to both patrons and the management — wider seats were installed for movie-going comfort, and the stage and organ areas were removed so that more seats could be fit into the auditorium. Nevertheless, some of the Capitol's picture palace elegance was lost. Most of sculptor Ferruccio Legnaioli's interior decorations were removed, including the urns, foliage, garden murals and porticoed ceilings along the theater's sides. Former Capitol usher Robert Willis recalled the renovations, but also the continuing touches of special service that made the Capitol so well-loved by its audiences:

> The big Wurlitzer pipe organ remained, but was no longer played. However, the ladies' lounge on the mezzanine was still attended by a maid in a black silk dress with white collar and cuffs, French style. [The auditorium] was midnight

SAMIS GROTTO TEMPLE MEETING HALL, *4026 MacArthur Ave., 2001.*

blue accented by ivory-colored furniture and deep blue carpet. We ushers wore crimson Eisenhower-type jackets fronted by gold buttons and fawn-colored trousers. Starched white dickies and black bow ties completed the uniform. Strict decorum prevailed at all times; every patron was shown to his or her seat by flashlight....At Saturday matinees, children were often accompanied by their nursemaids. No candy or, Heaven forbid, popcorn, was permitted....Sometimes, if a film was unusually popular, lines ran as far as the William Byrd [Hotel] and around the corner.[17]

The peak of the struggle between rival film exhibitors for dominance in Richmond came in 1937. Walter Coulter had expanded his interests from movie theaters into bowling alleys and dance clubs with his opening of the Tantilla Ballroom and Tinytown bowling alley complex in the West End in 1934. In 1937, he leased the Byrd and Brookland Theaters to Thalhimer's NTI. His partner Charles Somma became an NTI executive, and the company wisely chose to retain Robert Coulter as

manager of the Byrd. The Byrd and Capitol became twin centers of the NTI chain. From those two prominent and successful West End theaters, NTI next chose to expand even further westward, opening the Westhampton Theater in 1938.

The Westhampton, with 848 seats, was a neighborhood-sized theater compared to the larger Byrd, but it was far more elegant than any other suburban theater in Richmond. It was decorated in a Colonial Virginia theme, which was carried out from its brick exterior, to its lobby, laid out like a Williamsburg drawing room. Mrs. Morton Thalhimer selected antique furniture from Europe to adorn the lobby (this furniture was later donated to the Virginia Museum of Fine Arts.) Ushers and box office girls posed for pictures in Colonial costume. The theater auditorium did have a streamlined simplicity, but its walls were painted to resemble delicate Chinese silk wallpaper. A nod to the future was the incorporation of a large parking lot for automobiles behind the theater. While some local people were concerned that its location far from downtown would severely limit its patronage, the still-open Westhampton has long proved to be one of the most popular theaters in Richmond.

REGENT THEATER, *1205 Boulevard, Colonial Heights, 1941. This neighborhood theater, designed with Colonial decorative details similar to the Westhampton Theater in Richmond, was located in the heart of the commercial district.*

NTI also opened the Bellevue Theater on Rappahannock Avenue in the Bellevue-Ginter Park neighborhood in September 1937. Even before ground had been broken for the Bellevue, the Wilmer and Vincent chain announced plans to build a rival theater, the Ginter, across the street. The Bellevue Theater contained the latest word in Art Deco décor, both inside and out. It had 651 seats, and air-conditioning. Its first film was *Mountain Music*, a "hillbilly musical" featuring singer/comedienne Martha Raye. Bob Burchette remembers the Bellevue as a family-oriented theater that was a one-mile bicycle ride from his parents' home on Chamberlayne Avenue. It hosted neighborhood talent competitions, and the ubiquitous Saturday morning children's shows. Burchette was a Saturday morning regular, eating popcorn, Good n' Plenties and Juju Bees candy while soaking up the cowboy films. Warren Beatty and Shirley MacLaine, who lived with their parents on Fauquier Avenue, also attended this neighborhood theater during the war years. Burchette remembers the enormous wads of gum that accumulated under the Bellevue's seats, deposited by youthful moviegoers.[18]

The rival Ginter Theater opened across the street from the Bellevue in November 1937 with Ramon Novarro in *The Sheik Steps Out*. It had what was called a "unique" feature – a free parking lot with spaces for 300 cars. It also had a "crying room" where mothers could take fussy babies, which had a window through which the mothers could continue to watch the show without disturbing the other patrons. NTI was able to wrest away

POST OFFICE, *1205 Boulevard, Colonial Heights, 2001. The Regent was torn down to become the site of the Colonial Heights Post Office.*

control of the Ginter and the other to-be-constructed theaters from Wilmer and Vincent, and they closed the Ginter in January 1939. In 1937, Wilmer and Vincent had opened The Grove Theater up the street from the Westhampton Theater (it was located in what is today the Arcade); it too was closed in 1939. Wilmer and Vincent got as far as building the foundation of a theater on Brookland Park Boulevard in 1935 to rival the Brookland, but it was abandoned in 1938. The Patrick Henry, opened in 1933, and East End Theater, 1938, stood side by side on 25th Street in Church Hill. The Ponton on Hull Street, the Henrico Theater in Highland Springs and the Regent Theater in Colonial Heights were other suburban theaters that opened in the 1930s to serve Richmond's increasingly far-flung residential areas.[19] After a bruising battle, NTI emerged as Richmond's dominant film exhibitors by fending off Wilmer and Vincent's challenge, and absorbing the Coulter theater chain. After the dust settled, they had eleven movie houses in the area. Nevertheless, Wilmer and Vincent were still a factor, with five theaters, the National, Colo-

nial, Park, Carillon and Lee. They merged with the Fabian Chain of New Jersey in 1944, ending the hometown aspects of Richmond's theater rivalry.

During these years the film studios tightly controlled the distribution of their movies with the "block booking" arrangement. Theaters had to ally themselves with one studio and take all their products, good and bad. Loew's, of course, offered the films of its production studio MGM shown for the first time in Richmond. Loew's additionally ran some Paramount films. NTI theaters had the rights to play Fox studio films, along with some Warner Brothers products and the subsequent runs of MGM movies. Fabian theaters ran RKO movies. After its three-day "first run" in the swankiest downtown theaters with highest prices, a film was held out for 60 days, then it played across town at another theater. That was the "second run," and ticket prices at those theaters were cheaper because the exhibitor paid a lower rental fee on the film. Then the movie was held out again for three or four more weeks, and would be shown at a "third run" theater in yet another part of town, with even more af-

HENRICO THEATER, *305 E. Nine Mile Road, Highland Springs, 1938.*

HENRICO THEATER, SECOND FLOOR LOUNGE, *1938. Moviegoers of the 1930s and 1940s must have thought they stepped straight into the set of a Fred Astaire-Ginger Rogers musical when they entered this fantastically high style Art Deco-inspired upper lobby.*

fordable ticket prices. As Charles Wyatt recalls, "In the 1940s, westerns would first play in Richmond at the Grand Theater," and he would rush out to see them all. If the film starred one of his favorite cowboy actors, he would see it again three weeks later when it played at the Venus. Then he'd view it once more three weeks later at the Patrick Henry. If moviegoers were thrifty and patient, the films they wanted to see would eventually come to a neighborhood theater.[20]

Entertainment in Richmond's Black Community

In the 1920s, African-American amusement seekers in Richmond looked to the Hippodrome, Rayo and Globe theaters in Jackson Ward, owned by Charles Somma, and the Star and Lincoln Theaters on Hull Street for movie and vaudeville shows. Several theaters on Broad Street, the Strand (the former Bijou), Colonial and National,

had balcony sections for blacks and advertised their shows in the city's black newspaper, *The Richmond Planet*. Black Richmonders also had opportunities to attend musical concerts, plays and shows put on in local churches, schools and parks. One community theatrical highlight occurred in November 1932, when a local group of players put on a production of the folk morality play *Heaven Bound* at the City Auditorium before an audience of 1,600. It would subsequently be performed in local churches through the 1940s and 1950s as a fund-raiser.[21]

Jackson Ward's most famous theater was the Hippodrome, which was located on the 500 block of Second Street.[22] Second Street, called "The Deuce," was the center of black commerce in Richmond and the Upper South, with stores, banks, theaters, restaurants and hotels. It was the center of black city nightlife, which continued all night long. Waverly Crawley recalled that when

HENRICO THEATER, *305 E. Nine Mile Road, Highland Springs, 2001. This Art Deco gem served the Eastern Henrico County community for many years. Recently the County has begun renovation of the historic building to turn it into a community center.*

the Hippodrome's midnight show let out at 2:00 a.m., people spilled out into the street, headed for all-night restaurants and nightclubs.[23] Amanda Thorpe and Walter Coulter had built the 1,050-seat Hippodrome in 1914. In 1915, the Hippodrome featured vaudeville acts on stage, and played spine-tingling movie serials, like *The Million Dollar Mystery* and *The Exploits of Elaine*; printed versions of the serials ran as stories each week in the *Richmond Planet*. The Hippodrome was also a community center. In 1915, a large anti-segregation meeting was held in the theater's auditorium on a Sunday, and money was raised to fund attorneys who were arguing cases before the courts.

The Globe Theater was located at the other end of the block from the Hippodrome, and on busy nights the lines of people waiting to get into the next show completely filled the sidewalks. "The Hippodrome and Globe theaters – hot spots for movies – charged admission based on a person's height," Crawley recalled. If a youngster was small enough to get in at the lowest price, and still lacked a few pennies, he could hunt something to barter at the box office. "The streets were clean because people

could salvage cans and bottles and exchange them for theater admittance," Crawley remembered. In the 1920s, the Rayo Theater at Second and Marshall streets, built by John Mitchell, was also a popular movie theater.[24]

In the 1920s and 1930s, the *Richmond Planet* was filled with news about the black performing arts community in New York City during the Harlem Renaissance. Although far from Harlem's theaters, nightclubs and cabarets, Jackson Ward residents soaked up news of the latest publications, record releases and theatrical triumphs. Many followed the progress of two performers born in Richmond in 1878 who were big stars in New York – Charles Gilpin and Bill "Bojangles" Robinson. Gilpin first appeared on the stage in Richmond in 1890 at age 12. He left for New York at age 18, and after more than 20 years of working odd jobs and bit parts, he achieved great fame on Broadway in the early 1920s as the star of Eugene O'Neill's lengthy one-act play *The Emperor Jones*. He was the first African-American to be highly acclaimed as a serious actor on the Broadway stage. Bill Robinson discovered his love of tap dancing as a small boy when he performed outside the hotels in downtown Richmond

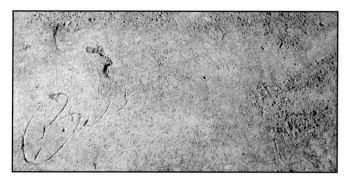

(Left) **BILL ROBINSON STATUE**, *Corner Of Leigh St. and Brook Ave., Jackson Ward, 2001.. The City dedicated a statue to Richmond's famous son, who became an internationally known tap-dancer and entertainer.*

SIDEWALK IN FRONT OF ROBINSON THEATER, *29ᵗʰ And Q Sts., Church Hill, 2001. In 1937, Robinson set his shoe prints and a signature in concrete in front of the box office at the dedication of the Robinson Theater, the spot saw so much foot traffic over the years that portions of the cement are worn smooth.*

for the pennies people would throw. He appeared in amateur contests and looked for any occasion to perform. Robinson also left home in his early teens, performing outside of theaters in Baltimore, hoping to be noticed. From the 1920s through the 1940s, Robinson was one of the biggest and most beloved stars in American entertainment, earning as much as $6,500 per week. He tap-danced and sang in Harlem nightclubs, and vaudeville, and in Broadway musicals like *Blackbirds of 1928* and *The Hot Mikado*, in movies and on the radio, where he hosted his own show.[25]

The heyday of the Hippodrome came in the 1930s and 1940s, when all the big stars performed on its stage, including Ethel Waters, Ella Fitzgerald, Ray Charles, Moms Mably, James Brown and comic "Pigmeat" Markham. Mably remembered in a 1974 interview that "the Hippodrome was part of a circuit operated by the Theater Owners Booking Agency, whose acronym TOBA also stood for 'tough on black artists,' because of the low wages and unfavorable working conditions on the black vaudeville circuit." She recalled that the Hippodrome was "one of the more agreeable stops on the TOBA circuit, largely because of the old Slaughter's Hotel across

the street, which was noted for its clean beds and beautiful food."

Robert Evans recalled his memories of the Hippodrome in the late 1940s: "Picture this: its Saturday morning. You're between the ages of seven and seventeen. You've got at least 15 cents in your pocket. What do you do? That's easy. You go to the Hippodrome Theater. You pay nine cents to get in and put your penny change in the peanut machine so you can have some peanuts to throw in the movies, mostly at the girls. Here's what you'd see: the coming attractions of next week's movies; a news reel or world events, plus the latest sports; two cartoons; two full length movies, usually a western and a gangster movie and a chapter in a serial continued from the previous week. If you look on the back row in the dark, occasionally you would see an entertainer sitting there like James Brown or Sam Cooke." In 1945, a four-alarm fire gutted the interior of the Hippodrome (local legend has it that a vaudeville performer at the theater fired a pistol and ignited the curtains). The theater was extensively rebuilt in 1946, and was primarily a movie theater afterwards.[26]

On June 4, 1934, entrepreneur Abe Lichtman, a film

HIPPODROME THEATER AND BOX OFFICE, *528 N. Second St., Jackson Ward, 2001. Rebuilt in Art Deco style after a fire in 1945, the Hippodrome is still occasionally in use today as a church and meeting center.*

exhibitor with a growing chain of theaters in Washington, D.C. and Norfolk, opened the first new movie theater in many years for black patrons in Richmond. The Booker T. Theater was housed in the old Empire/Strand Theater on Broad Street, which had been closed since a 1926 fire.[27] The Lichtman company announced that more than $20,000 was being spent in renovating the building into a first-class house, including installation of a lighted marquee extending over the sidewalk, new chairs and sound equipment. Lichtman was known in Washington's, and soon Richmond's, black communities for being a fair employer. Lichtman made a point of staffing his theaters almost entirely with black workers, providing much-needed employment in the neighborhood. The Booker T. was the Saturday morning theater of choice in the 1930s for Jackson Ward's young children, who were not allowed to roam down busy Second Street. Robinson Horne recalls the matronly lady ticket takers and the manager who walked about the theater to keep children from misbehaving during the show.

Dr. Francis Foster remembers that he would walk down early in the day to the Booker T. to assist the theater's maintenance man with his chores; then in the afternoons he would get in for free to see the "chapter pictures." Dr. Foster, a jazz enthusiast, recalls hearing Jimmy Lundsford and his band of Fisk University-trained

BOOKER T. THEATER, *116 W. Broad St, 1935. Renovated from the Strand Theater after a fire in 1926, the Booker T. opened in 1933.*

musicians perform at the Booker T., and the Delta Rhythm Boys, too. Dr. Foster was 13 when he saw a dancer performing on stage at the Booker T., Etta Moton, who subsequently had a long career as a dancer and singer. Young Francis was entranced and, determined to get her autograph, waited nervously behind the theater by the milk bottle building. He had never seen a woman with make up and décolletage in person, and he was speechless as she wrote "To Francis Foster, a very fine young man" in his book. He trailed a block behind her, totally fascinated, as she walked to the home of some friends on Clay Street, and he sat on the steps of the library several hours, then followed a block behind her as she returned to the theater for her next performance.[28]

Lichtman assumed control of the Hippodrome and Globe theaters in Jackson Ward. On December 31, 1936, Lichtman took over the long-closed Little Theater next door to the Booker T. to open the Maggie Walker Theater. A citywide contest was held to name the new movie

house, and Mrs. Mattie Booker won a $25 dollar prize for suggesting the winning entry.

Lichtman expanded his chain further by building a new facility in the Church Hill neighborhood, the 350-seat Robinson Theater, which opened at 29th and Q streets on September 29, 1937. It was named in honor of Bill "Bojangles" Robinson; a plaque beside the entrance honored "The World's Greatest Tap Dancer." A *Richmond Planet* article described the new theater's exterior as "cream California stucco with black alberene base, trimmed in a modern design of midnight blue. The theater front will be illuminated at night by a dazzling neon marquee. The interior decoration is strictly in the modern motif, the side wall treatment being four shades of rust with a background of peach."[29] Projection, sound and heating equipment were pronounced the most modern available. The gala opening featured executives from Lichtman Theaters, a delegation from the Southeastern Federation of the National Association of Colored

MAGGIE WALKER THEATER, *118 W. Broad St, 1943. The Maggie Walker Theater opened in the old Little Theater building next door in 1936.*

Women headed by president Ora Brown Stokes, Mayor Bright, and radio station WRTD, which broadcast the ceremonies across the area. The guest of honor was to have been Bill Robinson himself, but at the last minute he was called back to California on business, and so Fredi Washington, Robinson's co-star in the theater's opening film, *One Mile From Heaven*, appeared in person. Bojangles himself must have shown up soon afterwards for a second ceremony. Former State Delegate James Christian, Jr., who was doorman and assistant manager of the Robinson when it opened, remembers, "If you look today, in front of that building you'll see his footprint in that sidewalk. We left that section out until he arrived that night and they poured concrete in that night and he put his footprint in it."

Christian recalled the important role the Robinson played in the lives of Church Hill's children: "The theater was a social institution for the neighborhood. It certainly was a help to the youngsters in the community.

We sponsored a lot of talent shows. They would display their talents and we had prizes for them, for example. It became really a community interest especially on Saturday, so we had something going on for the youngsters all day on Saturday."[30]

Former governor Douglas Wilder recalled the Robinson Theater as part of the vibrant Church Hill community of his youth. Within a three-block radius of Wilder's home there were several churches, a hardware store, print shop, sawmill, laundry, candy store, bakery, drycleaner, butcher, barbershop, pool hall, drugstores and restaurants. Wilder commented that the neighborhood seemed to him to be a large, self-sufficient city. "Another thing that impressed me was the Robinson Theater. [Manager] George Clarke would stand out there with a cigar in his mouth and I would think he was a wealthy man. Those were the impressions of a child. People would go to the theater like they were going to a premiere on Broadway." [31] Dr. Jean Harris Ellis remem-

WESTHAMPTON THEATER, *5706 Grove Ave, 1938. The most elegant suburban theater in Richmond, located in the West End, the Westhampton initially drew speculation from skeptics that no one would drive so far out of town to go to the movies.*

bered the Robinson as "the principal source of recreation for the whole community. One could go to the movie and on Saturdays, all of us young people [were] off to watch the westerns." The Robinson Drug store, on another corner, was open late at night and was the place to go to get ice cream after a show.[32]

Carolyn Brown recalls the excitement she and her classmates felt when the word flew around school that a prominent African-American star, such as Lena Horne or Cab Calloway or Duke Ellington, was going to perform in an upcoming feature film at the Robinson Theater. The opportunity to see blacks on screen in Hollywood films was rare and thus precious. Occasionally a film created by a black filmmaker would be shown, and this was also greeted with great anticipation by the schoolchildren. Director Oscar Michaux's films were popular in Richmond in the 1920s and 1930s. The Lichtman movie theaters also featured performers live on stage – singers, dancers, jazz bands, comedians, and amateur talent shows; there was always something of great interest going on at the Robinson, Booker T., Walker, Lincoln, Hippodrome and Globe theaters.[33]

Special Events and Publicity Stunts

The theater manager's goal was to keep his movie house's name in the public eye as often as possible. Some of the best publicity-getters were special in-person appearances by film stars, but Hollywood was a long trip from Richmond in the days of travel by train. Nevertheless, Richmond had some celebrity sightings.

Freeman Gosden, co-star of the radio comedy series "Amos and Andy," was a Richmond-born celebrity. When an "Amos and Andy" movie was released in 1933, the Byrd Theater booked it, and the stars (Gosden and Charles Correll) made personal appearances on stage during the intermission between showings. In another celebrity sighting at Christmas, 1934, "Pete," the canine star of the "Our Gang" comedies, was in town. The ten-year veteran of motion pictures, who had also played an important role in Harold Lloyd's silent comedy *The Freshman*, appeared with his trainer Harry Luguenay, in a comedy skit on the vaudeville bill at the Lyric Theater for a week's engagement.[34]

On September 7, 1939, the legendary Mary Pickford (the biggest star of silent films and still the social leader of Hollywood) passed through Richmond on her way

WESTHAMPTON THEATER, *2001. Today the Westhampton is Richmond's art cinema, surrounded by the shops and restaurants of the Avenues of Libbie and Grove. Its balcony has been renovated into a second theater, but it still retains an air of elegance from its Williamsburg décor to the gourmet treats at the concession stand.*

the South Boston, where she was to be crowded Queen of the fifth annual National Tobacco Festival. Broad Street station overflowed with women in their 40's and 50's anxious to catch even a glimpse of their girlhood idol. Escorted through by Mayor Bright and state dignitaries all agog at their closeness to celebrity, Miss Pickford politely but firmly refused to sign any of the autograph books thrust out at her. Photographer Frank Dementi must have turned on the charm to convince Mary to autograph the news photo he sent her after her Richmond visit.[35]

Richmond hosted its first "world premiere" when the Paramount film *So Red the Rose*, a romantic drama set during the Civil War, held its opening at the Colonial Theater on November 15, 1935. Its star was Norfolk-born actress Margaret Sullavan, fresh from the New York stage, in her biggest screen role to date. The United

Daughters of the Confederacy were all atwitter. A reporter noted that "The UDC hostesses attempted to meet the 5:45 train yesterday afternoon to greet motion picture officials and newspaper and magazine critics, driving through the streets in an ancient surrey drawn by two horses and driven by a young man in Confederate uniform. But the plan went to naught when the fragile old surrey succumbed under the weight of the young ladies and crashed to earth."

That night at the premiere, more than 2,000 people, including many prominent Richmonders and a large number of New York, Washington, and Baltimore newspaper and magazine critics, filled the Colonial to the rafters. Thousands of other Richmonders listened in by radio. The lobby was filled with young men dressed in uniforms of the Richmond Blues, Greys, and Howitzers; banjo players, singers and women in hoop skirts (some

LOBBY OF THE WESTHAMPTON THEATER, *1938. Mrs. Morton G. Thalhimer chose the Westhampton's Williamsburg-style décor and she brought antique furniture over from Europe to adorn the lobby.*

of whom had presumably dusted themselves off after being unceremoniously dumped into the street earlier that afternoon.) Margaret Sullavan's mother, shy and plump, was brought up from Norfolk to greet the radio audience and beam at her daughter. Lieutenant Governor James Price and Mrs. Peery, the Governor's wife, gave welcoming speeches, followed by other local notables and film industry executives. The premiere was a big success, but it is not the Civil War film we most remember. *So Red the Rose* predated the wildly successful novel *Gone with the Wind* by a year, and is largely forgotten today. For a time, however, Sullavan was a front-runner for the film role of Scarlett O'Hara due to her performance in *So Red the Rose*, seen first in Richmond.[36]

Most publicity events did not have Hollywood stars upon which to draw. They required homegrown ingenuity, and Richmond's theater managers were expert showmen. They put on beautiful baby contests, bingo games, raffled off bicycles at Christmas, held amateur-night tal-

ent shows, co-sponsored promotions with local stores and newspapers, and tried every conceivable game, gag and giveaway. Being part of a movie-making empire gave the Loew's Theater certain advantages in the publicity department. Loew's mounted contests to allow lucky young Richmond women and children the chance to make a screen test. One such stunt prominently covered in the *News Leader* took place in November 1934. MGM's mobile screen test studio arrived and was parked next to Loew's for curious fans to explore. In Richmond, 1,200 applicants (local women between the ages of 18 and 28, and the parents of pretty children) submitted photographs. A group of 24 women and 20 children were chosen as semi-finalists, and from that group, seven lucky finalists made it to the Loew's stage: Ann Landon, Georgia Berry, Jean Moore, Julia West, and children Ruth Owen Baber, Dorothy Jean Weimar and Don Carleton Stearns. To wring the most publicity value from the stunt for Loew's Theater, the finalists had their screen tests

AUDITORIUM OF THE WESTHAMPTON THEATER, *1938. The auditorium's walls were painted to resemble Colonial-era Chinese silk wallpaper.*

shot right on the stage in front of the paying audience. Hundreds had to be turned away from the show that night. Ann Landon is shown here in a Dementi Studio photograph, rehearsing her lines from Norma Shearer's film *Riptide*. Instead of emoting, the children answered some questions on stage. One small contestant, asked if she would like to go to Hollywood, loudly answered "No!" and sent the audience into gales of laughter. The filmed results were shown on the big screen the next week. In a subsequent screen test competition that took place in 1937, the winner, 21-year old Miss Gillet Epps, won an all-expenses-paid 15-day trip to Paris. The experience for the contestants must have been quite a thrill. And it kept Loew's Theater name prominently on young people's minds.[37]

While the managers of Loew's Theater might not have been able to persuade Clark Gable to come to town to visit, Richmonders did get to see Leo the Lion, the "other" king of the MGM lot. The film studio spokes-

animal made a stop in Richmond with his handlers on a nationwide tour of Loew's theaters. While Leo was not the equal of Gable when it came to kissing girls and signing autographs, his face and trademark roars were known in movie theaters around the globe.

In 1936, Loew's and the *News Leader* sponsored the filming of a hometown home movie, *It Happened in Richmond*, described as "an all local talkie with an all local cast of over 300 boys and girls." The film's plot is apparently lost to the ages, but it is known that the brief movie had a high school setting, and University of Richmond football coach Glenn Thistlethwaite played a cameo role as Principal Dexter. *It Happened in Richmond* premiered at Loew's Theater on a rainy night, March 27, 1936. Although the storm prevented the use of outdoor Klieg lights to shine into the skies like a "real" Hollywood premiere, bright electric lights under the marquee flooded the theater front. "Through a public address system, the master of ceremonies described the affair and introduced

NATIONAL THEATER, *early 1930s. Long lines of young patrons wait to enter the National to see an aviation adventure film.*

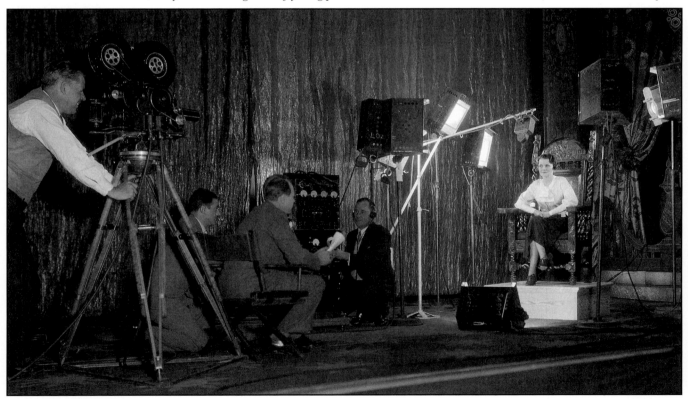

SCREEN TEST ON LOEW'S THEATER STAGE, *1934. A young woman participates in a Richmond publicity stunt – a contest to choose a talented young woman to go to Hollywood to seek a chance at stardom. Loew's audiences watched the filming and voted as the tests were screened the following week.*

MARY PICKFORD IN RICHMOND, *1939. Nicknamed "America's Sweetheart," the top star of silent film days was still beloved by legions of fans, and the personal appearance of a movie star in Richmond was always a major event.*

the celebrities and members of the all-local cast as they stepped out of their cars and forced their way through the waiting crowds," reported a newspaper account. "Photographers kept their cameras and flash lamps busy as the various players stepped up to the microphone and addressed the throng." At the conclusion of the showing of *It Happened in Richmond* in the jam-packed theater, the film's main players were introduced on stage one by one, to enthusiastic applause from the audience. The cast included Maurice Rosenbloom, Anne Byrd Sloan, Harold W. Philips, Jean Rigney, Thomas Duffy, Jr., Elizabeth Cavan, Broaddus Pitts, Vernon Holloway, Philip Cooke, Archer McDaniel, Guy Stinchfield, Jr., and Florine Gary. Richmonders were given a week, while the film ran on the Loew's program, to vote for their favorite performers. Rosenbloom was the runaway favorite for best actor, while there was a close contest between Rigney and Sloan for best actress. Coach Thistlethwaite received

27 write-in votes for best actor, as well. The winners were awarded trophies on the stage of the Loew's Theater the following Thursday evening.[38]

Richmond's theaters in the 1930s had seen the end of some traditions — such as theatrical touring companies, the vaudeville circuit, and silent film presentations — and the beginnings of others. The arrival of the "talkies" had made the movies an even more popular, and dominant, entertainment form. After the picture palace building boom of the late 1920s, there were no new large theaters built in the city during the decade of the 1930s. Nevertheless, the film exhibition system continued to evolve – more small movie theaters were built in Richmond's suburban neighborhoods, and the ownership of these theaters was consolidated into several large and powerful chains. Richmond's movie theaters continued to employ novel schemes to keep movie going a regular part of everyone's recreation habits, even dur-

MGM MASCOT MAKES AN APPEARANCE IN RICHMOND, *1930s. Leo the Lion was featured on the MGM logo, in stained glass on the Richmond Loew's marquee, and he also toured the country in person.*

CHRISTMAS TREE IN BYRD THEATER LOBBY,
*1946. The Byrd's staff worked hard to involve the theater in
community life, sponsoring charity drives, celebrating holidays,
publishing newsletters and holding Saturday morning
children's shows.*

ing the Depression. They established Mickey Mouse
Clubs and children's shows, employed organists to add
interest to programs, they installed air conditioning to
lure in patrons on sultry summer nights, and created
special publicity stunts to keep the theaters continually
in the public eye. The "golden age of movie-going" was
now in full swing, and by the time of the nation's entry
into World War II, motion pictures and movie theaters
were at the center of American entertainment. That
dominance would be threatened by the rise of a new
media form of the late 1940s — television. The theatrical
and performing arts community in Richmond was im-
paired in the 1930s by the decline of the tours of nation-
ally-known performers and plays. New initiatives coming from within the community, however, would help spur
the development of Richmond's local amateur and professional theaters, and the ballet and symphony, in the
years to come.

RICHMOND SKYLINE, *1960s*.

CHAPTER 4

Richmond Theater
1940-1970

As the war in Europe dominated the newsreels and newspapers in 1940, Richmond started the decade quietly waiting for whatever might come. The Depression was finally ending. Jobs were becoming more plentiful, and the movie theaters had full houses. After the attack on Pearl Harbor in December 1941, Richmond and the nation sprang into action. With active war industries bringing thousands of new workers to town (many from rural areas), and thousands of servicemen and moving through Richmond by train on their way to Norfolk, Petersburg and Washington D.C., Richmond's streets buzzed with activity. Theaters were packed with civilian and military patrons, hoping to see the latest war news, or to forget their worries in lavish musicals and clever comedies. "Professor" Jack Kaminsky and the Hal Sands showgirls graced the stage at the National Theater. Richmond theaters contributed to the war effort on the home front, too, holding War Bond drives and urging children to collect scrap metal. Across the nation, more than 90 million Americans attended the movies every week. It was a "golden age" of movie-going, when patriotic musicals, weepy women's pictures and battlefield dramas could be found at the city's more than two dozen theaters, and Saturday morning cowboy movie shows were a ritual for thousands of area children.

Gone with the Wind Blows through town

The long-anticipated film of Margaret Mitchell's 1936 best-selling novel *Gone with the Wind* premiered in Richmond at Loew's Theater on February 3, 1940. Jackie Samuels recalls standing in the cold rain, waiting in the long lines to purchase a ticket for the opening night and that her excitement in finally getting to see the film made her almost oblivious to the weather. Nikki Calisch Fairman was at the premiere, too, in the company of her mother, *Times Dispatch* film critic Edith Lindeman, and her father, brother and sister. She recalls the lines of people that stretched all the way from the box office down 6th Street to Broad Street. When Edith Lindeman arrived with her family in tow, the Loew's ushers ceremoniously cleared a path through the throng for them to enter the theater, like they were real celebrities. Edith rolled her eyes in amusement, Nikki remembers, but the young daughter thought that it was all very impressive.[1]

Gone with the Wind-themed balls were held across town, from a dance held at Loew's Theater at 11:00 p.m. after the premiere, to Junior and Senior Cotillions, to a grand ball at the John Marshall Hotel sponsored by the Richmond chapter of the United Daughters of the Confederacy. Dementi Studios took photos for the newspapers of a dozen debutantes and their mothers, modeling costumes they would wear at the big occasions. As Lindeman reported,

all the sweet young things swung their hoops and flaunted their shoulder curls and flirted with their beaux who were much more romantic and dashing in Confederate gray and ruffled shirt fronts. Scarlett's "fiddle-dee-dee" butters their conversation and they romped through the polka and the Virginia reel as gaily as they usually jitterbugged. But the youngsters weren't the only

PREMIERE OF *GONE WITH THE WIND* AT LOEW'S, *1940. Huge crowds battled cold drizzle to see the most-anticipated film of the decade.*

ones who succumbed to the romance of the '60s....Grandmothers whirled in the waltzes and polkas and many a baffled daughter worried over mother's blood pressure or bad heart.[2]

Geneva Thrower recalls saving up the 75 cents required to buy a matinee ticket to *Gone with the Wind*. For the first time in its history, Loew's Theater had instituted reserved seating and premium prices for this must-see movie. All seats for the evening and Sunday performances were $1.10, and the luxurious loge seats in the balcony cost even more. When films at neighborhood theaters might cost 25 cents and regular shows at the Loew's or Byrd cost 40 or 50 cents, 75 cents (let alone $1.10) was a lot to muster up. The newspaper advertisements warned, however, that "this production will be shown nowhere except at advanced prices, at least until 1941." The prospect of having to wait eleven more

months to see the most talked-about film of the decade caused anxious people, young and old, to scrounge up the money to go.[3]

Lucille Borden recalls that she and a cousin had pooled their money to purchase the book when it came out in 1936. They would take turns, reading one chapter, then passing it back and forth. Mrs. Borden remembers that the film version was so long, at nearly four hours, that people snuck in food underneath their coats, so that they would not miss their dinner, an infraction of Loew's strict policies barring any food in the auditorium. Dr. James Trice recalls that *Gone with the Wind* was the first film he'd ever seen that had an intermission. He remembers seeing people going out to stretch their legs and walk around on 6th Street, before returning to see the second half.

Stories that the Jefferson Hotel's 26-step red-carpeted marble staircase is the model for the one in Scarlett's

Atlanta mansion (which she tumbles down, at one point in the film) are, alas, untrue, but that has not stopped Richmonders from believing wholeheartedly in the myth. A 1976 newspaper article quoted Jefferson manager D. T. Oakes saying that 35 to 40 people a day came to the hotel specifically to see the *GWTW* staircase. Oakes proudly claimed that in the 1930s, the Jefferson's lobby "had such a wide spread reputation for elegance that a full camera crew was sent from Hollywood by the movie's producers to film 'the inspiration and the model for the staircase in *Gone with the Wind.*' " Hotel marketing director Rogers Rudd concurred, saying, "the movie's staircase prop was constructed from the film crew's footage with 'minor modifications.'" Rudd said that in 1972, the Gwaltney Meat Company sent a cast of 150 costumed actors to the Jefferson Hotel to film a "GWTW"-themed commercial on the staircase, but that the advertisement had never been aired.[4] (Did Rhett in the advertisement proclaim, "Frankly, Scarlett, I don't give a ham"?)

STAIRCASE, JEFFERSON HOTEL, *101 W. Franklin St., 1956. The Jefferson's grand staircase may not have been an inspiration for the one in* **Gone with the Wind,** *but that has not stopped many people from fervently believing it was true.*

FIFTH WAR BOND PARADE, *Sixth and Grace Sts, 1944.*

Despite all this wishful thinking over the years about the fame of the Jefferson's staircase, theater critic Edward Slipek firmly states, "it's apocryphal." He notes that "urban legend has it that David O. Selznick, the producer of *Gone with the Wind*, visited the West Franklin Street Jefferson Hotel sometime in the 1930s. He decided then and there the lower lobby would be the model for the hall staircase in Rhett and Scarlett's Atlanta townhouse....Apparently, in the 1970s when the set designer of the 1939 classic visited the hotel, he claimed he had never heard of the famed Richmond staircase."[5]

On the Homefront in Richmond

When the United States finally entered the war in December 1941, the nation faced a huge challenge – how to quickly shift gears to produce the mountains of planes, tanks, uniforms, guns, ammunition, foodstuffs and supplies that it would need to fight and win. Sixteen million men and women served in the armed forces. Many millions more worked in the factories producing much-needed goods. Every family was asked to contribute, either by taking a war job "for the duration," recycling scrap metal and cooking fats, rationing or doing with-

out a host of food products, shoes, cars, and clothing, growing "Victory Gardens," and putting up black out curtains. Many people worried about the fate of their family members and friends in the service, or about the progress of the fighting. At the same time, many were happy to have better jobs, more money and more opportunities.

Richmond's movie theaters, as well as its stores, banks and businesses, did their part for the war effort, participating in War Bond and saving stamp purchase drives. The Brookland Theater won an award for how many bonds it sold during one campaign. Movie stars like John Payne and Edward Arnold came through Richmond to support the War Bond drives.[6] The *News Leader* reported on December 7, 1942 that "In a special 'Avenge Pearl Harbor' War Bond drive this week, Richmond's motion picture theaters will join with about 15,000 other movie houses throughout the country with complete sales staffs for War Bonds and Stamps in lobbies of all showplaces....Showings of special movie shorts urging theatergoers to aid the war effort through purchase of Bonds and stamps will be given."[7]

Movie theaters also did their part to keep up morale

VENUS THEATER,
1412 Hull St., 1942. Richmond's movie theaters did their part to promote patriotism as well as comforting escapism during World War II.

WAR BOND SALES COMMENDA-TION, BROOKLAND THEATER,
115 Brookland Park Boulevard, 1946. Movie theaters joined stores, schools and community organizations in encouraging sales of war bonds and stamps.

NATIONAL AND STATE THEATERS, *1943. Nearby Camp Lee and the Norfolk naval bases brought soldiers and sailors through wartime Richmond, to attend the movies or even to perform in special fund-raising stage shows.*

with posters, slogans, jingles and sing-alongs. Even comic strip families pitched in, as the Venus Theater showed in *Blondie Goes to War*. Six Richmond theaters — Loew's, Westhampton, Bellevue, Capitol, Robinson and Hippo-drome — participated in a "Win with Tin" scrap metal drive during December 1942, offering free admission to a Saturday matinee to any child under the age of twelve who brought along ten flattened tin cans. A previous matinee in November had netted 56,000 cans from 5,600 Richmond children. The donation committee chairman admitted that the biggest difficulty he faced would be to secure enough railroad cars to haul the scrap metal away.[8]

One of Richmond's theatrical highlights during the war years was a performance of Clare Booth Luce's catty all-female farce, *The Women*, about a gaggle of New York society women scratching their way through divorces, affairs, female friendships and rivalries over men. The unique aspect of this Richmond production was its all-

male cast performing in drag. A group of Broadway-trained GIs who were stationed at Camp Lee training in the Special Services division mounted the show to benefit the Women's War Bond Committee. Audience members had to purchase at least one bond to get inside the Lyric Theater. Edith Lindeman recalled that "this wound up as the most unusual event of Richmond's theatrical history. Not only did the show bring in $80,000 in War Bond sales, but it was such a whopping success that it was repeated for the benefit of the Navy League." Photographers for *Life* and *Time* magazines took pictures that appeared across the nation. The gowns and accessories worn by the performers were auctioned off to bring in an additional $10,000.[9]

The 1940s were the National Theater's heyday as a movie house that also featured singing and dancing acts. Many Richmonders still fondly recall Jack Kaminsky's orchestra and the Hal Sands troupe. Bob Burchette rec-

PARK THEATER, *808 E. Broad St, 1943. The former Lubin and Isis Theater now showed wartime action films. The Park would meet with bad luck in the form of a fire and collapsed ceiling in subsequent years, causing some to label it a "Jonah" theater.*

ollects that when he was a boy, his father would take him to the National on Wednesday nights to see the performers and the Hal Sands girls. "They were hard-looking women," Bob laughs. James J. Kilpatrick was a young reporter for the *News Leader* during World War II; with many of the staff gone, he found himself pinch-hitting in various reporting roles around the city room, one of which involved him in the theatrical world, with unexpected results:

> I variously became business editor, outdoors editor, features editor and drama critic. I knew nothing at all of business and even less of the great outdoors, but it wasn't until I went into criticism that I got into trouble. The National Theater still featured vaudeville in those days, with Jack Kaminsky conducting a small orchestra in the pit. One evening I was assigned to cover the Girlie-Go-Round Revue. I began by recalling a team of wheel horses I had known at Fort Riley. Then my review continued: "For a moment

last night at the National Theater, we thought Astor Girl and Hannah had slipped the corral. Then the lights came up and it turned out to be a couple of girls in the stage show... There's not one good-looking girl in the outfit, and we'll draw a curtain of mercy down on their collective figures." The next day the entire chorus line, in abbreviated costumes, staged a protest in the city room. [Editor] Hamilton's keen sense of chivalry was touched. He directed me to write a second piece about the Girlie-Go-Round Revue. "The girls looked lots better in the News Leader's city room than they did on the National's stage." So much for valor. So much for discretion.[10]

While most theaters in Richmond thrived during the war years, some had troubles, such as the little Park Theater on Broad Street (which was originally the Lubin, then the Isis). Show business people labeled it a Jonah (a slang term for a person or place that seems to be followed by bad luck). In February 1943, a flash fire caused

HAL SANDS DANCERS, NATIONAL THEATER, *1940s.*

the screen to burst into flame during a Sunday night performance of a Bing Crosby film. More than 500 patrons were evacuated safely with the help of some soldiers in the audience who had been in town on leave from the Richmond Air Base. The soldiers reported back late, but once they explained themselves, they were commended by their officers and received passes for five-day leaves. Seven years later, on July 11, 1950, just as Leo the Lion's roar introduced the film *The Asphalt Jungle,* a 15x30 foot section of the building's roof caved in on the auditorium. Seventeen people sustained minor injuries, mostly cuts and bruises, and the rest of the audience escaped, frightened but unharmed. A news article at the time speculated that the might of Leo's roar could have caused the collapse. "City Building Commissioner William G. Wharton said such vibrations may have caused previously weakened parts of the ceiling to loosen and fall. 'It would have been on the verge of collapse for as long as two years, and almost anything might have caused it to fall,' Wharton was quoted as saying. 'A noise, vibration or even a change of temperature could have been responsible. What actually happened, I have no idea.'" The Park Theater was repaired, but closed in 1953. In 1957 it was remodeled into an insurance and banking office, becoming the first home of the Virginia Credit Union.[11]

As a young woman growing up in Richmond in the late 1930s and 1940s, Jackie Samuels felt that the city's neighborhood and downtown movie theaters were her second home. "I lived at the movies," she recalls. In the wartime years, she made a record of her movie-going experiences in a series of scrapbooks, carefully preserv-

ing ticket stubs, programs, and notes of what she saw and with whom, along with her mementoes of holidays, parties, vacations and good times with friends.[12] Jackie Samuels' affection for the movies had started at a young age. From the time she was three years old and living in Sparrows Point, Maryland, she recalls her mother, who was quite fond of films, taking her to see silent movies at Baltimore theaters and having to read the titles aloud to her. The backstage musical *Broadway Melody* was her first "talkie." She recalls seeing wonderful musicals, exciting dramas, vaudeville skits and stage shows with her mother at the at the luxurious Century, Howard and Hippodrome picture palaces in downtown Baltimore. Ruby Keeler and Dick Powell in *Forty Second Street* was her favorite childhood film.

In 1936, when Jackie was 14, her mother passed away and she and her father moved to Richmond's Fan district. Jackie soon located all the city's theaters and she began venturing out to the movies by herself, by trolley, bus and on foot. Jackie walked to the Lee Theater on Grace Street; it was a family-oriented, neighborhood theater showing "second run" movies in those days. She took the streetcar to the National, State, Colonial and Park theaters on Broad Street. She liked the stage revues at the National, and she also frequented the Byrd, Carillon, Bellevue, Brookland and Capital theaters. She rode to Loew's Theater on the bus to catch especially anticipated films, such as Jeanette MacDonald and Nelson Eddy's MGM musicals. In her high school years, Jackie often went to the movies with a group of girlfriends. Their favorite amusements included walking to the Byrd to see a show, going to "Y" or Eagle dances on Fridays, roller-skating, listening to

HAL SANDS DANCERS, NATIONAL THEATER, *1940s.*

TICKET STUBS, JACKIE SAMUELS SCRAPBOOK, *1943. Samuels memorialized many pleasant trips to Richmond movie theaters such as the Loew's, National, Carillon, Byrd, State and Bellevue.*

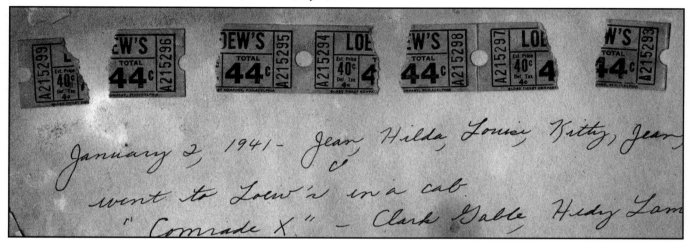

radio programs, and "hanging out" with other girls and boys at the Hanover Inn, drinking limeades and playing the jukebox. Jackie saved her money to get the 10-cent movie fan magazines like *Photoplay, Motion Picture,* and *Screenland,* for they kept her up to date on what the stars were doing and what new movies would be showing. Vivien Leigh, who had played Scarlett O'Hara to perfection, was Jackie's favorite actress of the early 1940s. And her favorite actor? "Lots – I loved them all", she laughs.

During World War II, "Richmond was heavenly for a civilian working girl," she remembers. "There were so many servicemen in town, there were plenty of jobs with good wages, and such exciting music and nightlife." "Richmond was not so heavenly for service folk on liberty," she adds, "no free nothing – no discounts on movies or band show tickets!" Jackie loved going to see big bands and popular vocalists at the Tantilla Gardens. But a girl needed to have a date to go there. Even a particularly dull blind date might be tolerated if it meant getting in to hear Jo Stafford or Tommy Dorsey in person. In 1944, she volunteered to join the WAVES, or Women's Auxiliary Naval corps.

Back in Richmond after the war, Jackie was relieved to find that the downtown theaters hadn't changed. Stars as such as famous crooner Frank Sinatra performed during a War Bond show at the Mosque in December, 1945. "Sinatra was so thin he could hardly hold the mike!"

she recalls. The drive-in movie theaters at the edge of town were a new treat. She could pile into her car with a date, or cousins, or girlfriends and their children and her dog, pack a big picnic dinner and drive out to the Broadway or Patterson drive ins. Throughout the 1950s and 1960s, she was a regular patron of the Byrd, Capitol, and Loew's, and the new Willow Lawn Theater, where she especially enjoyed seeing 1964's *The Sound of Music.* When cable television came to Henrico County in 1979, Jackie says she was the first customer to have it installed in her home. Since then, she has indulged in her love for the movies of her younger years on television. "I can still recite almost the complete dialog of my favorite movies," she marvels.

An Evening at the Movies

Friday and Saturday nights were the most popular times to go to the movies during the war years. The audiences were quite diverse – dating couples, families, soldiers, singles, friends, and people of all ages and economic backgrounds. The nightlife was exciting both at the first run picture palaces like Loew's or the National, and at second run theaters such as the Lee or Carillon. Harold Thrower recalls that the uniformed male ushers kept the long lines in front of the theaters moving in the right direction. It was not unusual to have the lines of patrons waiting to enter the National, State and Colonial theaters tangle up as they snaked down the sidewalk in front of Theater Row. Thrower's job was to keep the lines out of the middle of the sidewalk and keep the people patient as they waited to get in.

Seeing the feature film was only one part of the evening at the movies, which was a night filled with fun and a variety of entertainments. On Friday and Saturday nights, a comic's routine or a song and dance number opened the program while musicians played in the orchestra pit. At Loew's, the movie audience was treated to a performance by Eddie Weaver on the organ. Before the movie would begin, the lights dimmed and Weaver and his instrument, framed by a spotlight, emerged from under the stage. Boys used to snicker at a joke each one of them thought they had originated, that "the reason women go to the Loew's Theater is see Eddie Weaver's organ rise." Following the sing-a-long, viewers saw a cartoon, newsreel, comedy short and then the feature film. For the price of a ticket, it was entertainment that lasted all evening long.

Those on a budget waited in lines at theaters like the Lee and Carillon. The second-run houses were more affordable than the downtown theaters, but the experience was similar, for they too had ushers and polite ticket takers, and the audience members behaved themselves. For some movie fans, the opportunity to see films at Loew's or the National was a special and rare occasion. Not only were the admission prices higher downtown, but members of the audience, especially the women, were also expected to dress formally. Men needed suit jackets, and women always wore their hats and gloves.[13]

At both the first- and second-run theaters, the young men employed as ushers had the important job of controlling the crowds and insuring correct behavior among the audience members. Even the gangliest ushers looked professional in brimmed hats and spotless maroon uniforms trimmed with gold piping, which were provided by the theater. Theater managers made informal inspections of the ushers' uniforms at the beginning of the evening shift, some of them acting like drill sergeants. After managing the crowds outside, ushers guided the movie patrons to their seats. During the movie, ushers walked up and down the aisles, checking the behavior of the audience. They aimed their flashlights at those who talked during the movie. If an usher pointed his light twice at the same patron, he or she was asked to leave. The ushers were paid forty cents an hour for a 20-to-30 hour workweek, with no tipping allowed. Their shifts were six to eight hours long with fifteen-minute breaks. For a young man in high school, like Buddy Calisch or Harold Thrower, this was an ideal job: regular hours, uniforms and free admission to the movies and shows; all their

schoolmates were jealous. Few theaters hired female ushers, but young women like Geneva Thrower were able to get a position in the box office (she worked at the Carillon.) Managers assumed that a woman's voice answering the box office's telephone, and a "pretty face" at the ticket window, meant good business for the theater.

An usher's job was also the first rung on the career ladder of the movie theater business. In those days, many managers worked their way up from ushers. Stewart Tucker had begun as a water boy at the Bijou Theater in 1913, in the days of the Grayce Scott Stock Company. After a stint at the Mosque, he managed the State Theater for more than 20 years. Allen Brown started as an usher at the Loew's Theater as an 18-year-old just out of school; he figured it was better than being a grocery store bag boy. Three months later, he found himself at the Brookland Theater as doorman. He became manager of the Brookland at 19, and worked there for 21 years. When the Westover Theater opened in 1951, he moved over there to run it. Bob Hatcher climbed the career ladder from usher to doorman to student manager to relief manager, working late nights, weekends and covering for sick managers at other theaters, before eventually securing a manager's position at the Carillon and Lee.[14]

In Richmond, theater managers had incredible longevity in their jobs. Robert Coulter manned the helm at the Byrd for 43 years. George Peters managed the Loew's for 32 years. He did his job so well that in 1947, he was chosen to represent all film exhibitors across the nation in an article published in the *Saturday Evening Post*. Peters was profiled in the magazine's "Men at Work" series on the various jobs held by typical Americans. He was shown in a big color photograph dressed in his customary tuxedo, directing ushers and guiding gloved- and hatted-patrons along the roped-off entrance lines of the Loew's lobby.

Theater workers collected stories about the odd things that occurred around the movie house. George Peters recalled the "fabled ping-pong matches of theater organist Eddie Weaver and other back-and understage staffers." Movie patrons used to complain to him about strange tap-tapping noises that interrupted the quiet love scenes on screen. Former Byrd usher James Heslep remembered that George Stitzer, who was assistant manager for 43 years, loved to pull practical jokes. Heslep told of the time that Stitzer sent an usher down to clean up a mess around the seat of Mayor Fulmer Bright during a show. "There wasn't anything to clean up, and the mayor didn't know what to make of the young man crawling around the floor with dust pan and broom," he said. Heslep also recalled the time he fell into a basement puddle at the Byrd while mopping up after a flood and

USHER CORPS AT LOEW'S THEATER, *1940s. Dressed in crisp uniforms and trained to firmly maintain order in ticket lines and the auditorium, ushers had important jobs that brought young men needed wages, all the movies they could watch, and envy among their friends.*

had to hang his pants up to dry. Stitzer somehow engineered an errand which required Heslep to run outside and around to the front of the building clad only in uniform jacket and under shorts, much to the amusement of the people waiting in line to purchase tickets.

Duane Nelson and Miles Rudisill tell another of the Byrd staff's favorite anecdotes, about "a man who had a heart attack and died in his seat while watching a film.... To avoid causing a commotion, two ambulance attendants quietly walked down the aisle to where the man was sitting, slipped one his arms over each of their shoulders and walked the body to the lobby. Not one minute of the movie was interrupted."[15] The Loew's staff's favorite story was about the time a Richmond policeman heard shots inside when he was patrolling the alley behind the theater. "He called in [to police headquarters] and was told to wait for reinforcements. Instead, he came in and ran across the stage, in front of the screen, with his gun

drawn." There was a Western playing and the policeman's unexpected entrance caused a lot of comments.[16]

The 1940s also saw a change in the former prohibition on food inside movie theaters. As Leo Schario recalled of his movie-going experiences in Canton, Ohio (which had a sister theater in the Loew's chain),

When I first started going to the movies in 1926, all the great movie palaces were brand new, beautifully maintained and squeaky clean. No one would have even thought of bringing any food into the theatre. I remember how it first got started back around 1930. It was the Depression and theatres were desperate for any additional revenue. I was amazed one day to see a small candy machine over in the corner of the lobby of Loew's Theater. For a nickel you could make a selection from four candy bars. There was noth-

WORKERS AT STATE THEATER, *1940s. Behind the scenes at the movie theater, ushers had less-glamorous jobs such as scraping chewing gum off the carpets. Others changed the marquee and swept up before the next show.*

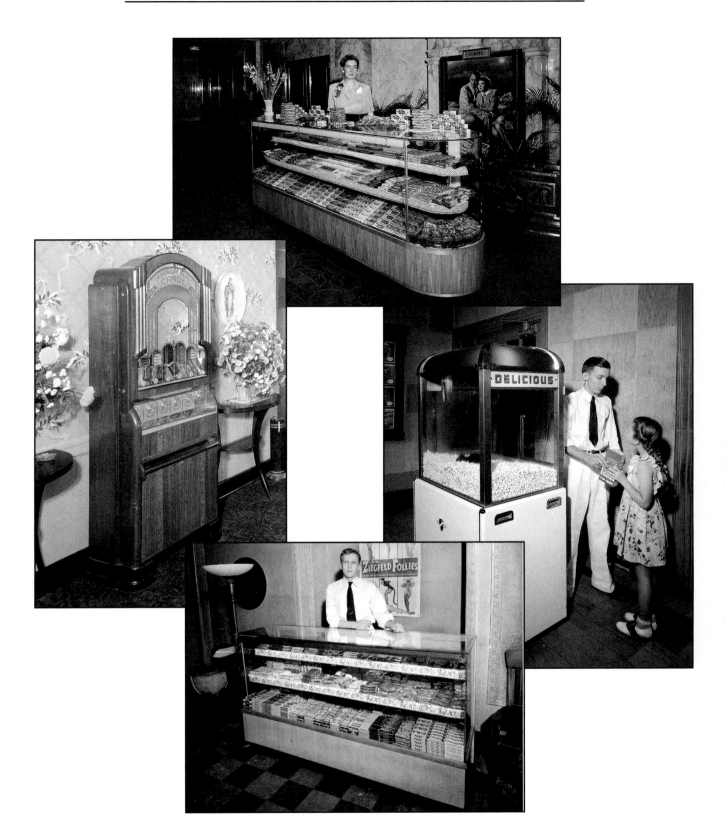

CONCESSION STANDS, *at the Byrd (top), Venus (right and bottom) and Regent (left) theaters, 1940s. Candy, popcorn and soda pop only entered Richmond movie theaters around World War II.*

CONCESSION STANDS, *at the Regal Short Pump, 2001 (left and top); Willow Lawn 1980s (right); and Commonwealth 20, 2001 (bottom). Candy and popcorn became increasingly popular with movie patrons. Theaters now offer a gourmet selection of treats, and cafes in the lobby.*

PROJECTION EQUIPMENT, *Westhampton Theater, 1938, Willow Lawn Theater, 1950s. Projectionists are unsung heroes whose fine work wrestling with these mechanical beasts is not noticed until the film breaks or sound or focus is faulty.*

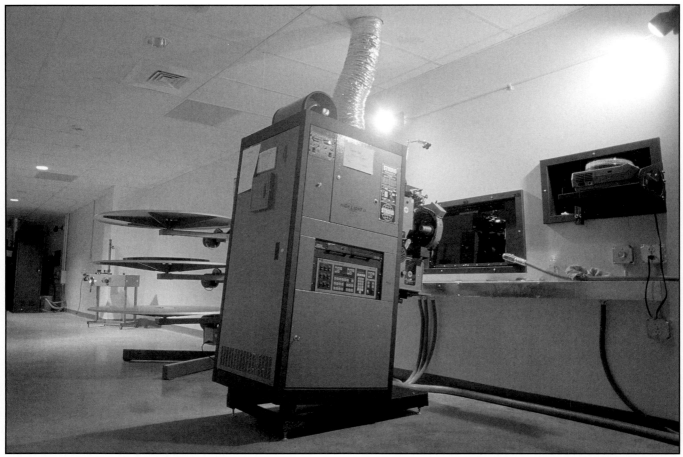

PLATTER PROJECTION SYSTEM,. *Commonwealth 20 Theaters, 2001. Today's complex equipment still offers the busy projectionist many challenges.*

ing else. But as Depression deepened and the war years came on, popcorn and real food was added as well as a very obtrusive and gaudy refreshment stand that was placed in the very center of the lobby or foyer.[17]

Edith Lindeman similarly recollected that in most Richmond movie theaters, "if you wanted popcorn, you had to get it outside the theater and sneak it in. Movie managers frowned on anything more edible than mint lozenges and cough drops."[18] In those days, popcorn had associations with less refined amusements like the tent show or circus. So instead, before or after the show, Richmond moviegoers stopped by places such as White's Ice Cream Parlor. There was one shop downtown by the Loew's theater, and another one on Cary Street near the Byrd. "Before we put in the concession stand, food was not allowed in the theater," recalled Byrd assistant manager George Stitzer; "We'd stop 'em at the door if they had a bag of popcorn."[19] In the early 1940s, Richmond's

theaters finally capitulated, realizing that they needed popcorn, candy and drink sales to boost their bottom lines. At the Byrd, the fountain and fish pool were taken out of the lobby and a concession stand was put in.[20]

The Saturday Morning Cowboy Shows
by Kristin Thrower

On Saturday mornings all across Richmond, doors opened as young boys, ages nine to fourteen, raced to their favorite movie theater to see the next installment of the current serial. Would the heroine be run over by a train or would the hero save the day at the last possible minute? These boys looked forward to Saturday mornings; it was a time to escape into the darkened theater and watch the stories unfold in front of them. Although World War II raged across the Atlantic and Pacific oceans, at home it was a golden era of movie-going. This was the time of the real cowboy heroes.

This generation of young boys went faithfully to the

NEIGHBORHOOD THEATERS, INC. 20TH ANNIVERSARY CELEBRATION, *1946. Posters, big cakes and cigarette girls help celebrate the success and growth of Morton G. Thalhimer's theater chain, which by the 1940s was a dominant force in local and statewide film exhibition.*

MOVIE POSTERS THEN AND NOW, *Brookland Theater, 1946 and Carmike 10 Theaters, 2001. Eye-catching promotions for upcoming films have always been a movie theater staple.*

PONTON THEATER, *1316 Hull St, 1944. Originally a nickelodeon opened in 1911, the Ponton was a small Southside house that played westerns and adventure films.*

movie theater every Saturday morning. For a young boy moving to Richmond, it took only one day to locate the theaters and which streetcar took you there. Movies were the most immediate connection to the neighborhood, the city and most of all, to your friends.

The morning adventure began with a ride. For seven cents, the streetcar took you to your favorite local movie theater. However, not all young children had the seven cents fare. A regular sight on Saturday mornings were gangs of young boys walking down Hull Street, across the railroad tracks and then across Cowardin Avenue in order to arrive at the Venus and Ponton theaters. Walking meant saving the seven cents for a possible treat at the theater or for the ride home.

The most important objective was meeting the ten-cent admission price, for which the youths were able to see a serial, a cartoon, newsreels and a full-length film, usually a western. Ten cents was thus the prized amount for these youngsters. If you were really lucky and had a

quarter, you purchased a ticket, bought candy and had enough left over for a streetcar ride home. A quarter also was the admission price to the first-run theater, Loew's, in downtown Richmond. The cost limited most boys on Saturday mornings to the second-run theaters, such as the Venus, Ponton, Bellevue, Patrick Henry, Robinson, and Grand.

The average child, however, did not have ten cents sitting in his pocket. Children were quite inventive in funding their Saturday adventures. To earn ten cents, boys ran errands for people, collected bottles and turned them in for deposit, or found scrap iron to sell. Movie theaters sometimes accepted a can of grease, an old tire, or a ball of tin foil in place of the dime. It was also known that occasionally, a movie ticket taker accepted bribes for the requested admission price, such as mother's homemade brownies. Boys also worked for their money by selling newspapers or taking their wagons to the local grocery store and carrying home people's groceries in hopes of

BROOKLAND THEATER, *115 Brookland Park Ave., 1936. Opened in 1925 on the city's Northside, the Brookland was popular with neighborhood children for Saturday morning cowboy shows.*

getting a big tip. The more inventive children hung out at the water fountain in Monroe Park. On particularly hot days, the children swam in the cool fountain waters. On very lucky days, servicemen walked by and tossed pennies, nickels and dimes into the fountain and watched the children dive and race for their treasures.

If all that failed, youngsters resorted to "bumming" for dimes, as Charles and Raymond Hughes did at the Grey Garnett Clothing Store on the corner of Cowardin Avenue and Hull Street. The two brothers entered the store and stood together beside the door, waiting without saying a word. Eventually, the clerk went to the register, opened the drawer and gave each boy his own dime. Charles and Raymond then ran to the Venus to watch the Saturday morning shows.

The last option was "hoodlumism." This was particularly popular at the expensive Loew's Theater. When a new movie came to town, the young boys were not always willing to wait for it to come to the second-run the-

aters. Twenty-five cents was a lot of money, however, so a collection was taken up among the gang of three to five boys to raise enough money for one ticket. Then one boy bought the ticket and entered the theater. Once inside, he found his way to the exit door on the side of Thalhimer's. When no one was looking, he opened the exit door and the rest of the gang sneaked in from the alleyway. After entering, each child sprinted in a different direction to decrease the chances of being caught. Eventually, the gang found each other and enjoyed the rest of the program together.

Having a dime, though, did not necessarily grant admission to the show. The theaters set different prices for different age groups, which became a problem to the young boy who was unfortunate enough to look older or be taller than most boys his age. The ticket taker then charged the higher adult admission rate. Thomas G. Wyatt ran into this problem with a certain ticket-taker. She did not believe him to be under twelve years old. In

HOPALONG CASSIDY AND YOUNG COWBOYS BRIAN DEMENTI AND FRIEND, *1943. The Western star made a personal appearance in Richmond and posed with his fans.*

order for him to continue to pay only ten cents, she required him to bring his birth certificate to the box office to prove his age. Other boys were able to take advantage of the age-set prices. If a young boy was smaller than most boys his age, he continued to pay that dime admission even at the age of thirteen. The most important thing about Saturday was the dime. Whether you worked, bummed or cried for your money, going to see the show was the most important thing.

The goal of these boys was to see the western full-length feature film and the next episode in the latest serial. They were so intent on seeing the films that there was no need to check the newspaper for the scheduled movie or times. Even arrival time at the theater was variable since entering in the middle of the feature film was okay. Saturday morning audiences stayed all day watching the same films several times over. Thomas Wyatt's father took him and his brother to the theater in the morning on Saturdays, and the boys stayed until dark, seeing the show through a mind-numbing five or six times. Westerns were the most popular film genre for the young boys. Most westerns contained the same revolving plot lines; cowboy stars ended up in wild rapid water rides, runaway stagecoach chases, and cattle rus-

THE GRAND THEATER, *1942. The Grand played the newest cowboy film releases first in town before they appeared at the suburban theaters.*

ROY ROGERS AND FAN OUTSIDE THE NATIONAL THEATER, *1942. Movie fan Bob Williams took this snapshot of his friend Albert Wilkerson shaking hands with the famous western movie star outside the National Theater when Rogers made a personal appearance in Richmond. Collection of Kathy Fuller-Seeley.*

tling fracases. The young fans were excited just to see the cowboy stars on the screen. A movie was even better if it featured two or more cowboy stars. Their favorites were Johnny Mack Brown, John Wayne, Lash LaRue, Tex Ritter, Bob Steele, Monty Hill, Fuzz Q. Jones, Wild Bill Elliot, Sunset Carson, and the Durango Kid. When a new movie came out that featured a favorite actor, the young fans followed the movie from theater to theater and eventually saw it several times. As the young boys matured and their tastes evolved, new names were added to the favorites list, like the singing cowboys Roy Rogers and Gene Autry. But when they were young, the western action stars were the boys' preferred heroes.

Western movies and serials influenced these young boys beyond their creative ways of earning the dime. Almost all young boys played cowboys and Indians or good and bad guys. Rarely did a boy assume the identity of an Indian, however, since other than sidekicks there were few strong Indian movie characters. Yet boys did choose the bad guy roles. To become a bad cowboy, a dirty handkerchief wrapped around the face suggested the part.

Guns assumed a major role in the "playing" of cowboys. Some boys were lucky enough to own toy guns while others used their imaginations by turning sticks into weapons. Play guns were worn to school in anticipation of the gunfights or showdowns certain to happen at recess. At the start of the school day, all guns were checked in to the teacher until recess. Gunfights rarely resulted in the death of the bad guy, a sure way to end the game. Most likely, the bad guy was shot and wounded, then the hero climbed aboard his horse and galloped away. Cowboy "horses" were created from broomsticks or fallen tree limbs. The boys carved spots on limbs so that they would resemble pinto ponies. Cowboy horses were off limits; it was considered extremely rude for one cowboy to touch another cowboy's horse. Oilcans collected from service stations added to the creative play. Boys crushed the cans and attached them to the bottom of their shoes. The crushed oilcans made a clopping noise, so when the cow-

LEE THEATER, *934 W. Grace St., 1936. The Lee offered family fare at inexpensive prices to moviegoers who lived in the surrounding Fan neighborhood.*

boy rode off into the distance he was accompanied by the sound of galloping hooves.

The influence of the on-screen cowboys was not limited to playtime. Hopalong Cassidy had a code of conduct that all of his fans had to follow. The code was quite simple — do not smoke, drink or curse. Good cowboys stars followed a similar code of high morals and values; negative habits symbolized bad cowboys. The western stars were father figures to the boys, teaching their young fans American values. There was good and bad, and wrong and right. If a cowboy's brother went over to the wrong side, the film centered on him being brought back into the fold. If the good brother was unable to save the bad brother by the end of the movie, the bad son was usually killed. Good always won in the end. Fairness, respect and good deeds were plentiful in these western pictures.

Occasionally, the cowboy heroes made personal appearances at Richmond movie theaters. There was usually no extra cost to see one's heroes in the flesh. Monty

Hill, Gene Autry, Lash LaRue, Bob Baker, and Tex Ritter were just a few of the cowboys to venture to Richmond. After the movie, the cowboy came out on stage to hand out free autographed pictures. Sometimes the cowboy even put on an exhibition. Lash LaRue gave out comic books at the Venus. Hopalong Cassidy came to Thalhimer's department store in the fall of 1950, where young fans had their pictures taken with him. Seeing their heroes in real life was the most exciting event these boys had ever experienced.

By mid-afternoon, the Saturday shows for children had ended. The ushers directed the young male audience out because it was time for the first evening performance. The evening's feature might even be a western movie, like *The Outlaw*, starring Jane Russell, or *Duel in the Sun*, with Jennifer Jones and Gregory Peck. Yet adults considered these movies too mature for the young western fans, to the boys' confusion and consternation at why their parents would not let them see those films.

GRACE STREET THEATER, *934 W. Grace St., 2001. The old theater gained a new community purpose when Virginia Commonwealth University purchased and renovated the Lee into a performing arts facility for its Dance Department.*

As time passed, the young fans aged and with that their movie habits also changed. The Saturday morning westerns were exchanged for the Saturday night movies with their girlfriends. The young woman often decided what movies the couple went to see. Now instead of seeing a John Wayne movie, a young man might see *Seven Brides for Seven Brothers*. But for these men who grew up watching the Saturday morning westerns and serials in the 1940s, nothing else could ever replace them. The old films bring back memories that still make many of the old cowboys smile. While most of the former cowboys still attend the movies, they all agree that there is something lacking today in the audience, the theaters, and the movies themselves. Children of today have too much vying for their attention, such as computers and television, whereas the young boys of 1940s had only the movies and to be able to attend them, they worked extremely hard. They got more than just a movie, the sing-a-long, live entertainment, newsreels, cartoons, feature films and a sense of shared community. They had managed to sit all day for that one dime.[21]

The Old Dominion Barn Dance
by Douglas Gomery

The Old Dominion Barn Dance, which ran from 1946 through 1957, was a well-known Saturday night country showcase broadcast live from the 1,300 seat Lyric Theater at 9th and Broad Streets over 50,000-watt WRVA radio. Its audience, which peaked at nearly a million listeners in 1950, stretched from Florida to Maine, from Virginia to Missouri. Its home, the Lyric Theater, had been built with 1,800 seats, but was modified to 1,300 for the radio shows.

WRVA radio, which first went on the air in 1925, was owned by the Larus and Brother Tobacco Company, which marketed Edgeworth Pipe Tobacco and Domino Cigarettes. Just as Prince Albert Tobacco benefited from its long association with *The Grand Ole Opry*, Larus and Brother used *The Old Dominion Barn Dance* as a radio country showcase to sell its products. The first WRVA studios were in the Larus and Brother Tobacco Building on Richmond's old Tobacco Row. In 1933 the station moved to the mezzanine of the former Hotel Richmond. No studio space at either site could hold the crowds *The*

LYRIC THEATER, *901 E. Broad St., late 1930s*.

Old Dominion Barn Dance would draw to its two Saturday night shows, and so they rented the close-by Lyric Theater, and renamed it the WRVA Theater in 1946.

The Old Dominion Barn Dance came to be when C. T. Lucy, general manager of WRVA radio, obtained the lease of the Lyric in 1946. Its official debut launched WRVA's 1946-1947 radio season in September 1946. The station also used the Lyric Theater for audience participation shows, and for public displays of broadcast election reports.

From the beginning the star and hostess of *The Old Dominion Barn Dance* was a local favorite — Sunshine Sue (Workman) – performing with her husband, John Workman, and brother-in-law, Sam Workman. Together the trio was known as Sunshine Sue and the Smiling Rangers. With Sunshine Sue as its hostess, *The Old Dominion Barn Dance* drew overflow crowds to see the Workmans sing the old standards as well as to listen and to watch guest stars such as now-members of the Country Music Hall of Fame Chet Atkins, the Carter Family, Grandpa

Jones, Flatt and Scruggs, plus on occasion rising local stars such as Patsy Cline and Roy Clark.

Virginia Governor William Tuck claimed he attended every show, and in 1949 he proclaimed Sue "Queen of the Hillbillies." The official state Chamber of Commerce magazine, *The Commonwealth*, profiled her, and told how she rejected labels as a folk or country artist, but just sang to the people, and was proud of her label "Queen of the Hillbillies." Standing against a painted backdrop of a barn and a big yellow moon, Sunshine Sue was the only female star to host a major radio barn dance. A veteran of small town radio and local barn dances from the 1930s through World War II, she and her family did stints at Louisville's WHAS radio, Chicago's *National Barn Dance* on WLS-AM, and *The Midwestern Hayride* from Cincinnati's WLW-AM before landing in Richmond.

Sue played the accordion, sang, and told homey stories that reminded city folk of mythic days back home on the farm. Her signature tune, *You Are My Sunshine*, opened and closed the show. She was literally on stage

WRVA THEATER, *1948. The vaudeville and playhouse, opened in 1912, became the home of the* **Old Dominion Barn Dance** *radio show when the Lyric Theater was purchased and renamed by WRVA.*

from 7:30pm to 11:15pm every Saturday night, with only a fifteen-minute break between the two shows. Sue also helped plan the shows, hire guest stars, organize tours around Virginia, and do a daily broadcast on WRVA promoting not only *The Old Dominion Barn Dance*, but also up-coming personal appearances. She and her husband leveraged their fame, and became entrepreneurs beyond what we might consider country music. For example, in the late 1940s and early 1950s, the Workmans booked touring Broadway shows into Richmond, including *Oklahoma*, and *Annie Get Your Gun*.

For a time in the early 1950s, *The Old Dominion Barn Dance* was even carried by the CBS radio network, and then later by the Mutual radio network. But *The Old Dominion Barn Dance* did not become a television show as WRVA-TV did not go on the air until late April 1956, in the waning days of *The Old Dominion Barn Dance's* popularity. Indeed, by the middle 1950s the Lyric was

no longer filled, and with the show losing money, WRVA management ended it's more than decade long run in 1957. Sunshine Sue was ready to call it a day. In a decade her family had become rich through wise investments, and she wanted to retire. Several months after the demise of the original, *The New Dominion Barn Dance*, created by Carlton L. Haney, was first broadcast on WRVA from the Lyric, featuring more bluegrass than country acts, and this re-incarnation, moving to the small stage of the north side's Bellevue Theater, lasted until 1964.

Post-War Changes in Movie-going

At the end of World War II in 1945, many Richmonders, like people across the nation, searched for the "good life" that had been so difficult to find during the long years of the Depression and the wartime emergency. By 1950, due to wartime growth and continuing manufacturing expansion, Richmond's population had grown by

***OLD DOMINION BARN DANCE* PERFORMERS,** *late 1940s.*

MOTHER MAYBELLE AND THE CARTER SISTERS, *late 1940s.*

Regulars on the **Old Dominion Barn Dance** *from 1946 to 1948, Maybelle Carter (center) and her daughters Anita (left) June [the future Mrs. Johnny Cash] (top), and Helen (right) posed for a publicity portrait. In 1927, Scott County (Va.) native Maybelle Carter and in-laws A.P. and Sara Carter formed the soon-to-be-legendary country music group, the Carter Family. After the original group dissolved in 1943, Maybelle performed with her daughters for three years on Richmonds' WRNL, before moving to the WRVA's* **Barn Dance**. *The quartet was accepted into the Grand Ole Opry in 1950.*

20 percent to 230,000 and the metro area as a whole was home to 350,000 people. The trend, however, was toward population growth out in the suburbs. Young families looking for homes with larger yards for their children to play in moved away from the inner city to new housing developments sprouting up south, north, east and west in surrounding Henrico, Chesterfield and Hanover counties.

New residential patterns also brought changes to the amusement-seeking habits of Americans; out in the suburbs with their young children, families increasingly gave up the long trips to the downtown movie theaters. Instead, they remained home to listen to radio shows and watch programs on that new invention, television, which was rapidly gaining popularity. Movie theater owners struggled to keep up with these changes, trying to lure patrons back by making the movies seem as different as possible from the black and white television programs shown on small, boxy sets, and combating the TV threat with Cinemascope, historical epics and color- saturated musicals. Retailers in Richmond began to address the new demographic trends in the 1950s, opening the first shopping malls farther out along Broad Street, Hull Street, and Midlothian Turnpike to reach the increasingly dispersed suburban customers. Similarly, to reach these same patrons, entrepreneurial film exhibitors opened drive-in theaters, creating a new form of movie going that took advantage of Americans' love affair with their automobiles.

The first of these new theaters in the Richmond area was the Open Air Movies Theater, which began operation a year before Pearl Harbor, on December 3, 1940; it was located in Midlothian at Route 147 Bon Air Road. A second early entrant into the drive-in market was the Autovue Theater, which opened October 1941 on Hopewell Road, just off the Petersburg Pike. War-time gasoline rationing severely curtailed business at these automobile theaters, but once the restrictions were lifted at the end of the war, attendance at the new outdoor theaters boomed and there was a rush to put up big screens, concession stands and an acre of car speakers set on poles on farmland all across the Richmond area. The Open Air changed its name to the Midlothian Drive-In Theater in 1947. The Bellwood Drive In opened in May 1948 four miles south of the Richmond city limits on Jefferson Davis Highway at Willis Road.

By the mid-1950s, drive-in theaters surrounded the city on its outskirts – the Broad Street, Patterson, Broadway, Airport, Sunset, Bellwood, Midlothian and Southside Plaza drive-ins all did good business. While they diverted some patronage from the downtown Richmond theaters, the drive-ins were very convenient for the 1950s and 1960s baby boom families who otherwise

SUNSHINE SUE, *late 1940. The hostess and star of the* Old Dominion Barn Dance.

might not have gotten out to the movies at all. To attend the drive-in, parents did not need to find a babysitter – they could bundle the kids in the car (often in their pajamas) with snacks and blankets, and go to a show knowing that their kids were safe. Drive-ins built playgrounds for children on the lawn underneath the giant outdoor screens, and concession stands offered hamburgers, hot dogs and drinks so enticingly advertised during the intermissions. Women and men did not have to worry about dressing up in suit jackets or hat and gloves, driving all the way into town, and finding a parking place, all just to go to the movies on Saturday night. They could attend a drive-in theater in their sloppiest work-around-the-house clothes, and no one minded if mom's hair was in curlers or dad hadn't shaved. Of course, that freedom from the scrutiny of the ushers, and the privacy of an automobile, made drive-ins especially popular with dating couples and teenagers. The steamed-up car windows common among cars at drive-ins gave the theaters the nickname "the passion pit." Drive-ins also served as excellent places for teenagers to gather in groups for friendship and fun,

SUNSHINE SUE WORKMAN AND GOVERNOR WILLIAM TUCK GREET ARTHUR GODFREY, *late 1940s.*
Sunshine Sue was Governor Tuck's favorite performer - he attended every broadcast. Here they meet renowned radio and television personality Godfrey.

and to watch the teen comedies and scary horror films that became frequent drive-in program fare. Some thrifty teens would try to cram their friends into the commodious trunks of the era's large cars to get the whole gang into the drive-in movies as cheaply as possible.

Only a few new "hard top" movie theaters opened during the period, but theater owners tried to make the new houses distinctive. The Neighborhood Theaters Inc. chain built the Westover Theater on Forest Hill Avenue in the close-by suburbs south of the James River; it opened on August 30, 1950. One of the Westover's most memorable film engagements was the big-budget film version of Cole Porter's musical *Kiss Me Kate*. Bob Burchette remembers viewing it wearing special "3-D" glasses (which others remember could give the viewer a terrific headache). Allen Brown, the Westover's manager, announced at its opening that, to combat the general trend in declining movie attendance, the Westover tried to integrate itself more than ever into the community's life:

At various times the Capitol, Westhampton, and Byrd have thrown open their doors on Sunday

mornings to accommodate congregations whose churches had burned or were in the process of rebuilding. The Bellevue at one time was the meeting place for women's organizations in the Ginter Park area, and several women's clubs still use the Westhampton regularly during the winter months. However, the Westover is the first local theater to be constructed with a preconceived plan for community service. It is a goodwill plan that will further cement the excellent public relationship between the city's people and all its local theaters.[22]

The Westover had a furnished lounge and small kitchen on the second floor. Ironically, this built-in space for community activities would help save the Westover after it closed in 1993. The New Canaan Baptist Church found that the rooms were suitable for church-use and the congregation settled in the former theater in 1997.

The National Theater brought in a "big screen television" to show a Jake LaMotta prizefight in July 1951, and the big event filled all 1,350 seats. The National's

BROAD STREET LOOKING WEST, *1950s. The glowing WRVA Theater sign beckons entertainment seekers amidst the lights and excitement of Broad Street at night.*

manager announced that he was very optimistic that souped-up television could be a boon to motion picture theaters.[23] In 1953, the Byrd Theater installed the first Cinemascope screen in the entire state for the local showing of the widescreen Technicolor biblical epic, *The Robe*. NTI opened the Willow Lawn Theater on November 15, 1956 at the new six million dollar suburban Willow Lawn shopping center in Richmond's West End. Called "the theater of the future," it had a single auditorium with a Cinemascope screen, showed 70mm films, and had the latest in retractable seats. Its first film was Judy Holliday's comedy The *Solid Gold Cadillac*. The 830-set house had the distinction of being the first theater in Virginia equipped to show movies in the Todd-AO process. *South Pacific* in Todd-AO premiered locally on the Willow Lawn's special large, curved screen, and broke all records for the longevity of its engagement, playing for five months. The Willow Lawn Theater was where most of the "blockbuster" films of the early 1960s played in Richmond. It had long runs for films like *Cleopatra, Dr. Doolittle*, and *Mary Poppins. The Sound of Music* stayed there for 87 weeks, winning the award for being the longest-running film in Richmond theater history. The Willow Lawn offered reserved seat tickets for the big films, and moviegoers came all the way from West Virginia and North Carolina. Super-wide screens, stereophonic sound, fabulous Technicolor, comfortable seats – all these features were inducements added by movie theater owners to lure movie patrons back out of their living rooms, but movie attendance kept declining and television became ever more popular.

The Rebirth of Local Theater in Richmond

Professional theater in Richmond was practically dead in the 1930s, for the resident stock companies and touring stage productions stopping here on "the road" had disappeared. However, the decade witnessed the blossoming of community theater in Richmond, sparked by the nationwide Little Theater movement of the late 1920s (Richmond's Little Theater League was active 1919-1930.) A dedicated core group of theater aficionados, with a great deal of hard work and dedication, kept the theatrical spirit alive for 30 years.

In 1927, Leslie Banks, a sixteen-year-old John Marshall High School graduate, who would become known as Richmond's "Mr. Theater," worked props in a Little Theater League production of Gilbert and Sullivan's *The Mikado*, with his high school sweetheart Rose Kaufman. The two decided to forge what would be a formidable partnership. "Rose and I went to North Carolina to attend the first Southern Association of Theaters Organization meeting and got married. It's the best thing I ever did," Banks recalled.[24] To finance their dreams of working in the theater in Richmond, Rose and Leslie Banks had to take other jobs to make ends meet. Leslie Banks was a stock boy at Thalhimer's, then an assistant buyer in the store's furniture department. Rose Banks found a position in the Richmond City Department of Recreation and Parks, and soon came to be superintendent of central activities for the department. Under her direction, the city became a prominent sponsor of school and community drama and dance productions through the 1930s, 1940s and 1950s. Rose Banks helped move the Department of Recreation and Parks offices to the Mosque Theater, which the city had taken over. The Mosque subsequently became the site of innumerable school plays, pageants and recitals. Richmond became one of the country's leading medium-sized cities to take such an active role in its cultural affairs.

In the 1930s, Rose and Leslie Banks were instrumental in supporting the city's amateur theater groups, including the Richmond Drama Guild, the Children's Theater and the Richmond Theater Guild. Leslie Banks' role was usually backstage, designing sets and lighting and working as stage manager. His firm, the Richmond Scenic and Lighting Company, handled a large percentage of local productions. The Richmond Theater Guild, directed by Bertram Yarborough from 1935 to 1940, mounted some memorable productions at the Lyric Theater, including 1937's *Berkeley Square*, which introduced Mallory Freeman to the local stage. Freeman, nephew of newspaperman and historian Douglas Southall Freeman, worked as an executive at the A. H. Robins Company, but he was smitten with the theater bug, too. He would be Richmond's most prominent community theater actor, with a career lasting more than 50 years in plays performed everywhere from school auditoriums to TheaterVirginia and the Barksdale. Recalling the scrapes that drama groups got into during those early years, Freeman especially remembered a Theater Guild production of a comedy set in the Colonial era, *The Pursuit of Happiness*, which contained a bit of stage business about young men and women indulging in the courtship practice of "bundling." (Courting couples of the 18th century could spend the night snuggled up together in a bed, so long as they remained fully clothed with blankets between them. It was community-approved romantic fun, but many marriages and babies resulted from it.) This bit of mildly risqué behavior on stage outraged a local woman who was president of the Virginia Society for the Prevention of Vice. She vigorously campaigned to have the production closed down. Freeman chuckled to remember all the free newspaper publicity that the protest brought. "Because of her, we packed the house," he said.

BELLWOOD DRIVE IN, *Jeff Davis Highway At Willis Road, 1947. The new drive-in movie theaters offered post-war Richmond dating couples and young families a night of entertainment under the stars without having to leave their automobiles.*

During and after World War II, Rose Banks, Margaret Eddington and their staff at the Department of Recreation and Parks put on War Bond sales rallies, and kept the city humming with a variety of community theater and dance activities. Leslie Banks ran a Civil Defense post in the Mosque's basement. The Shelton-Amos Players performed summer stock at the McVey Hall Theater at St. Catherine's School for several seasons, until gas rationing limited their audiences and the juvenile leads were called into the service. During the war, the Richmond Theater Guild died out, but the Richmond Opera Group gained prominence in the local theatrical community, mounting memorable production of such musicals as *The Vagabond King* and *Of Thee I Sing* at the Lyric. Leslie Banks managed scenery for their productions, working as stage carpenter and stagehand. Michaux Moody brought operatic productions, including performances of the Metropolitan Opera to the Mosque. In 1948, Rose Banks arranged for the city to purchase a huge collection of theatrical costumes from local designer Alma Cannon, who also joined the Department of Recreation and Parks as costume curator, designer and seamstress. The collection, housed in the Mosque's basement, grew to encompass 40,000 pieces, some donated from Richmond family attics and dating back to the 1890s, that created 10,000 complete outfits. It was possibly the largest collection held by any city in the nation. The beautifully detailed costumes added elegance and dashing theatrical spirit to the plays and pageants at schools, churches, Dogwood Dell productions, civic and community theater events for 50 years.[25]

City-sponsored productions overseen by Rose Banks included the annual Tobacco Gala Festivals and Christmas Pageants. The Tobacco Gala Festival, relocated from Bedford to Richmond in 1949 celebrated Virginia's most famous product. The Festival featured a big parade on Broad Street and the Boulevard with grand marshals like Frank Sinatra and Eva Gabor, the Tobacco Bowl football game played by rival Virginia universities, the crowning of a Tobacco Queen, and the performance of an elaborate play at the Mosque called *Tobacco-rama*, which involved seven or eight acts and more a cast of more than 500 people on stage. The annual tradition continued for 35 years.

The Nativity Pageants had begun in 1925 when a group sang Christmas carols at Capitol Square. Every

PLAZA DRIVE IN, *E. Belt Blvd., 1950s and 2001. Another popular suburban drive-in of the 1950s has its valuable land used for new purposes today.*

year the celebration became larger, and players posed on raised platforms placed atop the Capitol Square water fountain, while other performers staged scenes in the windows of office buildings for audiences to view as they walked past. Rose Banks is credited with creating the pageants in 1931 and directing them as they became increasingly elaborate; the city sponsored the programs until 1981, and the Richmond Nativity Advisory Committee has overseen it since 1985. In 1946, the festivities were relocated from Capitol Square to the Carillon in Byrd Park. Whole families participated each year, filling the 250 to 400 roles, and handing down the family line the costumes and roles of cherubs, townspeople, soldiers, travelers, and the 100-person-strong choir as part of the annual tradition. Because of the cold weather usually encountered on Christmas Eve, the costumes were made roomy enough that actors could wear warm clothes and overcoats underneath. Often as many as 10,000 people from several states journeyed to Richmond to enjoy the free pageant and carols performed on the Carillon's bells. The Freeman family has narrated the 30-40 minute pageant for its entire existence, with Douglas Southall Freeman doing the honors for about 15 years, Mallory Freeman for 30 years, and his son Allen for nearly 20 years more. A number of tiny performers who once played "Baby Jesus" have grown up to be chosen to play the Mary or Joseph roles in later years. Bob Burchette portrayed a Shepherd Boy for several years in the early 1950s. He remembers how proud he felt when he passed down Broad Street one year and noticed that Thalhimer's had decorated its store windows with large photographs of the Nativity Pageant players, including himself, pointing upward to the Star of Bethlehem.[26]

Community theater groups active in Richmond in the 1940s and 1950s included the Shakespeare Players, Living Room Players, the Catholic Theater Guild, and John Rolfe Players. In the 1940s, the Lyric Theater was home to the Richmond Opera Group, the Richmond Little Theater under the direction of Bertram Yarborough, the first iteration of the Richmond Ballet, the Richmond Musical Theater, and the Children's Theater.[27] An offshoot of the Drama Guild, the Children's Theater had been founded in 1927 by a coalition of parent-teacher associations and the Junior League of Richmond. For 59 years, it performed productions of young people's fairy tale favorites for hundreds of thousands of children in schools, community centers and at the Lyric Theater. The Aladdin Players, co-sponsored by the City Department of Recreation and Parks and the Richmond Junior League, and directed by Elizabeth Appley, had a reputation as one of the finest children's theater groups in the nation. The group's plays (three productions per year) were also performed at the Lyric Theater.

The Julia Mildred Harper and Eleanor Frye schools of dance held their annual student recitals at the Mosque each spring. From 1933 until the late 1970s, Julia Mildred Harper Marston put on her student productions, which were called *The Talk of the Town*, with 300 students displaying their modern dance, tap and ballet skills to delighted parents and squirming siblings. Marston, who had been teaching dance since she was 12 years old, operated her school in a studio building behind her home at 3511 Chamberlayne Avenue. "Dancing fundamentals are important, of course," she noted in 1952, "But even more so are certain social graces and good manners, which a

WILLOW LAWN THE-ATER, *Willow Lawn Dr., 1956. The first Richmond theater built in a shopping mall, the Willow Lawn's big screen played the blockbuster films of the 1950s and 1960s.*

dancing teacher can put across as nobody else can." The Frye school's annual programs were called *The Frylics*. Many Richmonders today can remember participating in those dance lessons and recitals, including Shirley MacLaine and Warren Beatty, who were young students at the Harper school in the 1940s. These organizations all gave talented young people exposure to the theater, dance and music, and nurtured a love of the arts among generations of the city's children.

In the 1950s and early 1960s, the Mosque again became a regular stop for touring musical road show companies, and Richmonders saw Broadway hits such as *Oklahoma, Annie Get Your Gun, "Carousel", The Music Man, My Fair Lady,* and *Hello Dolly.* The Mosque sponsored musical concert performances by internationally known orchestras, including Eugene Ormandy and the Philadelphia Orchestra, Leonard Bernstein, Leopold Stowkowski, George Szell and Andre Previn. Octogenarian Arturo Toscanini appeared at the Mosque in 1950, and nearly 5,000 people crowded the big auditorium to hear the maestro conduct the NBC Orchestra.[28] The Richmond Symphony was founded in 1956 and debuted before an audience 4,000 at the Mosque in October 28, 1957 (30 years to the day after the theater opened). Edgar Schenkman was the symphony's first conductor. Popular music also was well represented in Mosque concerts

over the years. Performers from big band crooners to jazz artists such as Louis Armstrong, Lionel Hampton, and Duke Ellington, to legends of rock and roll including Elvis Presley (who played the Mosque on July 2, 1956), Aretha Franklin and Jimi Hendrix have performed there.[29]

The Richmond Summer Theater, a signpost pointing toward the professional theater that would develop out of Richmond's community dramatic groups, began in 1945 as a joint project of Bertram Yarborough and a partner who provided the initial funding. Rose and Leslie Banks signed on as theater managers. Unfortunately, the organization was sputtering after only a season. Rose and Leslie Banks decided to take it over in 1947 and they ran this "straw hat" summer stock theater in the McVey Hall Theater at St. Catherine's School. With Leslie as stage manager and Rose doing the publicity, the Richmond Summer Theater mounted six productions each season. The group staged a new play every two weeks, starting three or four productions in rehearsal while performing another on stage. They put on five performances a week, Tuesdays through Fridays, before weekends and the River lured everyone out of town. The Summer Theater was quite successful; McVey Hall, whose seats were sold on a subscription basis, was filled every season. People from all the local theater groups pitched in for this summer

REGAL WILLOW LAWN CINEMAS 4, *Willow Lawn Dr., 2001. Remodeled into a modern four-screen multiplex, the Willow Lawn remains a popular moviegoing destination nearly 50 years later.*

effort. "We painted until 2:00 a.m.," Leslie Banks recalled. The scene designers and back stage crew were paid wages, but the actors worked for free. *Times Dispatch* theater critic Edith Lindeman also was a steadfast supporter of local theater all through the lean years. She attended the opening of every community production and critiqued them generously in her reviews. Lindeman always provided positive encouragement to the actors and crew in person and in the newspaper. Her whole family supported the local drama scene, as her daughter and husband often performed in local productions. Her husband Woolner Calisch was cast so often as a congressman or judge that he picked up the nickname "The Senator."

The support of community theater in the struggling years by dedicated individuals and the city bore fruit – it brought several new theatrical groups to Richmond in the 1950s to try their luck in attracting audiences to more elaborate productions. A group of six entrepreneurial young actors who had attended Wayne State University in Detroit chose the Richmond area because one member's mother lived here. In 1953 they pooled their money to purchase a dilapidated old country inn, fixed it up and put on a year-round series of plays. The Barksdale Theater's name honored a young woman they had known in college – Barbara Barksdale, who had been ill and wheelchair-bound, but whose deep love of the

theater, and her spirit and enthusiasm, inspired everyone she met. The innovative combination of plays and refreshments served in the Hanover Tavern fifteen miles north of Richmond gave the Barksdale the distinction of being the nation's first regional dinner theater. It was Edith Lindeman who suggested the idea of serving dinner to the patrons. Original group members David and Nancy Kilgore and Muriel McAuley would be with the Barksdale for 35 years.

The Virginia Museum Theater was organized in 1955 as the first performing arts group in the nation to be housed in an art museum. Leslie Cheek was its highly respected chief executive. Former director Bob Telford recalled that it was a heady time in which local theater tried not only to amuse, but to affect the local culture. "Everything we did at the Museum Theater was innovative," Telford remembered. "We broke the color barrier, for instance. It was state law that blacks and whites not appear together on stage. In Virginia, the message was 'Don't rock the boat.' There was 'massive resistance.' .... We did it in *You Can't Take it With You*, casting both the maid and her boyfriend with black actors. When they took their curtain calls, the applause was deafening."

In 1965, Richmond Professional Institute graduates and high school drama teachers Warner J. "Buddy" Callahan and his wife Betty Callahan took the advice of

RETAIL STORE BUILDING, *2820 W. Cary St, 2001. The old Carillon Theater gained a new lease on life by being renovated into shops.*

NEW CANAAN CHURCH, *4712 W. Forest Hills Ave., 2001. The former Westover Theater still serves the community as the home of a church congregation.*

ASHLAND THEATER, *209 England St., Ashland, 2001. The Art Deco Ashland is also finding new life, as it is being renovated into a community center.*

RPI professor Ray Hodges, who said "Don't rush to New York, go home to your hometown and start your own theater." The Callahans and Louis Rubin (a theater-loving optometrist) started the Swift Creek Mill Playhouse near Colonial Heights, in one of the oldest mill buildings in the nation (it dates from 1663). They drew on a pool of perhaps 100 local actors coming out of the University of Richmond and Virginia Commonwealth University (formerly RPI), as well as enthusiastic amateurs in the community. "We paid the actors $3 a night; dinner and theater cost $5," Buddy Callahan recalls.

In 1962, professionally organized, permanent theater companies were beginning to thrive in Richmond, so Rose and Leslie Banks decided it was time to close the Richmond Summer Theater. "When we started, there was very little theater here," Banks recalled. "Thirteen years later, the dearth of theater had ended. I'm proud of what we accomplished."[30]

The End of an Era, and the Beginning of Another

The 1960s would be the most difficult decade that film exhibitors ever faced. Population shifts, the flowering of alternative youth cultures and the generation gap fractured the great American film audience into many smaller interest groups. The television revolution and changing leisure habits took daily entertainment out of the theaters and into the home. The film production and movie theater industries went through a painful period of restructuring. In Richmond, as across the nation, most movie theaters were 30 to 40 years old and showing their age. A great many of the old theaters closed during the decade. By the late 1960s, some critics predicted the end of films and movie theaters as we knew them. But the 1970s and early 1980s would see tremendous change and growth in the movie business. New film genres, new theaters and new patterns of movie-going,

FRANK SINATRA, *1949. The popular singer and actor caused as commotion when he arrived in Richmond to serve as Grand Marshal of the first annual Tobacco Bowl Festival. He crowned Miss Dorothy Kirsten the Festival Queen.*

along with renewed interest in our theater legacy and the dedication of preservationists, breathed new life into Richmond's film theaters and entertainment scene.

In June 1961, Loew's Theater manager George Peters estimated that 29,296,000 tickets had been sold to movie shows at the Loew's since its opening 32 years before. Its projectionists had played an average of 453,600 feet of film, or 86 miles, each week. The venerable old theater was looking frayed around the edges, but it still had magical charms. Newspaper columnist Guy Friddell noted in the early 1960s that the special projected decorations were gone from the Loew's "sky" ceiling. One night at the theater, he asked George Peters, "where are the moon, clouds and stars?"

What happened, [Peters] said, is the moon wore out from all its revolutions across the sky, not to mention the clouds. The clouds and moon were painted on a silk screen mounted on two giant wooden wheels, three feet across, and hidden up front. One turning wheel would project the moon and her escorts half way across the ceiling, and then, as it let go, the other wheel would pick it up and carry them gently the rest of the journey. Through the years the paintings faded under the constant light of the projector. George was never able to find replacements. The stars are still there, though, on nights the balcony opens

.

Peters also shared the secret of the ceiling's stars. "They are lights encased in beer can-sized tubes poking through the ceiling, some 500 of them, and as you walk under them, passing out of the view of some and into the range of others, they just seem to twinkle."[31] A Richmond city ordinance in the late 1960s forbade movie theater marquees that extended out over the sidewalks, so the broad, curving Loew's theater marquee with the stained glass Leo, that had sheltered so many patrons from the rain while they waited to buy a ticket, was taken down May 5, 1969. The old theater received a "modernizing" face-lift in 1971, getting new seats and carpeting. Corporate headquarters deemed it too expensive and time-consuming, however, to renew and restore the decorative painting on the walls, so the entire interior was painted white, and the blue-sky ceiling was repainted red.

NTI purchased the 45-year-old Colonial and National Theaters from the Fabian chain in 1965 and 1966, giving them nearly complete control of Richmond's movie market. The two Theater Row stalwarts were redecorated; the National was "modernized" with a new steel marquee and a new name, "The Towne," the result of an area-wide contest. Its murals and plasterwork were painted over, as too expensive to restore. The Towne would be the last open movie theater downtown, operating until September 1983.[32]

Mirroring national trends, many of Richmond's older movie theaters closed in the early 1960s. Casualties here included the Brookland, Carillon, Venus, East End, Patrick Henry, Park and Grand. As Sam Bendheim noted at the Grand's closing in 1963, "Nobody wants to go to the action house anymore." They had westerns and serials enough to watch on TV at home. The Lee Theater on Grace Street closed in 1962; it had long ago moved from family movies to art films. Unfortunately, that audience was not large enough to keep a regular theater going. The Lee spent the next fifteen years as an X-rated movie theater. The Bellevue Theater in the Ginter Park neighborhood closed in 1963, but it subsequently found a new community role. The Samis Grotto Shrine purchased the building in February 1966 and made it their headquarters. The Shriners removed the seats from the auditorium, and 35 years later, they still hold dinners, dances and meetings in front of the stage that once framed the screen. Large palm trees are propped in the room corners for tropical-themed parties, and when not needed, the cardboard trees are pitched up into the balcony.

Across the South, the Civil Rights movement had been working since the mid-1950s to end segregation for African-Americans and achieve equality of opportunity for all, but change seemed to come at glacier pace. Film historian Douglas Gomery notes that " while Washington, D.C. theaters had integrated in 1954, and Maryland theaters followed in 1960, in Virginia things moved more slowly." In the spring of 1960, groups of college students re-energized the Civil Rights movement by bringing "sit in" protests to lunch counters and restaurants across the South. Virginia Union University undergradu-

"IT'S A TALULULU!"
—Walter Winchell

JOHN C. WILSON
presents
TALLULAH
BANKHEAD
in
NOEL COWARD'S BEST COMEDY
PRIVATE LIVES
with
DONALD COOK
BARBARA BAXLEY · WILLIAM LANGFORD

Staged by
MARTIN MANULIS

Settings by
CHARLES ELSON

WRVA THEATRE RICHMOND, VA.
4 Perfs. Only! — 3 Eves. and a Bargain Mat. on Wed.
MON., TUES., WED., NOVEMBER 28, 29 and 30

PLAYBILL, *1949. Theatrical and movie stars such as Tallulah Bankhead appeared in Richmond at the Lyric/ WRVA and Mosque theaters in the late 1940s, 1950s and 1960s in traveling company productions of their Broadway successes.*

ates, faculty and other activists held "sit-ins" at the lunch counters at Thalhimer's and Woolworth's downtown on Broad Street; their yearlong effort convinced storeowners to change their policies. Richmond's movie theaters, some of which had been segregated with "Jim Crow" balconies, but most of which had been restricted to white-only or black-only seating, were a more difficult challenge for Civil Rights protesters. "About a dozen Negroes tried unsuccessfully last night to attend a movie at Loew's, Richmond's largest theater," read a *Times Dispatch* news report in September 1961. "All ticket sales were stopped until the Negroes left."[33]

It took two more years to bring about changes in Richmond's movie theaters. Virginia Union University students conducted a month-long campaign in May 1963,

RICHMOND OPERA GROUP PRODUCTIONS, *1940s and 1956. Signaling a renaissance of local theater, Richmond performers appeared in productions of such musicals as* **The Vagabond King** *and* **Of Thee I Sing** *at the Lyric/WRVA Theater.*

LESLIE BANKS AND ROSE KAUFMAN BANKS, *1950s. This hardworking, dedicated couple did much to keep the spirit of local theater alive in Richmond throughout the 1930s, 1940s, and 1950s.*

during which 50 students peacefully picketed Richmond's four major downtown theaters every night. Joseph Dancy, Jr., student president of the VUU chapter of the NAACP, led the protests. He explained to reporters, "This deplorable situation has existed in Richmond for too long a time. It is obviously morally wrong. It is morally wrong from a practical point of view because it limits, to a degree, the intellectual and social growth of our youth, and deprives them of a safe, relatively inexpensive source of recreation. We are interested in doing something about this segregation."

"Our intention with the picketing," Dancy continued, "is not to cause trouble; merely to express our freedom of speech in a peaceful and orderly manner – which we have done. Our aim is to voice our protest to the status quo. And to call the attention to arouse the interest of the total community to the legal injustice being perpetuated here." The student leader expressed his delight

to reporters "at the large turn-out of participating students and appreciation to friends who lent their cars for transportation." He also thanked Major Frank S. Dulin and the Richmond Police Bureau for their cooperation in maintaining law and order during the group's picketing. "No agitators have been permitted to cause any disturbances as the pickets march peaceably and quietly carrying their placards of human dignity appeal," the *Richmond Afro-American* reported, noting that one counter-agitator had been arrested, but otherwise the events had gone quietly. The protest had wide support across the community, for as the reporter took in the scene, "Several passers-by spoke words of encouragement to the protestants and several white students refused to cross the picket lines."[34]

The students' picketing ceased by mutual agreement on May 28th, and student representatives, members of the NAACP, Richmond Citizens Advisory Committee,

RICHMOND SYMPHONY ONSTAGE AT THE MOSQUE, *1950s. Edgar Schenkman was the first conductor of the symphony, which was founded in 1956.*

and Virginia Council on Human Relations began to hold negotiations with theater executives. On June 11, 1963, Richmond's theater doors were finally open to all. The legal ending of theater segregation across the state came soon afterwards; the Federal District Court in Alexandria ruled on July 1, 1963 that Virginia's theater segregation law was unconstitutional.[35] Edith Lindeman noted at the time that "Once decided upon, the process was carried through quietly without incident. Movie managers report no falling off in their overall attendance, and no unpleasantness of note."[36]

The Hippodrome, Globe, Lincoln, Robinson, Walker, and Booker T. theaters, like other legendary restaurants, shops, banks and hotels in Jackson Ward, had served a generation of African-Americans before the Civil Rights movement brought desegregation to the city. Similar to what Richmond's other small, older theaters experienced, the Hippodrome's attendance declined swiftly after 1963, and it closed in 1967. The Booker T. and Maggie Walker theaters closed in 1969 (The Robinson had been remodeled into a pool hall in the mid-1950s). Urban road construction and suburbanization contributed to the decline of Jackson Ward's vitality as a retail center. But its heritage and promise remain alive. The

Robinson and Hippodrome theaters have been used for local performances and reopened for shows during the Second Street festivals, and the Hippodrome has also been used as a church. Hopefully, it can be restored to its former glory one day.[37]

While drive-in theaters still did good business in the first years of the decade, by the late 1960s, they too were in trouble, as drive-in exhibitors struggled to find enough family-friendly feature films to show among the shrinking number of productions released each year. Film producer and distributors favored the larger indoor theaters over drive-ins. Independent drive-ins theaters (those not part of large chains, which brought some protection) were hardest hit. Many drive-ins closed, for the land they sat on was now much more valuable for potential suburban development than when the drive-ins had been built "way out in the countryside" in the late 1940s and 1950s. The Bellwood Drive-In south of Richmond at Willis Road and Interstate 95 became the site of an open-air weekend flea market that draws bargain hunters from across the region. Other drive-ins sought alternatives so that they could remain open. The Rosebowl Drive-In was failing in July 1970 when it turned to X-rated films. *I am Curious Yellow* sold out two shows a night for 15 weeks; it was

MARK RUSSELL SMITH, *2001. Smith is currently conductor of the Richmond Symphony.*

the only theater in the area that would play this infamous film that so many people were curious to view. "It was a madhouse," recalled the manager. "On weekends, traffic was backed up for miles."[38]

In 1971, Robert Coulter, manager of the Byrd Theater since its opening 43 years before, retired. He nevertheless returned to work at the theater every day. The Byrd's second manager, George Stitzer, who had been an 18-year-old doorman at the theater's opening in 1928, said, "Mr. Coulter is the only man in town who knows how to operate every piece of equipment in this theater. He's even patched the big Wurlitzer organ but admits to not being an expert on organs." Coulter had trusted no one but himself to clean the chandelier, but the NTI executives would not let him climb the tall ladders and scaffolding any longer. He remained "resident engineer" for the aging heating, cooling and projection equipment.[39] A devoted core of Byrd Theater supporters and other preservationists successfully campaigned for the Byrd Theater to be declared a Virginia Historic Landmark in

1977, and the theater entered the National Register of Historic Places in 1979.

One of the last functioning downtown movie palaces in the entire United States in the 1970s, Loew's Theater celebrated its 50th anniversary quietly in 1978. Armand Doyle, who had purchased the theater's first ticket in 1928, returned to Richmond from his home in Chicago to be a part of the bittersweet celebration. *Times Dispatch* film critic Carole Kass spoke for many when she wrote, "From one fan, happy birthday, Loew's Richmond. Long may you stand. And may your spirit be eternal."[40] Lack of customers and changes in downtown finally took its toll, however, and the Loew's Theater closed in May 1979.[41]

By the 1970s, Richmond's old downtown theaters and retail stores had been totally eclipsed by the suburbs (a trend which overtook every American city), and familiar landmarks closed, one by one. But new ideas, new theaters and a renaissance in movie going and the theater lay ahead.

CHILDREN ON STAGE AT THE MOSQUE, *1940s. Richmond public schools, universities, dance classes, operatic and theatrical groups, and community organizations have put on productions at the Mosque/Landmark Theater for over seven decades.*

SWIFT CREEK MILL THEATER, *Jeff Davis Highway, Colonial Heights, 2001. This dinner theater company, performing in the nation's oldest standing mill building, has been in operation for more than 35 years.*

THEATRE VCU PERFORMING ARTS CENTER,
Virginia Commonwealth University, 922 Park Ave., 2001.
Strong theater programs at VCU, University of Richmond
other area schools add diversity to the local theatrical scene
and produce many of its talented actors.

RICHMOND SKYLINE, *2001.*

CHAPTER 5

A Renaissance — Richmond Theater
1970s to the present

Richmond's favorite entertainments have continually shifted over the past 200 years, from the vogue for Shakespearean tragedies at the Marshall Theater, melodramas and theatrical stars at the Richmond and Academy, stock companies at the Empire and Bijou, vaudeville at the National and Lyric, nickelodeon shows at the Lubin, picture palace splendor at Loew's, the Mickey Mouse Club at the Byrd, Saturday morning cowboy movies at the Venus and Hippodrome, *The Old Dominion Barn Dance* at the WRVA Theater, Cinemascope musicals at the Willow Lawn, opera and Broadway shows at the Mosque, to summer blockbuster films at the Virginia Commons 20 multiplex cinema.

While fashions in the theater, cinema and concert hall may come and go, our delight in the performing arts has endured. Young people of each generation have been entranced with the excitement of a show — from *Peter Pan*, action melodramas and handsome leading men on stage at the Academy, Bijou and Empire; Charlie Chaplin, Hopalong Cassidy and Judy Garland at the movie houses on Theater Row; Lena Horne on film and live acts on stage at the Booker T.; Frankenstein and Frankie Avalon at the Bellwood drive-in; and *Star Wars* and *E.T.* at the mall movie theaters; to *Peter Pan* at Theater IV, *The Nutcracker* ballet at the Landmark and *Annie* at the Carpenter Center.

The past 30 years has witnessed still another revolution in Richmond's entertainment scene. Cable and satellite television, videos and DVDs, computer games and the Internet have expanded our leisure options, bringing movies, theater and the arts into our homes and making them available all day and night. Richmond's geography has also changed greatly; the area in which we live, work, shop and play has grown to over 1,200 square miles spread out over the city and five surrounding counties, and a metropolitan population of nearly 800,000. Movie theaters are no longer clustered downtown, but have spread everywhere – today we have more than 120 screens in 15 theater complexes across the area. There has also been a theatrical renaissance in the city. The rise of local amateur theater in 1940s and 1950s spurred development of local professional theater in 1960s and 1970s. Today Richmond's thriving theatrical scene includes the Theatre IV, TheaterVirginia, Barksdale, Swift Creek Mill Playhouse and Firehouse Theater groups, plus community, school and university dramatic programs, and touring company productions.

The cultural core of the Richmond area, which connects the growing population, expanding communities and increasing number of entertainment choices in Central Virginia, is the wealth of performing arts facilities in the city of Richmond. Downtown's theaters, old movie houses and various performance spaces offer the legacy of 200 years of the history of the city and its people. Ambitious plans for a new Performing Arts Complex celebrate that continuity and promise to strengthen the core of our community. Rediscovering the beauty of our historic theaters, adding state-of-the-art modern entertainment facilities for the performing arts, and drawing more people in to a revitalized downtown will knit our diverse communities together even more, and will help make the performing arts even more popular in a city that has always loved them.

RIDGE CINEMAS I AND II, *1510 E. Ridge Rd., 1970s. This new style of dual-screen theater, opened in 1970, offered patrons an art gallery and large screens in a sleek modern setting.*

Changes in Moviegoing: Shopping Mall Theaters and Megaplex Cinemas

The majority of old movie theaters across the nation in 1970 were aging, worn, and hard hit by changing downtowns and the expansion of the far-away suburbs, and most of them closed. At the same time, however, a new generation of theaters was being built. Theater developers chose sites near the new shopping centers that were rising at the juncture of city limits and suburban development, a move that reunited entertainment with shopping, the way they had been connected when, for example, the Theater Row movie houses had been surrounded by the department stores, shops and restaurants of Broad Street's downtown retail corridor. The new theaters brought the latest technology to the moviegoing experience, such as wide screens, 70-mm film, improved sound and multiple speakers, but the builders focused much less than before on the theater building itself. There were economic reasons for the building of plain theaters of the 1970s; it was move to stem the ever-rising costs of theater construction. There were aesthetic reasons, too, for it was an era of simple, stark architectural forms. Movie going practices had also changed. Americans no longer attended the movies two to three times a week. Now they watched television and went to the movies only several times a year.

Neighborhood Theaters, Inc. opened the Ridge Cinemas I and II in November 1970 near the Regency Square Mall on Parham Road. Touted as the first new "hard top" movie theater to open in Richmond in 14 years, the simple but elegant theater complex contained an art gallery, coffee bar, automated projection equipment, two theaters with wide screens and 8-track stereo sound.

When the Ridge Cinemas expanded from two to four screens in 1975, it became the first "four-plex" in the state. It further expanded to seven screens in 1983. The Ridge quickly became Richmond's most prestigious cinema, where important films debuted. Other new theaters, such as the Cloverleaf Mall Cinemas 1 and 2, which opened in August 1972, were incorporated directly into shopping malls.

New movie theaters that opened during the 1970s had a spareness of design and size that harkened back to the earliest movie houses. Bill McCathern, architect of the Broad Street I and II twin theaters, which opened at 5314 W. Broad Street in May 1970, noted at their opening that, "The theaters' interior will be modern and simplistic in design. The gilded age is gone. The entire side walls will be draped for decorating and acoustics."[1] "Modern" movie theaters would have no more plaster nymphs, painted murals, stuffed parrots, or stars and moon on the ceiling. The new movie theaters were also "fully automated" – the projectors and lights were all run by computers and they required fewer projectionists to show the films on an increasing number of screens. The Litchfield Company opened cinemas in suburban locations like Chester and Midlothian; each of their six auditoriums under one roof seated only 100-204 people. The utilitarian interiors and small size made shopping mall movie theaters resemble nickelodeon theaters of 1907 like Amanda Thorpe's Dixie Theater. Six separate screens, however, offered exhibitors far more flexibility in scheduling movies than did just one larger auditorium. Theater managers still had to order their films far in advance, and now, depending on how a film drew with their local audiences, they could play a film in a larger

RIDGE CINEMAS 7, *2001.* *Today the Ridge multiplex has grown to seven screens.*

or smaller auditorium.

The 540-seat Biograph Theater opened on W. Grace Street near the VCU campus in January 1972, as the only theater in Richmond showing old Hollywood films, along with recent foreign films and art cinema. The Biograph's midnight showings of *Rocky Horror Picture Show* were a Richmond institution for young people from 1978 until 1982. The cult movie hit sold out Friday and Saturday night shows at least 190 weekends in a row. Many attendees interacted with the movie, dressing up as the film characters, and bringing with them props such as toast, squirt bottles of water and rice to throw at the screen during the wedding scene. The incursions of cable television and VCRs into homes in the 1980s, however, greatly changed the market for older films. When film lovers could watch classic films, foreign releases and even X-rated movies at home, movie houses like the Biograph and the Lee faded from the scene. The Biograph closed in 1987.[2]

A new phenomenon was born in the 1970s – the summer blockbuster. The movie *Jaws* played for three sold-out months at the Westhampton in 1975, and similar excitement occurred in subsequent years over *Star Wars, E.T.* and *Raiders of the Lost Ark.* The most anticipated and popular films of the year were now being released in summer, a time when theaters (like network television) used to show only minor films and re-runs. Teenaged fans and other viewers saw their favorite films again and again; its not unusual to find people who saw *Star Wars* 10 times when it was released in 1977. Children and their parents bought toys, books and clothing connected with the summer blockbusters, creating a marketing goldmine for studios, retailers and manufacturers. Fast food restaurants chimed in with children's meals

"tied-up" with summer hit films, even more so now that the children's film market has grown larger in the 1990s. Summer blockbusters are now responsible for a majority of a theater's ticket sales, while selling popcorn, sodas, candy and treats brings the bulk of movie theaters' profits, for most ticket sales proceeds go to the film's distributors.

Young people still gravitate to the movies similar to the way that children and teens of other decades flocked to action melodramas, cowboy films and musicals. Scott Terbush grew up as one such movie fan in the 1980s and 1990s. His neighborhood movie theater was the Chesterfield Town Center complex, which he reached by riding three miles on his bicycle. He performed chores around the house and saved his allowance to see matinee shows twice a month, more often in the summer. By his count, he has seen more than 1,000 films in theaters. Action, science fiction and fantasy films were the favored film genres for Terbush and his friends, boys' tastes not having changed much in a century of play- and moviegoing. Terbush, however, came of age in the era of the summer blockbuster, when fans latched on to one film to view repeatedly. With the help of merchandisers, young people created an entire fantasy world from the film story, reproducing favorite scenes and carrying on with the further adventures of their heroes in their creative play. Terbush estimates that when he was nine, he saw *Return of the Jedi* 15-20 times. As he grew older, joined the work force and married, Scott Terbush found, as did the cowboy fans of old, that his film-viewing situation changed. Asked how he thinks the movies have shaped his life, Terbush answers that they have expanded his imagination — "Movies gave me the answer to questions I didn't know I had. Movies show you worlds you didn't

FORMER BIOGRAPH AND GRACE STREET CINEMAS, *814 W. Grace St., 2001. Old theater buildings continue to see new adaptations, as the former Biograph/Grace Street Theater is undergoing renovation to become a coffeehouse to serve the growing VCU student community.*

know existed."[3]

Movie theaters have also continued to evolve since the 1970s. In the 1980s, a wave of mergers swept through the movie theater business. It became increasingly difficult to survive as a small chain of theaters when rivals were growing large so quickly. Richmond's hometown exhibitors, Neighborhood Theaters, Inc., merged with Cineplex Odeon. When that ambitious conglomerate fell apart, the executives of NTI bought the Richmond theaters back again; they merged with the Regal Cinemas chain in 1994.

The movie theater trend of the 1990s was a movement to build theater complexes that would recapture some of the elegance and fantasy of the old picture palaces, in new high-tech theaters that featured higher levels of patron comfort and convenience. Most striking is the massive size of the new complexes, which have ten, 15 and as many as 20 screens; the new theaters are called "megaplexes." The megaplex is a vaudeville-like experience, for there is "something for everyone" under one roof. Families and groups of friends can split up to see different films, then rendezvous in the lobby. The megaplex's many auditoriums, small and large, often have tiered "stadium" seating so that the latecomers who sit ahead of them never obscure patrons' view of the screen. Seats are large and comfortable, with built-in cupholders

for room for drinks and snacks. The latest advances in projection and sound technology bring viewers the ultimate viewing experience. The lobbies are dramatic and expansive, filled with neon, marble and brass. The concession stands serve a wide variety of food, from traditional buckets of popcorn and soda to nachos, sandwiches, and espresso. Café spaces and game rooms off the lobbies encourage families to linger at the theater. Ample parking lots and strategic locations near large shopping malls put the megaplexes at a central destination. In Richmond, the recent openings of the Virginia Center Commons 20, Commonwealth 20, United Artists 12, Carmike 10 and Regal Short Pump 14-screen megaplexes bring the return of opulence to Richmond's movie theater scene.

Richmond has been much more fortunate than other cities which have lost all of their old historic theaters to the wrecking ball. The Byrd, Westhampton, Empire, and the former Mosque, and Loew's, ranging from 65 to 90 years old, are still in use as theaters today. They have been well cared for architectural landmarks in a city that appreciates history. Several of the smaller neighborhood theaters have been adapted to new uses for their communities, such as the former Bellevue, Westover, Hippodrome, Lee and Carillon theaters. Some are being renovated into community centers, while a few others, like

AUDIENCE AT FLICKER SCREENING, 2001. *Viewers gather to watch short films and videos shot by Richmond-area independent filmmakers at programs sponsored by the Richmond Moving Image Co-op.*

the Brookland, Venus, Robinson and East End, are still standing, and ripe for redevelopment.

Times Dispatch film critic Carole Kass once noted that each theater in Richmond seemed to have its own personality. That is evident in the diversity of moviegoing experiences available today. The new megaplexes take on the feel of Disney World when crowds of children and their parents wait in line to purchase tickets to the newest animated film release. The Westhampton is like

an art gallery and still retains its Williamsburg ambiance for the patrons who view art films and foreign cinema there. It's like a huge high school party when the shopping center theater complexes like the Southgate and Chesterfield Town Center team with teenage viewers who include seeing the newest films into their pilgrimages to the mall. The unique experience of the giant, wraparound screen at the IMAX Theater at the Science Museum of Virginia makes groups of school children gape

Commonwealth 20 Theaters

Regal Short Pump 14 Theaters

Carmike 10 Theaters

PICTURE PALACES OF TODAY

Virginia Center Commons 20 Theaters

United Artists West Tower Theaters

PICTURE PALACES OF TODAY

CAFÉ TABLE IN THE LOBBY AND GAME ROOM, COMMON-WEALTH 20 THEATERS, *2001. Today's picture palaces offer gracious lobbies in which to enjoy snacks before the show, and video games for afterwards.*

at the wonders they view, and on weekend evenings, the concert films make adults and young people feel like they are in the midst of a huge rock and roll performance. A Flicker gathering has all the audience activity and delight in viewing and critiquing the locally-produced new films that nickelodeon audiences must have experienced nearly 100 years ago.[4]

The Byrd Theater has perhaps the most personality of all – it combines its picture palace past with the hip young character of the Carytown shops that surround it. The Byrd had closed in 1983 after George Stitzer's death, but a group led by Dr. Jearald Cable, who had renovated the Jefferson Hotel, restored it. Duane Nelson supervised the project as gold leaf was reapplied to the ceiling, varnish was stripped, marble and brass were polished, and floors were recarpeted. The Byrd reopened in April 1984 with the classic musical *Singin' in the Rain*. It now seats 914 on the main floor; its balcony seats 480 on weekend

nights. On Saturday evenings, crowds of dating couples, young adults and fans of the Byrd congregate to see second-run Hollywood releases at bargain prices, soak up the Cary Street atmosphere and listen to Bob Gulledge, (a former student of Eddie Weaver) play the famous Wurlitzer organ. A group of employees and friends lovingly care for the old theater, locating replacement vintage light bulbs, dusting the chandelier, maintaining the organ works, and patching the original wall decorations. The ghost of Robert Coulter, who is apparently still overseeing the building's care, assists them in their work. On several occasions, concession stand workers have reported seeing a tall gentleman in a suit sitting in the balcony section when it is closed. He has also been spotted at the theater's back doors, making sure they are locked after the last evening performance. If you ever encounter Mr. Coulter while at the Byrd, don't be alarmed; you will keep him happy if you follow the Byrd's

BOX OFFICE, REGAL SHORT PUMP 14 THEATERS, *2001. The neon lights and impressive size of today's box offices are reminiscent of the excitement and glamour of the old theaters.*

famous filmed reminder to pick up your litter: "This trash should not be in movie theaters — or anywhere else!"

Historic Theaters Are Renovated

The Richmond Symphony purchased the closed Loew's Theater in 1979 to renovate as their new home. The symphony rehearsed there all during the three-year restoration process, but not without a few mishaps. One account relates that: "During one rehearsal [in 1981], the conductor stopped proceedings to admonish the percussion section for not providing the proper beat. As the conductor explained his requirements, the orchestra members went from stifled grins to loud laughter. The banging of belabored steam pipes was the real culprit of the offbeat." Another rehearsal was washed out when open windows in the cupola above the stage let in a heavy wind that blew rain on the stage. The former Loew's had a gala reopening as the Virginia Center for

the Performing Arts on May 5, 1983. Opera diva Leontyne Price performed with the Richmond Symphony for three nights. It was renamed the Carpenter Center for the Performing Arts in 1985.[5]

The original Wurlitzer organ at Loew's had been donated to the Kennedy Center in Washington D.C. for "safekeeping" when the theater closed, but through a series of misfortunes, it was disassembled, sold, and left in a warehouse to gather dust. Cost estimates to repurchase and refurbish it ran as high as $125,000. Luckily, a more easily repairable replacement organ (which originally had been used at the RKO-Keith Theater in New York City) was donated to the Carpenter Center in October 1981. It is a 24-rank organ, nearly twice as large as the original 13-rank instrument. Restoration of the replacement organ still took 25,000 hours of work, all done by volunteers. Eddie Weaver played the "new" organ when it made its debut at the Carpenter Center in April 1992.

RICHMOND JAZZ SOCIETY PERFORMANCE, *2001. The rich cultural diversity of the city's performing arts groups enables Richmonders to experience a wide variety of entertainment.*

The State and Colonial Theaters along the old Theater Row on Broad Street had both closed in 1981, and they were sold to the city in 1992 and demolished. Pieces of the Colonial, however, continue to live on, in theaters around the city. The Colonial's lovely beige marble façade was preserved as the front of the new office building constructed on the Colonial site, which the city has leased to the state of Virginia. Miles Rudisill rescued the Colonial's stage curtains to replace worn out ones at the Byrd. The Valentine Museum took down a hunk of wall decoration, one of Ferruccio Legnaioli's plaster reliefs of cupids playing with a film reel surrounded by a wreath of leaves, for its collections, along with several seats, railings, stained glass exit signs, art deco-inspired mirrors and a vanity table that once graced the Colonial's ladies room.[6]

The National Theater, on the same block, was saved from the wrecking ball in 1989 by James M. Whiting and the Historic Richmond Foundation. Whiting and fellow volunteers have since invested years of sweat equity and the funds to repair holes in the ceiling and clean, refurbish and repaint the ornate plasterwork designed and sculpted in 1924 by Ferruccio Legnaioli. They have repainted friezes and murals, stripped wallpaper to find lovely artwork in a nursery room, restored lighting fixtures, polished marble walls and staircase and buffed the brass fittings. Original carpet from the Colonial was reinstalled at the National. With the building stabilized (and much refurbishing yet to do), a new life can hopefully be found for this jewel of Theater Row.[7]

In 1995 the aging Mosque, owned by the city of Richmond for 45 years, underwent a much-needed 15 month, $5.4 million dollar renovation, reopening October 28, 1995. It also received a new name; it is now known as Richmond's Landmark Theater. The spacious auditorium, with its seating capacity somewhat reduced to 3,600 seats, was scrubbed, re-gilded to its original faux-Oriental splendor, seats recovered and floors recarpeted. Only the theater portion of the cavernous building was restored, however; huge amounts of office space, meeting

RICHMOND BALLET HEADQUARTERS, *407 E. Canal St., 2001.*

rooms, swimming pool and hotel rooms still await a makeover. With its auditorium and lobbies lovelier than ever, the Landmark Theater has continued to host touring Broadway shows, concerts, lectures, the Richmond Forum, gubernatorial galas and graduations.

Several other recent projects aim to save Art Deco theater gems the Ashland Theater in Ashland, the Henrico in Highland Springs, and the Broadway Theater in Hopewell. Located in the hearts of their communities, these old theaters will hopefully have long new lives as community centers, renovated to draw the towns' people together in entertainment, education and fellowship.

Richmond's Theaters Thrive

Community and professional theater groups in Richmond, which were beginning to take off in the 1960s, have continued to expand. "Homegrown professional theater is the backbone of Richmond theater," *Times Dispatch* theater critic Roy Proctor has commented. "It keeps the city's sizable talent pools of actors, directors and designers intact. It stakes Richmond's credible claim to having more theater of a higher quality than any other American city of its size."[8] That's only half the story, for university and local area drama groups, and the touring companies of Broadway shows, also contribute a great deal to the vitality of the theatrical community in Rich-

mond. Today more than 250,000 people attend performing arts events in Richmond each year.

Theatre IV, founded in 1975 by Bruce Miller and Phil Whiteway, produces plays in the renovated, 90 year old Empire Theater on Broad Street, and in traveling companies that cross the nation. The group operates the country's second-largest children's theater in terms of attendance, serving more than 800,000 students in 37 states each year. It is also Virginia's largest residential theatrical organization, putting on productions ranging from *Peter Pan* to musicals like *Beehive* for both children and adults. In 1986 Theatre IV purchased the Empire/Strand/Booker T./Regency theater building and invested several million dollars in renovating the worn facility, bringing back theatrical productions to that theater after 65 years. The Empire is one of the oldest theaters in the state of Virginia still functioning as a playhouse. Since then, Theatre IV has also incorporated the old Little/Maggie Walker Theater building into the complex as dressing rooms and rehearsal space.[9]

TheatreVirginia, a member of the League of Resident Theatres, became a professional theater associated with Actors' Equity in 1972. For 45 years, the group has put on performances of classic and new plays, like the recent *Fair and Tender Ladies* by Virginia author Lee Smith. Now, after sharing space for its entire existence with the Virginia Museum of Fine Arts (although the

THEATREVIRGINIA, *2800 Grove Ave., 2001. A performance of* **Fair and Tender Ladies**, *a play by Virginia author Lee Smith.*

theater has operated independently of the museum since 1982), TheatreVirginia is poised to grow further (from the 5 or 6 productions per year that they can mount at the Museum theater, and the 10 or 12 they would like to produce each year). To do this, TheatreVirginia intends to build a home of its own, a new state of the art facility at the Virginia Performing Arts Complex downtown on Broad Street in a facility that is connected in part to the Carpenter Center.

The Swift Creek Mill Theater is Richmond's largest commercial playhouse. Now celebrating more than 35 years of operation, the group's productions of musicals like *Forever Plaid* and other popular shows continue to take place in the nearly 350-year old Swift Creek grist-mill-theater complex that is located south of the city on US Highway 1 just north of Colonial Heights.

The Barksdale Theater presented plays for nearly 45 years in the 199-seat basement performance space that group members constructed in the historic Hanover Tavern, 15 miles north of the city. The old building is now being renovated and the Barksdale has moved to town, to a large playhouse created at the Willow Lawn shopping complex in Richmond's West End. The Barksdale Theater became a non-profit organization in the mid-

NATIONAL THEATER, *704 E. Broad St., 2001. During renovation of the National, the theater is occasionally opened for special events such as silent film screenings with live musical accompaniment during the James River Film Festival.*

1980s. Its musical production of *Joseph and the Amazing Technicolor Dreamcoat* was one of the most successful and longest-running shows in Richmond theatrical history.

The Firehouse Theater Project is an active non-profit drama group founded in 1993. It performs contemporary American plays such as the recent production of *Heads*, written by Virginia author Philip Bly, at the turn of the century fire station at 1609 W. Broad Street.

Other active local dramatic groups include the Chesterfield Theatre Company (formerly the John Rolfe Players) sponsored by the Chesterfield County Department of Parks and Recreation; the Chamberlayne Actors Theatre, formed by the North Chamberlayne Civic Association in 1963; the Lee Playhouse at Ft. Lee, founded in 1968; the Mystery Dinner Playhouse; the Encore! Theatre Company's Richmond Shakespeare Festival, whose plays are produced in an appropriate period setting at Agecroft Hall; Ashland Stage Company; Henrico Theatre Company; Richmond Triangle Players; the Jazz Ac-

tors Theater, directed by Ernie McClintock, which is an affiliate program of the Richmond Department of Recreation and Parks; and the Theatre at the Bolling Haxall House at the Richmond Woman's Club on Franklin Street, the nation's only theatre devoted exclusively to drawing room comedies.

Theater programs at VCU and the University of Richmond are among the premiere sources of dramatic and musical talent in Richmond. Their institutional affiliations allow them to put on productions that range from the classics to experimental works that might not be successful in commercial theaters. Theatre VCU traces its roots back to 1940 and Professor Raymond Hodges's program at the Richmond Professional Institute. A theater on campus is now named in his honor. VCU has also renovated the Lee Theater into the Grace Street Theater, which is used for Dance department programs, classes and lectures. The University Players and other performing arts troupes mount their productions at the

BROADWAY THEATER, HOPEWELL, *1920s. This postcard depicts the new theater building soon after its completion. Collection of Kathy Fuller-Seeley.*

University of Richmond's recently built Jepson Theater at the Modlin Center for the Arts.

Road shows also come to town to perform at the Carpenter Center and Landmark Theater, from the "Broadway Under the Stars" series of five productions per year to individual touring companies. Richmond sees about 15 road show companies in town annually.

The city's Department of Recreation, Parks and Community Facilities is celebrating the 45th anniversary of its annual summer theatrical productions (two plays and a large-scale musical) which are put on during the Festival of the Arts at the Dogwood Dell in Maymont Park. The Festival's free plays, concerts and art shows are seen by 150,000 or more people each year.

The Richmond area also enjoys a wealth of concerts and performances put on each year by local organizations such as the Richmond Symphony, the Elegba Folklore Society, Ezibu Montu African dance and music company; the Richmond Ballet; the Virginia Opera; the Richmond Boys Choir and the Richmond Jazz Society. The city's Alliance for the Performing Arts represents more than 60 local arts organizations.

Hollywood on the James

During Hollywood's "golden age," nearly all movies were filmed in California, where scenic artists in the studio could recreate any location, no matter how exotic. On rare occasions, film crews journeyed across the country to capture authentic settings, and at least two feature films of that era contain scenes shot in Richmond.

The 1924 silent film *America*, directed by D. W. Griffith, was a romantic drama set during the American Revolution. Griffith, his cast and crew stayed at the Jefferson Hotel, and they filled two ballrooms with 300 costumes brought down from New York, and a row of electric sewing machines for wardrobe fitters to use. Griffith shot scenes at the Westover mansion for several days in November 1923, and members of the Richmond Little Theater League appeared as extras in the movie.[10]

On September 5, 1940, *The Howards of Virginia*, another Revolutionary War-era drama starring Cary Grant and Martha Scott, which had been shot in Williamsburg the previous May, made its world premiere in Richmond. So many people clamored to attend the debut that simultaneous showings were held at the Byrd, Westhampton and State theaters. The film's producer/director Frank

BEACON THEATER, *401 N. Main St., Hopewell, 2001.* *The old movie theater is undergoing renovation to become a cultural center for the community.*

Lloyd and Miss Scott made personal appearances across the city and participated in numerous publicity events.[11]

After the Hollywood studio system's decline in the 1960s, however, movie and TV producers and directors began shooting on location far more frequently. They sought more authentic filming sites, and production places where expenses were lower than in Los Angeles and New York.

In the past 25 years, Virginia, and Richmond in particular, has increasingly served as a location for scenes in films and television movies. The State Capitol building often stands in for the White House, which it closely resembles. The Richmond area offers diverse settings – antebellum churches, downtown business district, colonial-era mansions, large railroad passenger stations, parklands, cobblestone streets and more — that filmmakers can transform into many different time periods or places.[12]

To encourage more film and TV productions to shoot more often in the Commonwealth, Virginia political and media leaders lobbied to open a state film office, as other states such as North Carolina and Florida were successfully doing. Governor Gerald L. Baliles started the ball rolling in 1979 as a member of the Virginia House of Delegates when he sponsored legislation and budget amendments to create the Virginia Film Office, now affiliated with the Virginia Economic Development Partnership and the Virginia Tourism Corporation.

The Virginia Film Office is a marketing organization that acts as a catalyst to attract film and video production, enhancing the state's economy and employment opportunities. Under the leadership of director Rita McClenny, the film office works with media producers to bring their projects to the Commonwealth, to scout locations, facilitate production, and act as a liaison with local government officials. It also works to support

NEW MILLENNIUM STUDIOS,
Petersburg, 2001.

**TIM REID AND DAPHNE
MAXWELL REID,** *2001.*

FORMER GOVERNOR GERALD BALILES , *2001. Governor Baliles was instrumental in the establishment of the Virginia Film Office in 1979.*

Virginia's own growing film and media industry, compiling an annual *Virginia Production Services Directory*. Since 1980, more than 200 major media projects have been shot in Virginia, bringing more than $500 million into the state.

The Virginia Film Office and the Commonwealth of Virginia further encourage media production in the state by offering economic incentives. Since 1995 film companies have been exempt from Virginia state sales tax on the purchase or lease of goods related to the production. Expenses add up quickly and this promotion can result in significant savings. The Virginia Film Office's co-ordination of the biennial Governor's award competition for screenplays produced by Virginians also nourishes the talent pool of local writers and brings the recipients national attention.[13]

Besides its scenic locations, the Richmond area also boasts the availability of the state's only full-service film and television production facility, New Millennium Studios, located in Petersburg. Prominent film and television actors Tim Reid and Daphne Maxwell Reid founded New Millennium Studios. A Norfolk native, Tim Reid is realizing his dream of building a first-class production facility in his home state.

The 60-acre site holds a full-service film and TV studio that features a 15,000 square foot sound stage, a 25-acre backlot, and state-of-the-art post-production facilities that offer filmmakers capabilities to produce digital effects, virtual reality and computer animation. New Millennium has forged a supportive partnership with the city of Petersburg, which, with the assistance of a grant from the Governor's Opportunity Fund, has invested a half-million dollars in the project through purchasing the land site for the studio.

Since the $11 million complex's opening in July 1997, New Millennium Studios has produced two feature films

AUDIENCE AT LEGEND BREWING CO. PUB, *321 W. Seventh St., 2001. Reminiscent of the open-air movie theaters at Idlewood and Forest Hill Parks in 1905, moviegoers today enjoy watching films under the stars at this local restaurant.*

(including *Asunder*, starring Petersburg native Blair Underwood, which was directed and produced by Tim Reid), two CBS network television movies, and more than 40 commercials and music videos. The Reids produced and starred in a series for the Showtime cable TV network, *Linc's*, at the studio. New Millennium has also hosted numerous other television and film company productions that were shot there in whole or part. One of the studio's most recent projects is *American Legacy* a syndicated television documentary special and series in development that profiles significant people and events in 20th century African-American history.

As director of operations at New Millennium Studios, Daphne Maxwell Reid is one of Virginia's most prominent businesswomen. She wears many hats each day, managing budgets, overseeing construction projects, running sales meetings and negotiating contracts.[14] The facility bustles with the activities of student interns, sea-

soned industry professionals, and energetic young filmmakers and digital artists drawn from across Virginia. New Millennium Studios enthusiastically rises to the challenge of succeeding as an independent production facility in a world of media conglomerates.

Alongside the commercial film and media activities in the area, a local independent film community has also been developing in Richmond, creating in turn a growing audience interested in seeing new works made by area film and video-makers. In 1997, the first Flicker film screening was held, to showcase independently made 16mm films and videos produced by Richmond filmmakers. More than 170 short movies and videos made by 125 filmmakers have been screened at subsequent Flicker events. Experimental, avante garde and art films old and new are screened during the annual James River Film Festivals, which have been held at VCU and at theater spaces around the city. Last year's festival screened

BROWN'S ISLAND FILM FESTIVAL, *2001. Movie fans watch the Hollywood classic* **Singin' in the Rain** *at the annual summer outdoor series, sponsored by Downtown Presents.*

silent films at the historic National Theater, undergoing renovation. Recently the Flickers group has joined with the planners of the James River Film Festival to form the Richmond Moving Image Co-Op, a non-profit organization which supports local media artists and enthusiasts by providing a regular scheduled series of public film screenings, holding classes and training workshops, providing access to equipment and resources, and awards small grants to aid the work of local filmmakers.

Just as enthusiastically as it has embraced watching movies for the past 100 years, these days the Richmond community is becoming increasingly involved in the making of feature films, TV programs and independently produced short videos. Locally filmed movies and videos not only bring pride of place to hometown audiences, and create publicity that draws viewers from all over the world to Richmond as tourists. The media production process also generates significant income for the businesses, services and people of the region.

ELEGBA FOLKLORE SOCIETY, *2001.*

A Vision for the Future — The Virginia Performing Arts Complex

Professional and community theater, concert groups, symphony, ballet and smaller arts organizations in Richmond have an exciting future ahead of them. The Virginia Performing Arts Foundation has been created to develop a Performing Arts Complex for Richmond, which is now envisioned to thrive along the Broad Street corridor downtown.[16]

The city's famous theaters, the Landmark, Empire, Carpenter Center, and National are poised to become, more than ever, the centers of Richmond's cultural life as they become the centerpieces of the new complex. enhanced with up-to-the-minute facilities to benefit the performers and audiences. The plans call for Richmond's

Landmark Theater to be renovated and upgraded to contain larger loading and docking spaces for traveling companies (for the current space is inadequate for many of today's groups); the Landmark could gain larger dressing rooms, and enhanced restrooms and other public areas. The Carpenter Center is to gain an expanded lobby space by better utilizing the small retail shop spaces that had been incorporated into the Grace and Sixth Street sides of the old Loew's Theater building. Additional space for the stage, dressing rooms, and loading and docking facilities behind the original theater will add significantly to its usefulness for today's concerts and productions. Then, the innovative plans for the Virginia Performing Arts Complex call for a multi-story facility to be built on the site of the old Thalhimer's building. A 600-seat the-

EXECUTIVE COMMITTEE OF THE VIRGINIA PERFORMING ARTS FOUNDATION, *2001. First row: Bob Mooney, Jackie Stone, Jim Ukrop. Second row: Stephanie Micas, John Sherman, Brad Armstrong, Phil Bagley. Not pictured: John Bates, Booty Armstrong, Jim Murray, Jerry Shechan, Mac McDonald.*

ater on the first floor and a second story 250 seat "black box" theater, along with dressing rooms and rehearsal spaces would become the new home for TheaterVirginia. The 600 seat Empire Theater would be renovated, and an adjoining 250 seat theater would be added for performance, rehearsals and use by other community performance groups. Additionally the National Theater would be renovated to serve as a venue for concerts and film festivals. The Virginia Performing Arts Complex is being planned to draw together performance spaces for the Richmond Symphony, Richmond Ballet, Theater IV, Elegba Folklore Society, Jazz Actors Theater, Richmond Jazz Society, and a host of other local arts groups.

This vision for the future of performing arts in Rich-mond includes an ambitious plan to bring all these facilities under the common ownership and management of one organization, the Virginia Performing Arts Foundation. Working closely with the Alliance for the Performing Arts (which represents the performing arts organizations), this foundation will help the city's major performing arts groups become even more cohesive and creative. The end result can be an even richer Richmond entertainment and cultural scene, a re-creation of Broad Streets' famous "Theater Row", that will help rejuvenate the downtown area. In many ways, the performing arts groups and the city are building on the strengths of the past, and the best is yet to come.

Movies and Television programs filmed in the Richmond area:

2001 – *Mickey* feature film written by John Grisham.

2000 – *Hannibal* feature film starring Anthony Hopkins and Julianne Moore.

2000 – *Hearts in Atlantis* feature film starring Anthony Hopkins.

1999 – *Sally Hemmings*, CBS TV mini-series.

1998 – *Asunder* feature film starring Blair Underwood, produced by Tim Reid.

1998 – *Linc's* Showtime TV series starring Tim and Daphne Reid.

1997 – *The Love Letter* Hallmark Hall of Fame TV movie.

1996 – *G. I. Jane* feature film starring Demi Moore.

1996 – *The Jackal* feature film starring Bruce Willis and Richard Gere. The special effects crew made downtown Richmond buildings appear to blow up in this espionage thriller.

1995 – *First Kid* feature film starring comedian Sinbad.

1995 – *The Shadow Conspiracy* feature film starring Charlie Sheen, Donald Sutherland and Linda Hamilton. Sheen careening up Franklin Street the wrong way in a Jeep caused much interest on the VCU campus.

1994 – *Kingfish* TNT network TV movie.

1994 – *Tad* Family Channel TV movie starring Kris Kristopherson and Jane Curtin.

1992 – *Dave* feature film starring Kevin Kline and Sigourney Weaver.

1991 – *Miss Rose White* Hallmark Hall of Fame TV movie.

1991 – *Doc Hollywood* feature film starring Michael J. Fox.

1990 – *Love Field* feature film starring Michelle Pfeiffer.

1989 – *My Name is Bill W.* Hallmark Hall of Fame TV movie.

1987 – *The Murder of Mary Phagen* – NBC TV mini-series starring Jack Lemmon. City Hall was among the sites that stood in for Atlanta in the 1910s.

1987 – *Gore Vidal's Lincoln* NBC TV mini-series starring Sam Waterston, Mary Tyler Moore and John Houseman.

1985 – *Roanoak* PBS TV mini-series.

1985 – *Dream West* CBS TV mini-series starring Richard Chamberlain. Scenes were filmed at the Monumental Church.

1984 – *Finnegan Begin Again* HBO TV movie starring Robert Preston, Mary Tyler Moore, Sam Waterston and Sylvia Sidney. The *Times-Dispatch* news-room, Richmond Memorial hospital and Hollywood cemetery were used as locations.

1983 – *Kennedy* NBC TV mini-series starring Martin Sheen and Blair Brown. The state capitol stood in for the US capitol, and the assassination in Dallas was filmed along Semmes Avenue.

1982 – *Nancy Astor* BBC TV mini-series.

1980 – *My Dinner with Andre* feature film directed by Louis Malle. Shot at the then-closed Jefferson Hotel. [15]

1979 – *The Henderson Monster* CBS TV movie.

1977 – *Rollercoaster* feature film starring George Segal, Richard Widmark, Henry Fonda and Timothy Bottoms. Filmed in part at Kings Dominion.

1973 – *The Last Detail* feature film starring Jack Nicholson. The West Broad Street railroad station was used.

1940 – *The Howards of Virginia* feature film starring Cary Grant and Martha Scott, filmed in Williamsburg, world premiere held in Richmond.

1924 – *America* feature film directed by D.W. Griffith. Scenes filmed at Westover, with local actors in the background.

HISTORIC AREA THEATERS
1780-1970

Richmond Theaters

Academy of Music – 105 N. Eighth St. Playhouse, 1,160 seats. Opened 1886. Burned 1927.

Airport Drive-In – Williamsburg Rd. Open 1950s-1980s.

Albion Theater – 211 N. Third St. Movies, 350 seats. Opened 1914. Closed 1918.

Ashland Theater – 209 England St., Ashland. Movies, 350 seats. Opened 1948. Closed 1990s. Still standing; now being renovated as a community center. Also, Cab Theater — Opened in 1927. Closed 1958.

Autovue Drive In – Hopewell Road. Opened 1941. Closed 1950s.

Auto-View Drive In — Nine Mile Road, Highland Springs. Opened 1940s, closed 1960s.

Barton's Opera House –Eighth and Broad Sts. Vaudeville. Open in mid-1880s. Also called Ford's Opera House; remodeled into the original Bijou/Colonial Theater in 1899.

Beacon Theater, 401 N. Main St., Hopewell. Movies, 500 seats. Formerly Broadway (1920-1930). Open 1930. Closed 1970s. Still standing, now being renovated as a community center.

Bellevue Theater – 4026 MacArthur (Rappahannock) Ave. Movies, 622 seats. Opened 1937. Closed 1965. Still standing, renovated as Samis Grotto Shrine meeting hall.

Bellwood Drive-In – Willis Road at Jeff Davis Hwy. Opened 1948. Closed 1970s. Partially standing, now site of Bellwood Flea Market.

Belmar Theater – 307 ¹/₂ Louisiana St. Nickelodeon. Opened 1909. Closed 1910.

Bijou Theater (original) – 714 E. Broad St. Vaudeville. Opened 1899 in renovated Barton Opera House. Closed 1905, re-opened as original Colonial Theater.

Bijou Theater — 810 E. Broad Street. Vaudeville, movies, 1,488 seats. Opened 1905. Closed 1933. Renovated and reopened as Strand Theater 1933-1938. Now site of Library of Virginia.

Biograph Theater – 814 W. Grace St. Movies. Opened 1971. Closed 1991. Re-opened as the Grace Street Theater 1992-1995. Still standing.

Bluebird Theater – 620 E. Broad Street. Movies, 600 seats. Opened 1920. Closed 1933, renovated and re-opened as Grand Theater.

Booker T. Theater – 118 W. Broad St. Movies, 842 seats. Opened 1934, formerly Empire and Strand Theaters. Closed 1974. Became Edison Theater in 1970s. Still standing, now renovated and re-opened as the Empire Theater, home of Theater IV.

Broad Street Cinemas – 5410 W. Broad St. Movies. Opened 1970. Closed 1990.

Broadway Open Air – Broad St. at Wistar. Drive-In. Opened late 1940s. Closed 1960s.

Broadway Theater – 712 E. Broad St. Movies, 668 seats. Opened 1919. Closed 1933, reopened as the State Theater.

Brookland Theater – 115 Brookland Park Ave. Movies, 634 seats. Opened 1925. Closed 1957. Still standing.

Byrd Theater – 2905 W. Cary St. Movies, 1,396 seats. Opened 1928. Briefly closed in 1983 but still operating today.

Capitol Theater – 2525 W. Broad St. Movies, 678 seats. Opened 1926. Closed 1984.

Carillon Theater – 2820 W. Cary St. Movies, 517 seats. Opened 1934. Closed 1958. Still standing, renovated as retail shops.

Carpenter Center for the Performing Arts – 600 E. Grace St. Playhouse, 2,043 seats. Opened 1983, formerly Loew's Theater. In operation today.

Casino Theater – Beverly St. Open-air vaudeville and nickelodeon. Opened 1903. Closed 1911.

Casino Theater – 1912 Hull St. Movies. Opened 1920. Closed 1920s.

Casino Theater – 300 W. Broad St. Nickelodeon. Opened 1915, formerly Pekin Theater. Closed 1916.

City Auditorium – Linden and Cary Sts. Concert hall, 3,608 seats. Opened 1890s, formerly meat market. Closed 1950s. Still standing, renovated as gymnasium by Virginia Commonwealth University.

Colonial Theater (original) – 714 E. Broad St. Vaudeville and Movies. Formerly original Bijou. Opened 1902. Closed 1920. Demolished to become site of new Colonial Theater.

Colonial Theater – 714 E. Broad St. Movies, 1,307 seats. Opened 1921. Closed 1981. Partially standing, façade preserved as front of an office building.

Cozy Corner Theater — 1814 Hull St. Nickelodeon. Opened 1909. Closed 1910.

Dixie Theater — 18 W. Broad St. Nickelodeon. Opened 1907. Closed 1921. Still standing.

Dixie Drive-In — Belt Blvd., Midlothian. Opened late 1940s. Closed 1960s.

East End Theater – 418 N. 25th St. Movies, 850 seats. Opened 1938. Closed 1970. Still standing.

Empire Theater – 807 Second St. Nickelodeon. Opened 1908. Closed 1909.

Empire Theater – 118 W. Broad St. Playhouse, 1,050 seats. Opened 1911. Closed 1915. Re-opened as Strand Theater 1915-1927, Booker T. 1934-1974. Still standing, renovated and re-opened as Empire Theater, home of Theatre IV.

Fifth Street Theater – 500 E. Broad St. Movies, 330 seats. Former Theato. Opened 1923. Closed 1927. Re-opened as Rex Theater 1927-1928.

Gaiety Theater – 221 E. Broad St. Nickelodeon. Opened 1908. Closed 1910.

Gem Theater – 2 W. Broad St. Nickelodeon. Opened 1909. Closed 1910.

Ginter Theater – 4011 Rappahannock Ave. Movies, 754 seats. Opened 1937. Closed 1939.

Globe Theater – 1005 N. First St. Nickelodeon. Opened 1909. Closed 1913.

Globe Theater – 528 N. Second St. Nickelodeon and movies, 408 seats. Opened 1909. Closed 1950s.

Grand Theater – 620 E. Broad St. Movies, 576 seats. Formerly Bluebird. Opened 1933. Closed 1963.

Grove Theater – 5604 Grove Avenue. Movies. Opened 1937. Closed 1937. Still standing, remodeled as Arcade Shops.

Henrico Theater – 305 E. Nine Mile Road, Highland Springs. Movies, 900 seats. Opened 1938. Closed 1962. Reopened several times since, still standing and being renovated as a community center.

Hippodrome Theater – 530 N. Second St. Vaudeville and movies, 850 seats. Opened 1914. Burned and remodeled 1945. Closed 1970. Reopened several times since.

Ideal Theater – 700 W. Broad St. Nickelodeon. Opened 1909. Closed 1910.

Idle Hour Theater – 122 E. Broad St. Nickelodeon. Opened 1909. Closed 1910.

Isis Theater – 808 E. Broad St. Movies, 577 seats. Formerly Lubin Theater. Opened 1916. Closed 1929. Renovated and re-opened as Park Theater in 1938.

Landmark Theater – Laurel and Main Sts. Playhouse and concert hall, 4,035 seats. Formerly the Mosque. Renovated and reopened 1996. In operation today.

Leader Theater – 1002 Hull St. Nickelodeon. Opened 1908. Closed 1913.

Lee Theater – 934 W. Grace St. Movies, 588 seats. Opened 1935. Closed 1962. Re-opened as Lee Art Theater 1962-1993. Still standing, renovated and re-opened by Virginia Commonwealth University as the Grace Street Theater, 1995.

Lennox Theater – 514 Louisiana St. Movies. Opened 1948, formerly Star Theater. Closed 1950s.

Lincoln Theater – 1919 Hull St. Movies. Formerly Star Theater. Opened 1934. Closed 1960s.

Little Theater – 110 W. Broad St. Movies, 330 seats. Opened 1914. Closed 1920. Renovated and re-opened as Maggie Walker Theater, 1936. Still standing, now incorporated into Empire Theater.

Loew's Theater – 600 E. Grace St. Movies, 2, 043 seats. Opened 1928. Closed 1979. Still standing, renovated and re-opened as Carpenter Center for the Performing Arts, 1983.

Lubin Theater – 808 E. Broad St. Vaudeville and nickelodeon, 577 seats. Opened 1909. Closed 1916 and renamed Regent (1916), Isis (1916-1929) and Park (1938-1953).

Lyric Theater 1720 E. Main St. Nickelodeon. Opened 1909. Closed 1910.

Lyric Theater – 903 E. Broad St. Vaudeville, movies and playhouse, 1,576 seats. Opened in 1914. Closed 1946. Re-opened as WRVA Theater in 1946. Closed 1963.

Maggie Walker Theater – 114 W. Broad St. Movies, 330 seats. Formerly Little Theater. Opened 1936. Closed 1963. Briefly re-opened as Edison Theater. Still standing, renovated as part of Empire Theater.

Majestic Theater – 23 W. Broad St. Nickelodeon. Opened 1908. Closed 1910.

Marshall Theater – 701 E. Broad St. Playhouse. Opened 1823. Renamed Richmond Theater 1860. Burned 1862 and rebuilt as New Richmond Theater.

Midlothian Drive-In Theater – Bon Air Road, Midlothian. Formerly Open Air Movies Drive In. Opened 1947. Closed 1960s.

Mosque Theater – Laurel at Main Sts. Playhouse, movies and concert hall, 4, 035 seats, Opened 1927. Purchased by city of Richmond, 1940. Renamed Richmond's Landmark Theater, renovated and re-opened 1996.

National Theater – 704 E. Broad St. Vaudeville and movies, 1,393 seats. Formerly site of Rex Theater. Opened 1923. Renamed Towne Theater 1968. Closed 1983. Still standing.

New Theater – 206 E. Broad St. Movies, 440 seats. Opened 1915. Closed 1918.

Odeon Theater – 211 N. Sixth St. Movies, 500 seats. Formerly Superior Theater. Opened 1916. Closed 1927.

Orient Theater – 300 W. Broad St. Nickelodeon. Opened 1909. Closed 1910, renamed Pekin Theater.

Park Theater – 808 E. Broad St. Movies, 577 seats. Formerly Lubin and Isis theaters. Opened 1938. Closed 1953. Renovated as office building, first site of Virginia Credit Union.

Pastime Picture Show – 1435 Hull St. Nickelodeon. Opened 1910; moved to 1224 Hull St. in 1911; became Pastime Photoplay in 1912. Closed 1915.

Patrick Henry Theater – 404 N. 25th St. Movies, seats 748. Opened 1933. Closed 1953.

Patterson Drive-In – Patterson Ave., Western Henrico County. Open 1950s. Closed 1980s.

Pekin Theater –300 W. Broad St. Nickelodeon. Formerly Orient Theater. Opened 1910. Closed 1915.

Plaza Drive-In – E. Belt Blvd. Opened late 1940s. Closed 1980s.

Ponton Theater – 1316 Hull St. Movies, 464 seats. Formerly Victoria Theater. Opened 1931. Closed 1950s.

Putnam's Theater – 1313 E. Franklin St. Burlesque and vaudeville. Formerly Theater Comique. Opened 1870s. Renamed Lyric Theater 1907, closed 1908.

Rayo Theater – 111 N. Second St. Movies. Opened 1921. Closed 1923.

Regent Theater – 1205 Boulevard, Colonial Heights. Movies, 419 seats. Opened 1937. Closed 1950s. Now site of Colonial Heights post office.

Rex Theater – 700 E. Broad St. Nickelodeon and movies, 250 seats. Opened 1909. Closed 1920. Became site of Colonial Theater.

Richmond Theater – 1300 E. Broad St. Playhouse. 600 seats. Opened 1800. Burned 1811. Now site of Monumental Church.

Richmond Theater – 701 E. Broad St. Playhouse Formerly Marshall Theater. Opened 1860. Burned and rebuilt 1862. Closed 1899.

Robinson Theater – 2901 Q St. Movies, 350 seats. Opened 1937. Closed 1960. Still standing, occasionally used for community performances.

Rosebowl Drive-In – Rt. 1, Ashland. Opened late 1940s. Closed 1980s.

Royal Theater – 923 N. 29th St. Nickelodeon. Opened 1909. Closed 1910.

Royal Theater – 1435 Hull St. Nickelodeon. Opened 1909. Closed 1910.

Shirley Theater – 1224 Hull St. Movies. Formerly Pastime Photoplay. Opened 1925. Closed 1930s.

Star Theater – 512 Louisiana St. Nickelodeon and movies, 196 seats. Opened 1909. Closed 1948, renovated and re-opened as Lennox Theater, 1948.

Star Theater – 1919 Hull St. Nickelodeon. Opened 1912. Closed 1916.

State Theater – 712 E. Broad St. Movies, 668 seats. Formerly Broadway Theater. Opened 1933. Closed 1981.

Strand Theater – 810 E. Broad St. Movies, 1,488 seats. Formerly Bijou. Opened 1933. Closed 1938. Now site of Library of Virginia.

Strand Theater – 118 W. Broad St. Movies, 1,050 seats. Formerly Empire Theater. Opened 1915. Closed 1927 after a fire. Renovated and renamed Booker T. Theater in 1934. Still standing as Empire Theater.

Superior Theater – 211 N. Sixth St. Nickelodeon, 500 seats. Opened 1913. Closed 1915, renovated and renamed Odeon Theater.

Theato – 500 E. Broad St. Nickelodeon and movies, 350 seats. Opened 1908. Closed 1923, renamed Fifth Street Theater 1923-1926.

Theatre Comique – 1313 E. Franklin St. Burlesque. Formerly Metropolitan Theater. Opened 1860s. Closed 1890s and renamed Putnam's Theater.

Towne Theater – 704 E. Broad St. Movies, 1,393 seats. Formerly National Theater. Opened 1968. Closed 1983. Still standing.

Venus Theater – 1412 Hull St., Movies, 843 seats. Opened 1925. Closed 1950s. Still standing.

Victor Theater – 800 E. Broad St. on ground floor of Massey Building. Movies, 300 seats. Opened 1914. Closed 1920.

Victoria Moving Picture Show – 1316 Hull St. Nickelodeon and movies, 350 seats. Opened 1911. Closed 1925. Re-opened as Ponton Theater.

Virginia Theater – 1018 W. Cary St. Nickelodeon. Opened 1909. Closed 1910.

Virginia Theater – 711 E. Broad St. Nickelodeon, 320 seats. Opened 1913. Closed 1915.

Westhampton Theater – 5506 Grove Ave. Movies, 848 seats. Opened 1938. Still in operation today.

Westover Theater – 4712 Forest Hill Ave. Movies. Opened 1947. Closed 1995. Still standing, renovated and used as a church.

Willow Lawn Theater – Willow Lawn Dr. Movies, 830 seats. Opened 1956. Closed 1981. Demolished, rebuilt and re-opened as four screen theater, 1990.

Wonderland – 1313 1/2 Hull St. Nickelodeon. Opened 1909. Closed 1910.

WRVA Theater – 901 E. Broad St. Concert hall and playhouse, 1,500 seats. Formerly Lyric Theater. Opened 1946. Closed 1960.

Petersburg Theaters

Academy of Music Theater – W. Bank Street. Playhouse. Open 1880s-1920s.

Barney's Theater – 109 Harrison St. Movies, 390 seats. Open 1930s-1960s.

Bluebird Theater — 16 N. Sycamore St. Movies, 617 seats. Formerly Columbia (1900) Colonial (1921). Open 1929-1960s.

Century Theater – 249 N. Sycamore St. Movies, 878 seats. Open 1930s-1960s. Moorish style decoration, the grandest movie theater in town.

Cockade Theater – 248 N. Sycamore St. Movies, 300 seats. Open 1930s-1940s.

Gem Theater — 222 Halifax St, Movies, 415 seats. Open 1930s-1960s.

Idle Hour Theater — 116 Halifax St. Movies, 390 seats. Open 1920s-1960s.

Lombard Theater – Bank St. Playhouse. Mrs. Poe performed here.

Palace Theater — 143 N. Sycamore St. Movies, 473 seats. Formerly Lyric Theater (1900) and Bluebird (1919). Open 1929-1960s.

Rex Theater — 245 N. Sycamore St. Movies, 396 seats. Open 1930s-1960s.

NOTES

Prologue

1 Roy Proctor, "How 'Up' Are You on Richmond Theater's Past?" *Richmond Times Dispatch* [*TD*], Sept. 19, 1987.

2 Patricia Click, *The Spirit of the Times: Amusements in 19th Century Baltimore, Norfolk and Richmond* (Charlottesville: University Press of Virginia, 1989), p. xiv.

3 James Dormon, Jr., *Theater in the Ante Bellum South, 1815-1861* (Chapel Hill: University of North Carolina Press, 1967); Edith Lindeman, "Playhouses Created Tragic History," *TD* Feb 14, 1971.

4 Click, p. 34.

5 Earle Lutz, *A Richmond Album: A Pictorial Chronicle of an Historic City's Outstanding Events and Places* (Richmond: Garrett and Massie, 1937), p. 22. Gilbert Hunt eventually gained his freedom, journeyed to Liberia, returned to Richmond, and lived to be 90, dying in 1863.

6 Ophelia Johnson, "Shedding New Light on Very Old Church," *TD* Feb 22, 1996. The Historic Richmond Foundation acquired the church in 1983.

7 Marie Tyler McGraw, *At the Falls: Richmond, Virginia and Its People* (Chapel Hill: University of North Carolina Press, 1994), p. 146.

8 Eric W. Barnes, *The Lady of Fashion: The Life and Theater of Anna Cora Mowatt* (New York: Scribner's, 1954).

9 Mary Wingfield Scott, *Old Richmond Neighborhoods* (Richmond: William Byrd Press, 1950), p. 129.

10 Edith Lindeman, "Jenny Lind in 1850, Toscanini in 1950; City Has Full Theater History" *TD* Oct 22, 1950, p. 18; Vera Palmer, "Richmond Man Paid $105 to Hear Jenny Lind," *TD* January 6, 1924.

11 Ernest Furgurson, *Ashes of Glory: Richmond at War* (New York: Knopf, 1996), p. 102-103.

12 George Rogers, "Of Jake Wells...And a Trunk Strap...and Amateur Night at the Bijou," *NL* June 2, 1952; Earle Lutz, "Bat Strap Leads to Big Theater Combine," *TD* Jan. 6, 1924."

13 Click, p. 54.

14 Thomas C. Leonard, "The Theatre and Its History in Virginia," *TD*, n.d., Richmond Public Library.

15 Proctor, "How 'Up' Are you on Richmond Theater's Past?"

16 Bruce Chesterman, "Walls of Historic Playhouse Preserved as 7th and Broad Building is Remodeled," *TD* October 12, 1936; Roy Proctor, "The Battle of the Bells," *TD* March 4, 1982.

17 *Richmond Times Dispatch [RD]* March 4, 1876.

18 George Rogers, "City Witnessed a Boom in Theater Houses 40 Years Ago, Most Have Gone Now, But Show Business Goes on Forever," *TD* June 3, 1952.

19 George Rogers, "Downtown Demolitions Area Once Knew Some Lively Times," *News Leader* [*NL*], Nov 16, 1953.

20 *RD* October 7, 1889.

21 James K. Sanford, ed., *A Century of Commerce, 1867-1967* (Richmond: Chamber of Commerce, 1967), p. 56.

22 "They Want the Theater," *Richmond State* Dec. 21, 1892.

Chapter 1

1 McGraw, *At the Falls*, pp. 244-248.

2 Edith Lindeman, "Days When the Flicks Really Flickered, Local Theaters Gave Free Handkerchiefs," *TD* Feb 11, 1971.

3 "Early 1900s Found Silver Screen Battling Spoken Drama" *NL* May 29, 1934.

4 G. Watson James, Jr., "Regular of Peanuts Roost Recalls Academy's Heyday," *TD* August 11, 1963.

5 Proctor, "How 'Up' Are You on Richmond Theater's Past?"

6 *RD* Aug 28, 1898, Sept 18, 1898.

7 Rogers, "City Witnessed a Boom in Theater Houses."

8 Roy Proctor, "Norfolk Theater: Alive and Wells; Granddaddy of Stage Dragged Richmond Out of the Dark Ages," *NL* Jan. 22. 1987.

9 "Probe Circumstances of Jake Wells' Death," *NL* March 17, 1927.

10 *News Leader* October 10, 1908.

11 Rogers, "City Witnessed a Boom."

12 Rogers, "City Witnessed A Boom."

13 Lindeman, "Jenny Lind in 1850."

14 Harry Tucker, "Harry Tucker Recalls," *TD* November 15, 1931.

15 "To Exhibit the Cineograph" *Richmond Dispatch*, April 25, 1897.

16 Neil November, "I Remember When," n.d. clipping at Valentine Museum.

17 *RD* Oct 15, 1899.

18 "Richmond's First Movie," n.d. clipping at Valentine Museum; Q&A, *TD*, March 10, 1942; "Harry Tucker Recalls."

19 Tucker, "Harry Tucker Recalls."

20 "Cheap Theaters Must Be Safer," *TD* March 13, 1908 p. 10.

21 "Robert Coulter Dies," *TD* Jan. 28, 1978.

22 Lindeman, "Days When Flicks Flickered."

23 November, "I Remember When."

24 Tucker, "Harry Tucker Recalls".

25 Eckhardt, Joseph, *The King of the Movies : Film Pioneer Siegmund Lubin* (Madison, N.J. : Fairleigh Dickinson University Press , 1997).

26 "Lubin's Theater," *NL* December 7, 1908; *TD* Dec 6, 1908

27 November, "I Remember When."

28 Lindeman, "Jenny Lind in 1850."

29 "Leo Wise, Academy Veteran, Tells of Old Theater Days" *NL* October 18, 1944.

30 "At the Theatres" *TD* September 11, 1904. The reporter thought that the young women really wanted to see the male actors, but that their courage failed them, and they did not wish to risk the social embarrassment of having others see them "in the attitude of man-gazing."

31 Lindeman, "Days When Flicks Really Flickered."

32 Neil Downe, "She was a True Jewel in Those Days, Was the Old Bijou," *NL* Nov 13, 1952.

33 *NL* July 5, 1913.

34 Lindeman, "Days when Flicks Really Flickered."

35 "They See John Bunny," *NL* August 18, 1914.

36 *Richmond Planet* March 27, April 10, May 1, May 17, 1915.

37 "*The Birth of a Nation*," *Richmond Planet* October 30, 1915.

38 *NL* October 26, 1915, *TD* October 26, 1915.

39 *Richmond Playgoer*, December 1911.

40 *Screenland*, November 13, 1916.

Chapter 2

1 Frances Watson, "Amanda Ellen Thorpe: Richmond Motion Picture Pioneer," *Richmond Quarterly* 1:2 Fall 1978, p. 39-40.

2 "New Colonial Theater Will Open Today at 2" *TD* October 12, 1921

3 Interview with Bob Burchette, November, 2000.

4 "Handsome New Colonial Theater Will Be Opened Next Wednesday," *TD* Oct 9, 1921; "New Colonial Thrown Open," *TD* October 13, 1921.

5 "Theatre Adopts Policy from Popular Canvas," *NL* Nov 12, 1923.

6 Bill Jenkins, "The Capitol Theater – Historical Significance," unpublished paper, 1995. "Richmond Sculptor Decorative Artist," *TD* November 7, 1926.

7 "Richmond Sculptor Decorative Artist"; Betsy Powell Mullen, "Richmond's Renaissance Man Remembered; Efforts Made to Preserve Work of Artist Who Helped Give City Its Unique Look" *TD* July 23, 1994.

8 Richard McCann, "Ghosts and Gila Monsters: Richmond's Theaters," *Richmond Mercury*, July 3, 1974.

9 "Voice Failing Her, Viola Dana Can Only Wave to Big Crowd," *NL* February 24, 1922.

10 "Griffith's *America* Greatest He Has Tried; Noted Motion Picture Here in Connection with Filming of Play." *NL* November 2, 1923, *NL* Dec. 22, 1923.

11 "Charleston Winners Are Awarded Cups by Crowd; The News Leader's Contest at Colonial Witnessed by Thousands, Hundreds Turned Away," *NL* March 15, 1926.

12 Elroy Quenroe, "Movie House Architecture, Twenties Style," *Arts in Virginia*, 1976; Carpenter Center playbill, 1986; *TD* April 8, 1928.

13 Carole Kass, "Capitol Theater to Be Demolished," *TD* April 15, 1984.

14 "Willow Lawn is Firm's 45th Film House," *NL* November 7, 1956.

15 "Musicians Skeptical on Talking Pictures" *NL* August 15, 1928

16 "Amateur Singers New Movie Pest," *NL* August 31, 1929.

17 Lindeman, "Days When Flicks Flickered."

18 "Action Letters," *NL* May 13, 1968.

19 U. Troubetzkey, "City's Mosque of the Mystic Shrine," *NL* November 21, 1954.

20 Ben Hall, *The Best Remaining Seats*, (New York: Bramhall House, 1961).

21 Carpenter Center program, 1986.

22 Annette Burr, "Loews's Theater" clipping, August 8, 1979, Carpenter Center archives.

23 "Loew's Opens with Fine Picture," *NL* March 10, 1928; William J. Mann, *Wisecracker: The Life and Times of William Haines, Hollywood's First Openly Gay Star* (New York: Viking, 1998).

24 "Charles A. Somma Has Made Signal Record as Virginia Showman," *The National Exhibitor* December 12, 1928.

25 Steve Clark, "Movie Palace Fit for a King," *NL* December 19, 1978; Alton Williams, "Theater Veteran to Retire," *NL* Sept 28, 1971. Robert Coulter died at age 83 in 1978.

26 Helen DeMotte, "New Byrd is a Place of Beauty," n.d. clipping in Richmond Public Library.

27 Carly Trader, "A Grand Old House," *Inside Richmond,* Sept. 15, 1992.

Chapter 3

1 "1930 Marked Vaudeville's End in City" *NL* Dec. 20, 1955.

2 Edith Lindeman, "Entertainment Has Changed in 30 Years," *TD* May 31, 1964.

3 Peples, "Lyric's Heyday Impels Ballad," *TD* January 3, 1989.

4 Lindeman, "Jenny Lind in 1850."

5 "1930-1939 Begins in Depression, Ends with Start of a New World War," *TD* October 22, 1950.

6 "Movies Not to Rival Churches," *NL* May 22, 1936; "Its finally official now – the Byrd is a Landmark," *TD* June 8, 1980.

7 Kathryn H. Fuller, *At the Picture Show: Small Town Audiences and the Creation of Movie Fan Culture* (Washington: Smithsonian Press, 1996).

8 Interview with Dr. E. Randolph Trice, October, 2000.

9 "Pipe Organ is a Mighty Affair, with 1229 Different Pipes Unified," *TD* April 5, 1937.

10 "Weaver to Play Film Classic" *NL* March 20, 1982; "Eddie Weaver," *NL* Sept 3, 1960; "Of Eddie Weaver and Pickled Peppers" *TD* Sept 12, 1948; "Eddie Weaver to Do Show Over WRNL" *TD* April 23, 1950.

11 "Weaver Ready to Reinaugurate Famed Organ," *TD* March 29, 1992; "Eddie Weaver Celebrates His 83rd Birthday on November 1" *Oh Magazine* 1991, clipping, Library of Virginia.

12 Liz Hart, "Loew's Brought Stars from Hollywood Here," *NL* April 29, 1983.

13 "Eddie Weaver" *NL* Sept 3, 1960; "Weaver to Play" *NL* March 20, 1982.

14 Interview with Dr. Trice; Edith Lindeman, "Eddie Weaver to Quit Loew's" *TD* Nov 26, 1960.

15 Guy Friddell, "The Moon is Through," *NL* Feb 28, 1963.

16 Clarke Bustard, "Weaver Let Good Times Roll More than 50 Years," *TD* January 28, 2001.

17 "Usher Relives Capitol Memories," *TD* Dec 30, 1995.

18 Interview with Bob Burchette, November 2000.

19 Interview with Jack W. Lively, September 30, 1982, Church Hill Oral History Project, VCU Library.

20 Carole Kass, "Movies Have Come Long Way in Richmond Over the Years," *TD* July 21, 1974; Dan Neman, "The Good, the Bad and The Western: He's an Expert in Horse Operas," *TD* May 3, 1996; Interview with Haywood Baugh, Virginia Black History Archives, Education Oral History Project, VCU Library.

21 Interview with Carolyn Brown, October, 2000.

22 "That Anti-Segregation Meeting," *Richmond Planet*

March 27, 1915.

23 "Crowds Return to the Deuce" *TD* October 7, 1990; "The Heyday of 'the Deuce': Second Street Gala Revives Old Times, Old Smells, Old Attire," *TD* October 5, 1997.

24 Tom Mitchell, "Second Street Was the Hub of Life and Hope for Richmond's Blacks," *TD* March 13, 1989.

25 Roy Proctor, "Celebrities Through the Century by Way of Richmond," *TD* November 28, 1999.

26 Charles Gerena, "Polishing a Jewel of Jackson Ward," *TD* January 16, 1998.

27 Robert Headley, *Motion Picture Exhibition in Washington D.C.* (Jefferson, NC: McFarland, 1999).

28 Interview with Dr. Francis Foster, March, 2001; interview with Robinson Horne October, 2000.

29 "The New Robinson Theater to Throw Open its Doors Sept. 29" *Richmond Planet,* Sept 25, 1937.

30 Interview with James S. Christian, Jr., September 30, 1982.Church Hill Oral History Project, VCU Library.

31 Interview with Douglas Wilder, September 29, 1982, Church Hill Oral History Project, VCU Library.

32 Interview with Dr. Jean Harris Ellis, September 29, 1982, Church Hill Oral History Project, VCU Library.

33 Interview with Carolyn Brown.

34 "'Pete' Visits," *NL* December 24, 1934.

35 "City and State Fathers Turn Out to Welcome "America's 'Sweetheart' Here," *TD* Sept. 7, 1939.

36 "MGM to Bring Real Film Studio Here to Make Tests in Search for New Talent," *NL* November 6, 1934; "Seven Chosen for Film Test," *NL* November 16, 1934; "World Premiere of Film Here has Pomp of Broadway Debut," *TD* November 15, 1935.

37 "Richmond Finalists Ready for Screen and Voice Tests," *NL* November 17, 1934; "Gillet Epps Winner of Talent Contest," *NL* July 21, 1937.

38 "Premiere of Local Talkie Enthusiastic Despite Rain," *NL* March 28, 1936.

Chapter 4

1 Interview with Nikki Fairman, February 1, 2001.

2 "Richmonders are Costumed for the *GWTW* Ball," *NL* February 2, 1940; Edith Lindeman, "*Gone with the Wind* Here, Lives up to all its Promotion," *TD* February 3, 1940; "City Succumbs to *GWTW*, Likes Epic of Lost Cause," *NL* Feb 3, 1940.

3 *NL* Feb 2, 1940.

4 "Many Still Visit 'Film' Staircase," *TD* Nov. 11, 1976.

5 Edward J. Slipek, "Hollywood on the James," *StyleWeekly*, n.d. clipping at Valentine Museum.

6 Interview with Lucille Borden, September 2000.

7 "Theaters Join in Bond Drive," *NL* December 7, 1942.

8 "Six Theaters to Take Part in Second Tin Can Drive" *NL* December 10, 1942.

9 Edith Lindeman, "Nostalgic Touch in *The Opposite Sex.*"

Nd clipping in Valentine Museum archives.

10 James J. Kilpatrick, "'Small-town' Paper Still Allowed a Newsman Many Opportunities," *TD* Dec 25, 1988.

11 Dean Levi, "Lion's Roar Could Have Set Off Ceiling Collapse," *NL* July 19, 1990; n.d. clipping, Richmond Public Library.

12 Interview with Jackie Samuels, September, 2000; Jackie Samuels scrapbooks, Collection of Kathy Fuller-Seeley.

13 Liz Hart, "Loews brought the Stars" n.d. clipping, Valentine Museum archives.

14 *TD* June 19, 1951.

15 Carly Trader, "A Grand Old House."

16 Clarke Bustard, "Those were the days, at Loew's," *TD* November 10, 1980; Carole Kass, "George R. Stitzer: The Byrd was his home," *TD* April 11, 1982; Carole Kass, "Loew's Movie Palace Moves into History," *TD* May 14, 1979.

17 Leo Schario, "Food Never Brought into Great Film Palaces," n.d. clipping, Stark County Historical Society, Canton, Ohio.

18 Edith Lindeman, "Entertainment has Changed in the Past Three Decades," *TD* May 31, 1963.

19 Clark, "Movie Palace Fit for a King."

20 Interview with Dr. Trice.

21 Interviews with: Harry Daniel, Harry Stanley, Thomas G. Wyatt, Tommy Sammons, Charles E. Hughes, Paul Webb; James Harold Thrower and Geneva Thrower Woodrum, October, 2000.

22 Edith Lindeman, "Westover Theater Features Furnished Lounge for Use of Community Groups Free," *TD* August 30, 1950.

23 *TD* July 2, 1951.

24 "Leslie Doyle Banks, a.k.a. 'Mr. Theater' Dies," *TD* April 1, 2001.

25 Roy Proctor, "City's Imperiled Stock of Costumes is 'A Real Gem' Says its Caretaker," *TD* March 12, 1988.

26 Tedde Thompson, "Hallelujah! Unto Us a Nativity Pageant is Given," *TD* Dec. 23, 1993; Will Jones, "A Star Returns: Richmond Community Christmas Pageant is Tonight," TD Dec. 24, 2000.

27 "Children's Theater Has Closed," *TD* June 20, 1986.

28 Lindeman, "Jenny Lind in 1850."

29 Clarke Bustard, "The Mosque: Orphan to jewel in 50 Years," *TD* Dec. 25, 1977.

30 Roy Proctor, "When Daddy Longlegs Showed Up, Little Leslie Banks Didn't Fall Asleep," *NL* Sept 3, 1988.

31 Friddell, "The Moon is Through."

32 "Colonial Theater Is Sold," *TD* May 15, 1965.

33 "Negroes Denied Loew's Entrance," *TD* September 26, 1961.

34 "Picket Line at Theaters," *Richmond Afro American* May 18, 1963, p. 1, 2.

35 Douglas Gomery, *Shared Pleasures: A History of Movie Presentation in the U.S.* (Madison University of Wisconsin Press, 1992) p. 166-1677; *Motion Picture Herald*, 10 July 1963, p. 4; *Motion Picture Herald*, p. 7 August 1963, 7.

36 "Theaters Reportedly Integrated," *TD* June 11, 1963; Edith Lindeman, "City's Entertainment," *TD* Dec. 29, 1963.

37 Clarke Bustard, "Hippodrome Reopens As a Movie Theater" *TD* December 30, 1982.

38 N.d. clipping, Richmond Public Library.

39 Williams, "Theater Veteran to Retire."

40 Carole Kass, "Loew's Quietly Observes 50th Birthday" *TD* April 16, 1978.

41 Kass, "Loew's Movie Palace Moves into History."

Chapter 5

1 "Twin Screen Theater Work to Start," *NL* May 1, 1970.

2 Carole Kass, "Midnight Show: Party Time" *TD* July 28, 1978.

3 Interview with Scott Terbush, December, 2000.

4 Carole Kass, "Each Theater Has Its Own Personality," *TD* October 5, 1990.

5 Clipping, April 1981, Carpenter Center archives.

6 "Final Scene," *TD* December 7, 1991.

7 Carole Kass, "National Theater," unpublished mss., 1993.

8 Roy Proctor, "Other Stages: Road, Campus, Community Shows Aplenty," *NL* January 11, 1992.

9 Roy Proctor, "Scraping, Screaming, Seasoning, Succeeding," *TD* May 14, 1995.

10 "Continue Filming of Scenes in *"America"* at Westover Today," *NL* November 5, 1923.

11 "Film Premiere to Attract Many Visitors," *TD* Sept. 4, 1940; Edith Lindeman, "Martha Scott is Welcomed by Richmond; Actress and Director Make Many Friends," *TD* Sept. 5, 1940.

12 Slipek, "Hollywood on the James."

13 Gary Robertson, "Dreaming the Hollywood Dream: State Competes, Gains Momentum," *TD* March 25, 2001.

14 Lorraine Blackwell, "Reid's Breaking a Leg on a New Sort of Stage," *TD* December 14, 1997.

15 "Filmed in Virginia," Virginia Film Office publication, 2001.

16 Roy Proctor, "Arts in the Heart of the City; Theater Groups Applauding Plan," *TD* June 24, 2001.

BIBLIOGRAPHY

Specific newspaper article sources are cited in the notes. This is a general bibliography of sources I consulted.

Alicoate, Jack, ed. *Film Daily Yearbook.* New York: Film Daily, 1929-1957.

Ayers, Edward. *The Promise of the New South: Life After Reconstruction.* New York: Oxford University Press, 1992.

Barnes, Eric W. *The Lady of Fashion: The Life and Times of Anna Cora Mowatt* New York: Scribner's, 1954.

Bowers. Q. David. *Nickelodeon Theaters and Their Music* Vestal, N.Y.: Vestral Press, 1986.

Butsch, Richard. *The Making of American Audiences: From Stage to Television, 1750-1990.* New York: Cambridge University Press, 2000.

Click, Patricia. *The Spirit of the Times: Amusements in 19ᵗʰ Century Baltimore, Norfolk and Richmond.* Charlottesville: University Press of Virginia, 1989.

Dorman, James. *Theater in the Antebellum South, 1815-1861.* Chapel Hill: University of North Carolina Press, 1967.

Fuller, Kathryn H. *At the Picture Show: Small Town Audiences and the Creation of Movie Fan Culture.* Charlottesville: University Press of Virginia, 2001; Smithsonian Press, 1996.

Furgurson, Ernest. *Ashes of Glory: Richmond at War.* New York: Knopf, 1996.

Gomery, Douglas. *Shared Pleasures: A History of Movie Presentation in the United States.* Madison: University of Wisconsin Press, 1992.

Hall, Ben. *The Best Remaining Seats.* New York: Bramhall House, 1961.

Headley, Robert K. *Motion Picture Exhibition in Washington, D.C.: An Illustrated History of Parlors, Palaces and Multiplexes in the Metropolitan Area, 1894-1997.* Jefferson, N.C.: McFarland, 1999.

Kimball, Gregg D. *American City, Southern Place: A Cultural History of Antebellum Richmond.* Athens: University of Georgia Press, 2000.

Levine, Lawrence. *Highbrow/Lowbrow: The Emergence of Cultural Hierarchy in America.* Cambridge: Howard University Press, 1988.

Lutz, Earle. *A Richmond Album: A Pictorial Chronicle of an Historic City's Outstanding Events and Places.* Richmond: Garrett and Massie, 1937.

Mann, William J. *Wisecracker: The Life and Times of William Haines, Hollywood's First Openly Gay Star.* New York: Viking, 1998.

McGraw, Marie Tyler. *At the Falls: Richmond Virginia and Its People.* Chapel Hill: University of North Carolina Press, 1994.

Peiss, Kathy. *Cheap Amusements: Working Women and Leisure in Turn-of-the-Century* New York. Philadelphia: Temple University Press, 1986.

Richmond City Directory. 1895-2001.

Sanford, James K. *A Century of Commerce, 1867-1967.* Richmond: Chamber of Commerce, 1967.

Scott, Mary Wingfield. *Old Richmond Neighborhoods.* Richmond: Whittet and Shepperson, 1950.

Stokes, Melvyn, and Maltby, Richard, eds. *American Movie Audiences: From the Turn of the Century to the Early Sound Era.* London: British Film Institute, 1999.

Waller, Gregory A. *Main Street Amusements: Movies and Commercial Entertainment in a Southern City.* Washington D.C.: Smithsonian Press, 1995.

INDEX

RICHMOND SCREENLAND

Published in Richmond, Virginia, Every
Two Weeks by the Byrd, Capitol,
Venus, Brookland and
Bluebird Theatres

Printed in Richmond by Appeals Press, Inc.

Vol. 1   November 8, 1932   No. 2

Richard Powell Carter, Editor